Essays in the Unknown Wittgenstein

Essays in the Unknown Wittgenstein

Morris Lazerowitz and Alice Ambrose

Prometheus Books

700 East Amherst St. Buffalo, New York 14215

Published 1984 by Prometheus Books
700 E. Amherst Street, Buffalo, New York 14215
Printed in the United States of America

ISBN 0-87975-234-3
Library of Congress Catalog Card No. 83-62923

Contents

Foreword

Wittgenstein was capable of profound insights into academic, reasoned philosophy, insights that can lead to the explanation of its central enigma: the intrinsic irresolvability of its disagreements which attaches to every one of its claims. Some of Wittgenstein's work has made it possible to look with understanding, if not with ego gratification, at conventional philosophy. There can be no room for doubt that his mind was in conflict with itself, that the traditional although extraordinarily original thinker was in conflict with the iconoclastic thinker. This perhaps is one reason why he never developed his insights, and why he scattered them so thinly in his later writings, where they lie concealed like uncut diamonds on a pebbled beach. He left them in a state which reduced their value to conversation pieces.

Two of these iconoclastic observations will be briefly remarked on here. One is that "philosophical problems arise when language *goes on holiday.*"[1] The other is, "The confusions which occupy us arise when language is like an engine idling, not when it is doing work."[2] The first implies that philosophers use ordinary language but not in the usual, accepted ways. They use it to play games with terminology. To illustrate, the claim advanced by W. V. Quine that there are no synonyms makes a holiday use of "synonym." He plays a game with it, and is not using it, as he seems to be, to make a statement about the actual use of the term "synonym" in the language. One implication of Wittgenstein's second remark is that the philosophical use of language is not intended to communicate a fact or transmit a message or express a wish, etc. Its work is something else. Thus, for example, the Parmenidean statement that it is impossible to think of what does not exist does not express a claim about what we cannot think or imagine. Neither does it present a claim about the actual use of the expression "imagines a nonexistent creature." In these respects the Parmenidean utterance is like an engine idling. It is natural, however, to take it to be about what can or cannot occur. But it may well be that part of its work is to create this impression.

---

1. *Philosophical Investigations* (ed. by G. E. M. Anscombe and Rush Rhees; trans. by G. E. M. Anscombe. Oxford: Basil Blackwell, 1953), p. 19.
2. Ibid, p. 51.

If this is the case, we have within our means the possibility of understanding why the disputes surrounding it are so durable.

The essays in this collection have a common orientation, which is to bring to light the thoughts behind Wittgenstein's cryptic remarks. The topics were chosen independently, and were determined by the interests that preoccupied the writers at the time. The essays were discussed and criticized by both contributors, but were individually written. Morris Lazerowitz contributed essays I, II, IV, V, VII, X, XI, XV, and XVI; Alice Ambrose contributed essays III, VI, VIII, IX, XII, XIII, and XIV.

Smith College
Northampton, Massachusetts   Morris Lazerowitz

Introduction

Wittgenstein's Iconoclastic Breakthrough

Wittgenstein's thought, after his *Notebooks, 1914–1916*, falls into three periods. The first is the period in which he worked on his *Tractatus Logico-Philosophicus*. At that time, he was concerned primarily with conventional philosophical problems, which he looked at through the spectacles of logical positivism. As with Hume, Wittgenstein's main object was to eliminate metaphysics from intelligible discourse and, following Bertrand Russell, to give logical respectability to philosophy.

The second period, which marks an iconoclastic departure not only from the *Tractatus* but from traditional ways of looking at philosophy, fell into a small number of years after his return to Cambridge University in 1929. It is at this time that he dictated the material now published under the title *The Blue and Brown Books*. There was also in existence *The Yellow Book,* a set of notes taken by Margaret Masterman and Alice Ambrose, the title of which was widely known, although its contents were not. With the appearance of a book of lecture notes from the years 1932 to 1935, edited by Alice Ambrose, most of *The Yellow Book* has now been made public.[1] It is in this period that G. E. Moore, Alice Ambrose, and John Wisdom attended Wittgenstein's lectures and, to a greater or lesser degree, fell under his intellectual influence. Roughly speaking, the years after 1936 represent a partial return to the pre-*Blue Book, Tractatus* period. His *Philosophical Investigations,* which he wrote in these years, is given over in part to what amounts to a philosophical critique of doctrines in the *Tractatus.*

Different views are current about the connection between these three periods. Von Wright, the successor to Wittgenstein's chair at Cambridge and one of his literary executors, holds that the second period is a puzzling discontinuity in Wittgenstein's thought, that it is something which really does not belong. In his own words: "I myself find it difficult to fit the *Blue Book* into the development of Wittgenstein's thought."[2] The suggestion — one might say the plain implication — of his words is that the period is not representative of the "real" Wittgenstein. The overtone of von Wright's

11

remark is that it is the thirteenth floor at which the elevator should not stop. Other of Wittgenstein's later followers consider the philosophy he did in this period to be his "false philosophy." To their minds, it is an aberrant period in his intellectual odyssey and should therefore be discounted. One cannot help thinking of these followers as metaphysical morticians who have come to praise Caesar in order to bury his heresies. There is still another view about the connections between these periods. Some well-known philosophers maintain that there is no discontinuity in Wittgenstein's development; they deny that the second period exists. For them the thirteenth floor is not even a possible elevator stop. These philosophers are the true lotus-eaters, who erase from their minds by self-induced somnambulism Wittgenstein's disquieting perceptions into the hidden workings of philosophy.

Wittgenstein's middle period represents a fundamental breakthrough in the history of philosophical thought. Philosophy has been a Lorelei for more than 2,000 years, but underneath it lies an enigma to our understanding. For if we resort to the device Ulysses used to circumvent the sirens and take a careful look at philosophy, what we shall see is a highly respected discipline that has not produced a single firmly established result in the whole of its long history. The glaring fact that technical philosophy, which professes to be a demonstrative science, has no secure results is a riddle for which conventional philosophy provides no answer. The work of Wittgenstein's middle period shows the way to an understanding of this strange absence of uncontested propositions. His explanation of the nature of philosophical utterances may not be entirely correct, but without it we would remain completely in the dark. It may be unkind but nevertheless true to say that too many philosophers act on the assumption that what is emotionally unpalatable is either false or does not exist. But Wittgenstein's explanation must be unappealing to philosophers, since the fact on which it throws light is one that they prefer not to see. The following excerpts from Wittgenstein's writings will make it clear why a philosopher would tend to ignore an important side of his thought. Nevertheless, they throw light on what is otherwise opaque, although admittedly arresting. The risk that improving our understanding of technical philosophy may in fact dissolve it has to be taken by those who wish to discover the reason for the intractability of its disputes.[3]

Before discussing the excerpts, it is important to call attention to Wittgenstein's change of attitude toward psychoanalysis. For the insights he had into the workings of philosophy are like the perceptions that a psychoanalyst has into the forces that produce a neurosis, a dream, a reverie, a surrealist painting, a fairy tale. The central motive of his middle period was the linguistic unmasking of philosophical utterances, utterances parading as statements about the inner nature of things, about space and that which lies beyond its boundaries, about time, causation, and so on. In a Socratic metaphor, the implication of some of Wittgenstein's later insights is that philosophical statements are semantic wind-eggs represented as having ideational substance.

When Wittgenstein first learned about psychoanalysis and read some of the writings of Freud, he was filled with admiration and respect. His reported observation was: "Here is someone who has something to say." Later he turned against psychoanalysis and rejected it as a harmful mythology. A remarkable thing took place, however, something that might be described as the hidden, displaced return of the rejected. Wittgenstein imbued his philosophical talk with a kind of psychoanalytical atmosphere. It is as if, for him, philosophy had become a linguistic illness from which people needed to be relieved, and this could only be done by laying bare the illusion-creating tricks that were being unconsciously played with language. The impression one gets from reading the later Wittgenstein is that he had become, without being aware of it, the psychoanalyst of philosophy, the background formula perhaps being: I don't need analysis, philosophers need it; I am the psychoanalyst, philosophy is the illness from which philosophers need to be cured by getting them to see what they are doing with language. It is perhaps within the bounds of reasonable speculation to think that Wittgenstein would never have had his remarkable insights into philosophy if the need for analysis had not been deflected away from himself and projected onto philosophy. A number of philosophers seem to have divined his role with respect to philosophy when they describe him as a therapeutic positivist. Indeed, Wittgenstein explicitly stated that his "treatment of a philosophical question is like the treatment of an illness."[4] "The philosopher," he said, "is the man who has to cure himself of many sicknesses of the understanding before he can arrive at the notions of the sound human understanding."[5]

The following excerpts represent an extraordinary intellectual breakthrough:

> The confusions which occupy us arise when language is like an engine idling, not when it is doing work.[6]

> The fallacy we want to avoid is this: when we reject some form of symbolism, we're inclined to look at it as though we'd rejected a proposition as false. . . . This confusion pervades all of philosophy. It's the same confusion that considers a philosophical problem as though such a problem concerned a fact of the world instead of a matter of expression.[7]

These remarks are so transparent that it is hardly necessary to elaborate on them. Their implication is that a philosopher changes language in one way or another under the illusion that he is expressing a proposition about what there is and about the nature of what there is. The further implication is that the revised piece of language is semantically idle, i.e., that it has no actual use to communicate information.

An example taken from classical philosophy will make Wittgenstein's point clear. Heraclitus maintained that everything constantly changes, that nothing remains the same. You cannot on his view step into the same river twice or sit on the same bench twice, because there is no such thing as the same river or the same bench — or even the same you. There is an apochryphal tale that a debtor of Heraclitus refused to make repayment on the grounds that the present Heraclitus was not the Heraclitus from whom he had borrowed the money, and that he was not the original borrower. In linguistic terms this "view" amounts to withholding the application of the phrase "remains the same," while retaining in the language the antithetical term "changes." Without its antithesis "remains the same," the phrase "undergoes change" no longer serves to distinguish between things, and thus, to use Wittgenstein's word, it becomes linguistically "idle." The meaning of the phrase "thing which undergoes change" vanishes into the meaning of the word "thing," so that in the sentence "All things are things that undergo change," the term "undergoes change" loses its use and becomes semantically functionless. The meaning of the sentence contracts into that of the tautologically empty sentence "Everything is a thing." Nevertheless, banishing "remains the same" from the language while artificially retaining "undergoes change" creates the deceptive illusion that the sentence "Everything changes, nothing remains the same" expresses a theory about the nature of things.

M.L.

NOTES

1. *Wittgenstein's Lectures, Cambridge 1932–1935* (Totowa, N.J.: Rowman and Littlefield; Oxford: Basil Blackwell, 1979; Chicago, Ill.: University of Chicago Press, 1982).

2. G. H. von Wright, "Ludwig Wittgenstein, a Biographical Sketch," in Norman Malcolm's *Ludwig Wittgenstein, A Memoir* (London, New York: Oxford University Press, 1967), p. 14.

3. In lectures Wittgenstein talked of philosophical problems having *dissolutions* rather than solutions; and one contemporary philosopher, Gilbert Ryle, has coined the verb "meta-evaporate."

4. *Philosophical Investigations,* p. 91.

5. *Remarks on the Foundations of Mathematics,* ed. by G. H. von Wright, Rush Rhees, and G. E. M. Anscombe; trans. by G. E. M. Anscombe (New York: The Macmillan Co., 1956), p. 157.

6. *Philosophical Investigations,* p. 51.

7. *Wittgenstein's Lectures, Cambridge 1932–1935* (Alice Ambrose, ed.).

I

Wittgenstein's Philosophical Odyssey

I shall light a candle of understanding in your heart which shall not be put out.

II Esdras

Ludwig Wittgenstein was one of the most original philosophers of this century, and there can be no doubt that the impact of his perceptions regarding the nature of philosophical problems will radically and permanently change the course of philosophy in the future. Unfortunately, the influence of his thought has been retarded. Apart from a paper in the *Proceedings of the Aristotelian Society* and his famous *Tractatus Logico-Philosophicus,* he did not permit any of his work to be published during his lifetime, although some of his lectures were mimeographed and circulated privately among a selected group of his students. According to all accounts, Wittgenstein was a man of compelling personality who tended to gather a circle of favored students around himself. An aura of mystery, not untinged with religion, was thus created around both his work and his special group of students. Understandably, such an atmosphere might well, and in fact did, have consequences somewhat less than desirable from an intellectual point of view. Fortunately, time has already begun to disperse the emotional mists and to clear the air. Now that Wittgenstein's work is being made publicly available, it should make itself felt widely and objectively in the doing of philosophy. Without stretching a metaphor unfairly, philosophy up to the present may be described as an expanding museum of exhibits, a sort of Madame Tussaud's, to which new figures are constantly being added but from which no figures are ever removed. But some things that Wittgenstein said will plant a seed in the minds of philosophers, which in time will grow into an improved understanding of the workings of philosophy, and enable us to look at it in a new way. And the explanations of theories and arguments flowing from this understanding will not become just additional exhibits: instead they will place these exhibits in a light that will enable us to see them for what they are. An observation by Professor John Wisdom is worth quoting here: "What Wittgenstein and others following him said did not by any means make everything as clear as one would wish. There was plenty of room for improvement. And a renewed look at what went before Wittgenstein can be a help in going forward from Wittgenstein. But one may recognize this without trying to do philosophy like one blind to the change Wittgenstein made."[1] It may be that a philosopher *must* do philosophy like a person who is blind to what Wittgenstein saw.

Over the years, philosophy presented itself to Wittgenstein in a number of different guises. Some of these were the usual ones that all of us know, while others were not. It is, of course, the later ways in which he saw philosophy that are so enlightening and helpful; but to realize how enlightening these are, some of the earlier ways need to be looked at. Before considering these, however, it is important to notice a connection between some of the things G. E. Moore did and the insights into philosophy that Wittgenstein arrived at later. As is well known, Moore brought philosophical theories (or some of them, at least) down to earth from the Platonic "heaven above the heavens" where they were protected against our understanding. Placed in the light of the ordinary sun, they could be scrutinized under less distorting conditions. Such a general philosophical view as that of F. H. Bradley, e.g., that physical things are not real, or that they are mere appearances, Moore would translate into (perhaps it would not be far off to say, *deflate* into) its concrete implications: for example, that he was not really wearing a waist-coat or that he was mistaken in believing that there was a sheet of paper on which he was writing with a fountain pen. Moore's ostensible purpose in effecting his translations into the concrete was to force on our attention the consequences of an abstract philosophical theory, consequences which we apparently tend to avoid noticing. The point of doing this was, frequently if not always, to refute a theory by subjecting it to "trial by example." But what could not fail to emerge, whether grasped consciously or unconsciously, was that, given Moore's translations, the theories were altogether too plainly false for anyone to have failed to see *for himself* that they were false. A further puzzling feature attaching to Moore's translations is that many philosophers who became acquainted with them did not give up their views. The idea that inevitably suggests itself is that such a philosophical view as "physical things are unreal" is not what it is taken to be. The question could not but arise whether the view is actually *incompatible with* a factual proposition, for example, that Moore is wearing a waistcoat and is writing with a fountain pen. Surprising as it might seem, Moore's translations into the concrete, if they showed anything, tended to show that the theories he opposed were not open to his translations. The problem then becomes one of understanding rightly how a philosopher is using language when he says, "Physical things are not real," or "Physical things exist but are mere appearance." Wittgenstein's later work shows us the way to a correct understanding of such statements.

In one place Moore observed that it would seem as though ordinary everyday language was "expressly designed to mislead philosophers."[2] With the same complaint apparently in mind, Wittgenstein said that "Philosophy is a battle against the bewitchment of our intelligence by means of language,"[3] and "A philosophical problem has the form 'I don't know my way about.'"[4] Moore resorted to one procedure, that of careful analysis of the meanings of words, to free philosophers from their bewitchment. Wittgenstein also used this procedure to help them find their way through the maze of language. According to Wittgenstein: "A main source of our failure to understand is that we do not *command a clear view* of the use of our words. Our grammar is lacking in this sort of perspicuity."[5] To express the matter with the help of his arresting metaphor that has captured the imagination of many philosophers, what will help the fly escape from the fly-bottle is an analysis of usage, i.e., getting straight about how we ordinarily use words. There is, however, a difference in the procedure of Moore and Wittgenstein, which it will be useful to look at. This difference might very well have led Wittgenstein to say that a philosopher of Common Sense ("and that, *n.b.,* is not the common-sense man"[6]) is himself captive in the fly-bottle but favors a special corner in it; in trying to refute positions that go counter to Common Sense, he also "does not know his way about." Moore's disagreements with philosophers result in *philosophical* stalemates, stalemates as old as those between Parmenides and his opponents.

It will be recalled that Moore's attempted defense of Common Sense against the attacks of philosophers — attacks sustained throughout the long history of philosophy — has been rejected as begging the question, and Moore has been criticized as being dogmatic about the "truisms" he lays down. And in bringing them, unsupported by chains of reasoning, against the counterclaims of philosophers who back their own propositions with analytical arguments, Moore has, in the opinion of many thinkers, begged the very questions that are in debate. Moore's familiar expletives, "nonsense," "absurd," "obviously false," etc., may momentarily silence a philosopher who goes against Common Sense, but it does not affect the way such a philosopher continues to think about the "errors" of Common Sense. Long ago Parmenides said, "Heed not the blind eye, the echoing ear, nor yet the tongue, but bring to this great debate the test of reason." We might restate this philosophical recipe without antecedent prejudice to the question as to whether or not our senses are reliable sources of information: Disregard the eye, the ear, and the tongue (for we all pretty much hear the same, taste the same, and see the same), but bring only reasoning to a philosophical investigation. Moore's defense does not do this. Thus, for example, Moore allows that he neither gives nor attempts to give an argument for *the premises* of what he puts forward as proofs for the existence of external things; and a philosopher who does give arguments against Common Sense claims that we have knowledge of the existence of things can, with the appearance of justification, charge that Moore is dogmatic and begs the question. Indeed, Moore does need to explain why it is that calling philosophers' attention to the truths of Common Sense has not brought them back to it nor made them give up their wayward attacks. But perhaps an explanation can be found only by looking at philosophy from an external vantage point, that only from such a standpoint will it be possible to see rightly the nature of philosophical stalemates.

It can with justice be said that Wittgenstein has been read with too much haste in recent years, and that some of his ideas have been slid over, while others have been put into the service of the private needs of philosophers, with resulting gaps and distortions in our understanding of his later work. In the present connection it is important to read with particular care one of Wittgenstein's passages in which he discusses what happens when we philosophize, and how we are brought back from philosophy to Common Sense without at the same time being brought back to philosophy. The passage also shows how his procedure differs from Moore's. Moore, on the whole, represents the philosopher who departs from or attacks Common Sense as having made an error of fact. Wittgenstein frequently represents him as having made an error of language, and identifies the mistake with the aim of effecting a remedy. The following is the passage:

> When we think about the relation of the objects surrounding us to our personal experience of them, we are sometimes tempted to say that these personal experiences are the material of which reality consists. How this temptation arises will become clearer later on.
>
> When we think in this way we seem to lose our firm hold on the objects surrounding us. And instead we are left with a lot of separate personal experiences of different individuals. These personal experiences again seem vague and seem to be in constant flux. Our language seems not to have been made to describe them. We are tempted to think that in order to clear up such matters philosophically our ordinary language is too coarse, that we need a more subtle one.
>
> We seem to have made a discovery—which I could describe by saying that the ground on which we stood and which appeared to be firm and reliable was found to be boggy and unsafe.—That is, this happens when we philosophize; for as soon as we revert to the standpoint of common sense this *general* uncertainty disappears.
>
> This queer situation can be cleared up somewhat by looking at an example; in fact a kind of parable illustrating the difficulty we are in, and also showing the way out of this sort of difficulty: We have been told by popular scientists that the floor on which we stand is not solid, as it appears to common sense, as it has been discovered that the wood consists of particles filling space so thinly that it can almost be called empty. This is liable to perplex us, for in a way of course we know that the floor is solid, or that, if it isn't solid, this may be due to the wood being rotten but not to its being composed of electrons. To say, on

this latter ground, that the floor is not solid is to misuse language. For even if the particles were as big as grains of sand, and as close together as these are in a sandheap, the floor would not be solid if it were composed of them in the sense in which a sandheap is composed of grains. Our perplexity was based on a misunderstanding; the picture of the thinly filled space had been wrongly *applied*. For this picture of the structure of matter was meant to explain the very phenomenon of solidity.

As in this example the word "solidity" was used wrongly and it seemed that we had shown that nothing really was solid, just in this way, in stating our puzzles about the *general vagueness* of sense-experience, and about the flux of all phenomena, we are using the words "flux" and "vagueness" wrongly, in a typically metaphysical way, namely, without an antithesis; whereas in their correct and everyday use, vagueness is opposed to clearness, flux to stability.[7]

Looking at a philosophical utterance in this way is enormously helpful, but it is not enough. And Wittgenstein did go beyond this point of view to deeper insights into the way philosophy works. This is shown, for example, when he characterizes a philosophical problem as one arising "when language goes on holiday,"[8] or "when language is like an engine idling, not when it is doing work."[9] The plain implications of these observations, and of many other things Wittgenstein has said, is that a philosophical problem is not a mere verbal muddle to be cleared up by analyzing usage; rather, it is the expression of a special kind of game that can be played with language. On this construction of what doing philosophy consists in, to solve a philosophical problem is just to understand the game that is being played with terminology.

To go back to his earlier work, in the *Tractatus* Wittgenstein states a number of views about the nature of philosophy, or of some of its parts. The following statements give the most important of the views he advanced:

(1)   Most of the propositions and questions to be found in philosophical works are not false but nonsensical. Consequently we cannot give any answer to questions of this kind, but can only establish that they are nonsensical. . . . And it is not surprising that the deepest problems are in fact *not* problems at all.   (4.003)

(2)   Philosophy is not a body of doctrine but an activity. A philosophical work consists essentially of elucidations. Philosophy does not result in "philosophical propositions," but rather in the clarification of propositions. (4.112)

(3)   All philosophy is a "critique of language." . . .   (4.0031)

(4)   The totality of true propositions is the whole of natural science (or the whole corpus of the natural sciences).   (4.11)

> Philosophy is not one of the natural sciences.
> (The word 'philosophy' must mean something whose place is above or below the natural sciences, not beside them.)   (4.111)

The inconsistencies among these different things Wittgenstein has said about philosophy are not inconspicuous, and there must be an explanation to account for the fact that they have gone unnoticed. But bringing out inconsistencies is not important here. What is important to see is that philosophy could present such different faces to Wittgenstein. About his own statements in the *Tractatus*, presumably those concerning philosophy, he said: "My propositions serve as elucidations in the following way: anyone who understands me eventually recognises them as nonsensical, when he has used them—as steps—to climb up beyond them. (He must, so to speak, throw away the ladder after he has climbed up it.) He must transcend these propositions, and then he will see the world aright" (6.54).

This pronouncement, which many people have found exciting, is odd, to say the least; and the excitement it arouses must derive from some sort of hidden message it conveys. Perhaps, like the Delphic oracle, it "neither speaks nor conceals, but gives a sign." On the surface the pronouncement seems to imply that his own statements are nonsensical *elucidations,* and also, according to his own words, that nonsensical elucidations can lead one to see the world aright. The underlying implication would seem to be that philosophers do not see the world aright, and that they can be led by nonsense to see it aright. It must be granted that nonsense seems at times to have remarkable curative powers, but it is hard to think of it as being a "specific" for philosophers. However that may be, the series of views Wittgenstein advanced explicitly or by implication about philosophy are the following: (a) Most philosophical utterances are devoid of literal intelligibility, in the way in which "The good is more identical than the beautiful" is without literal intelligibility. (b) No philosophical proposition is true. This follows directly from (4) above, and parallels something he said at a later time: "What the philosophers (of whatever opinion) say is all wrong, but what the bedmaker says is all right."[11] He also seems to have held, (c), that some philosophical propositions are true. Thus, he came out for one of Hume's views about causation: "Belief in the causal nexus is *superstition*" (5.1361); and he also came out for the view that a proposition about the future is a hypothesis: "It is an hypothesis that the sun will rise tomorrow: and this means that we do not *know* whether it will rise" (6.36311). (d) He held, furthermore, that in philosophy no propositions are advanced. According to one way philosophy presented itself to him, it was just analytic clarification and had no propositions of its own to put forward: there are no "philosophical propositions" as there are scientific ones.

The claim, (a), that most philosophical utterances are devoid of literal intelligibility is usually linked with the so-called Verifiability Principle, which requires some comment. Moritz Schlick formulated the following principle for determining whether an indicative sentence that does not express an *a priori* proposition has or lacks literal significance: "Stating the meaning of a sentence amounts to stating the rules according to which the sentence is to be used, and this is the same thing as stating the way in which it can be verified (or falsified). The meaning of a proposition is the method of its verification."[12] This version of the principle is usually attributed to Wittgenstein and it probably originated with him. Those who have adopted the principle as well as those who have rejected it commonly consider the Verification Principle to have eliminated metaphysical sentences from the class of literally meaningful sentences constructible in a language, and in this way to have rid philosophy of its most spectacular if also its most unsatisfactory branch. This understanding of the job of the criterion fits in with a number of statements in the *Tractatus,* but a careful scrutiny of the criterion brings to light the curious fact that it does not eliminate metaphysics and certainly contains within itself the possibility of the return of the rejected. For the criterion, as it is worded, does not preclude the possibility of there being supersensible verification, which would be the kind of verification appropriate to a statement referring to a nonsensible reality. That is, as phrased (and the phrasing cannot be supposed the result of a merely accidental lapse), the criterion is open to the specification, "The meaning of a metaphysical proposition is the method of its verification." The criterion does not rule out of court the claims of a philosopher like Edmund Husserl, who wrote: "Under the title of 'A Pure or Transcendental Phenomenology' the work here presented seeks to found a new science — though, indeed, the whole course of philosophical development since Descartes has been preparing the way for it — a science covering a new field of experience, exclusively its own, that of 'Transcendental Subjectivity.'"[13]

In the present connection, it is particularly interesting to notice that one idea about philosophy expressed in the *Tractatus* (4.113) is that it "settles controversies about the limits of natural science." This would seem to imply the view that at least one task of philosophy is to settle territorial disputes between science and religion. The underlying idea, from which perhaps Wittgenstein never completely freed himself, is that the metaphysician is able to survey reality in all its parts, supersensible as well as sensible, and, like the guide at the maze in Hampton Court, is able to help those who get lost in the cosmic labyrinth. This idea may have considerable connection with the fact that a number of Wittgenstein's later students have returned to metaphysics. It should be mentioned, however, that at least one follower of Wittgenstein has taken a different course, also consonant with the criterion. According to him one task of philosophy, perhaps its only task, is to bring to light modes of verification appropriate to different sorts of propositions. Interestingly enough, logic has a similar function, according to Aristotle. W. D. Ross describes Aristotle's conception of logic as not being "a substantive science, but a part of general culture which everyone should undergo before he studies any science, and which alone will enable him to know for what sorts of proposition he should demand proof and what sorts of proof he should demand for them."[14]

Let us return to the four different and incompatible views of philosophy to be found in the *Tractatus*: (a) most philosophical utterances are senseless; (b) philosophical propositions are not truths; (c) some philosophical propositions are truths; (d) there are no philosophical propositions. These lie comfortably enough alongside each other, and there is no evidence that Wittgenstein ever attempted to sort them out and select from among them. Nevertheless, it cannot be supposed that in Wittgenstein's active and original mind they could continue indefinitely to live in amity with each other. Their existence shows unmistakably that one of his main preoccupations, perhaps his central one, was to get clear about the nature of philosophy. In his later thinking Wittgenstein did not completely free his mind from his earlier views about philosophy. A few examples will suffice to show this. In *Philosophical Investigations* he writes: "The results of philosophy are the uncovering of one or another piece of plain nonsense and of bumps that the understanding has got by running its head up against the limits of language,"[15] and also, "My aim is: to teach you to pass from a piece of disguised nonsense to something that is patent nonsense."[16] In *The Blue Book,* Wittgenstein sometimes seems to represent philosophers as individuals who make false empirical claims, although in this connection he disagrees with Moore as to how they are to be corrected. He wrote:

> There is no common sense answer to a philosophical problem. One can defend common sense against the attacks of philosophers only by solving their puzzles, i.e., by curing them of the temptation to attack common sense, not by restating the views of common sense. A philosopher is not a man out of his senses, a man who doesn't see what everybody sees; nor on the other hand is his disagreement with common sense that of the scientist disagreeing with the coarse views of the man in the street.[17]

At times Wittgenstein represents philosophers as making mistaken claims about the use of terminology, claims which his own investigations are designed to correct. He describes what he does in the following words:

> Our investigation is therefore a grammatical one. Such an investigation sheds light on our problem by clearing misunderstandings away. Misunderstandings concerning the use of words, caused, among other things, by certain analogies between the forms of expression in different regions of language. —Some of them can be removed by substituting one form of expression for another; this may be called "analysis" of our forms of expression, for the process is sometimes like one of taking a thing apart.[18]

Also:

> When philosophers use a word—"knowledge," "being," "object," "I," "proposition," "name"—and try to grasp the *essence* of the thing, one must always ask oneself: is the word ever actually used in this way in the language-game which is its original home?—
>   What *we* do is to bring words back from their metaphysical to their everyday usage.[19]

At times he seems to represent the philosopher as making two different kinds of mistake simultaneously: one a factual mistake, to be removed by looking or introspection; the other a linguistic mistake, to be removed by noting what an expression is normally applied to. Thus in *The Blue Book* Wittgenstein says: "Examine expressions like 'having an idea in one's mind,' 'analyzing an idea before one's mind.' In order not to be misled by them see what really happens when, say, in writing a letter you are looking for the words which correctly express the idea which is 'before your mind.'"[20] We may gather from this that the Platonist, for example, is led by a common form of words into holding a false factual belief about what is before one's mind; he is misled by a linguistic analogy into forming a wrong notion of the actual application of the expression, "analyzing an idea before one's mind" (compare with "analyzing a substance before one's eyes"). This in turn results in a false belief regarding what *is* before one's mind when one conducts an analysis. The impression gained is that both errors are to be corrected by looking at the facts, both the erroneous idea about usage and the erroneous idea about what takes place when we "have an idea before our mind." But plainly the "linguistic mistake" of the Platonist, who appears to think that there are special refined objects designated by the phrase "idea before one's mind," is not like that of a person who thinks the word "horse" is normally used to apply to cows, or like that of a person who sees a horse but thinks he sees a cow or thinks he sees what in fact does not exist. Wittgenstein could not have failed to realize this, and, indeed, a new insight into philosophy had begun to develop in his mind.

The direction of his thinking became more and more oriented toward the notion that philosophical problems are muddles, verbal tangles to be straightened out by recourse to ordinary usage, with the help of a special device he called "language games." A philosopher develops a "mental cramp," and the therapy for removing it is to bring him back to ordinary usage. The following passage from *The Blue Book* will make this clear. In considering the question as to whether I can know or believe that someone else has a pain, Wittgenstein wrote:

> But wasn't this a queer question to ask? *Can't* I believe that someone else has pains? Is it not quite easy to believe this?— . . . needless to say, we don't

feel these difficulties in ordinary life. Nor is it true to say that we feel them when we scrutinize our experience by introspection. . . . But somehow when we look at them in a certain way, our expression is liable to get into a tangle. It seems as though we had either the wrong pieces, or not enough of them, to put together our jig-saw puzzle. But they are there, only all mixed up; . . . .[21]

The thing to do to get straightened out, to cure our verbal malady, is "to look how the words in question *are actually used in our language.*"[22] When Wittgenstein observed that to call what he did "philosophy" was perhaps proper but also misleading, and that what he did was one of the "heirs" of philosophy, he certainly had in mind the technique of examining the actual usage of expressions in the language for the purpose of "dissolving" philosophical problems. It is worth noticing, in passing, that he conceived his work as beneficially destructive. "Where does our investigation get its importance from, since it seems only to destroy everything interesting, that is, all that is great and important? (As it were all the buildings, leaving behind only bits of stone and rubble.) What we are destroying is nothing but houses of cards and we are clearing up the ground of language on which they stand."[23]

To return to the question as to whether Wittgenstein's work could appropriately be called philosophy, he had in mind not only the procedure of attempting to settle controversies by examining usage—so as to bring philosophers down to the linguistic realities—but also, possibly, the new notion that was beginning to take form. It must be allowed that he did not give much expression to the insight into the linguistic structure of philosophical theories that gave rise to this notion, nor did he elaborate and develop it; but he did give some expression to it and he did make some application of it. In *The Blue Book* there occurs this important paragraph:

The man who says "only my pain is real," doesn't mean to say that he has found out by the common criteria—the criteria, i.e., which give our words their common meaning—that the others who said they had pains were cheating. But what he rebels against is the use of *this* expression in connection with *these* criteria. That is, he objects to using this word in the particular way in which it is commonly used. On the other hand, he is not aware that he is objecting to a convention. He sees a way of dividing the country different from the one used on the ordinary map. He feels tempted, say, to use the name "Devonshire" not for the county with its conventional boundary, but for a region differently bounded. He could express this by saying, "Isn't it absurd to make *this* a county, to draw the boundary *here*?" But what he says is: "The *real* Devonshire is this." We could answer: "What you want is only a new notation, and by a new notation no facts of geography are changed." It is true, however, that we may be irresistibly attracted or repelled by a notation. (We easily forget how much a notation, a form of expression, may mean to us, and that changing it isn't always as easy as it often is in mathematics or in the sciences. A change of clothes or of names may mean very little and it may mean a great deal.)[24]

The idea that quite unmistakably comes through from this passage is that a philosophical theory is the misleadingly phrased introduction of an altered piece of terminology. The form of words in which a philosopher presents his remodeling of conventional language is the form of words ordinarily used to state a matter of fact; and in presenting his renovated terminology in this way the philosopher makes himself dupe to what he does, as well as anyone who either sides with him or opposes him. The philosopher imagines himself to be expressing a matter of fact or a theory, i.e., to be delivering himself on what really is the case or on what exists or on what cannot exist; and his mistake lies in the construction he places on what he is doing, not in his understanding of the actual use of terminology. He is mistaken about what he does with conventions of usage, not about what the accepted conventions are: "The fallacy we want to avoid is this: when we reject some form of symbolism, we're inclined to look at it as though we'd rejected a proposition as false. It is wrong to compare the rejection of a unit of measure as though it were the rejection of the proposition, 'The chair is 3 feet instead of 2 feet high.' This confusion pervades all of philosophy. It's the same confusion that considers a philosophical problem as though such a problem concerned a fact of the world instead of a matter of expression."[25]

This view as to the nature of philosophical statements, and of what might be called the "fallacy of philosophy," quite plainly has great explanatory power. The position that philosophical utterances are about states of affairs—about reality—does not, for one thing, square with the analytical arguments philosophers use to support their theories; neither does it explain, for another thing, how a philosopher can hold his views while not being, to use Wittgenstein's words, "a man out of his senses, a man who doesn't see what everybody sees." The position that philosophical utterances use language improperly, or are misdescriptions of actual usage, does not explain why a philosopher is not corrected by bringing terminology back to its "original home." It does not explain why a philosopher who is made to feel embarrassed by being shown the correct use of language nevertheless does not give up his claim, or, if he does give it up, is able to return to it later. The view that philosophical utterances are nothing more than pronouncements embodying covertly revised criteria for the use of expressions explains both these things, and it also explains other eccentricities attaching to philosophical theories. To use Wittgenstein's imaginative metaphor, it explains why the fly cannot be shown the way out of the fly-bottle. The fly cannot be led out, because it does not want to be led out. The fly-bottle is only superficially its prison. At a deeper level, the fly-bottle is its home—a home it has built for itself out of language.

A somewhat extended passage from the unpublished part of *The Yellow Book* would seem to indicate plainly enough that this was the direction Wittgenstein's thinking took regarding the nature of philosophical theorizing, i.e., about what goes on when we think in a "philosophic moment," to use Moore's expression. It should be remarked immediately that the passage does not indicate this direction unambiguously and in so many plain words, without indications of other directions. But Wittgenstein's mind does not seem to have worked in straight lines. What follows is the passage, and it is well worth a careful reading:

> Suppose now I call my body by the name of Wittgenstein. I can now say, "Wittgenstein has toothache," just as I can say, "Shaw has toothache." On the other hand I should have to say, "I feel the pain," and I might feel it at a time when Wittgenstein has no toothache; or when Shaw had. It is only a matter of fact that Wittgenstein has the toothache when I feel the pain.
>
> If I use "I" and "Wittgenstein" thus, "I" is no longer opposed to anything. So we could use a different kind of notation. We could talk of pain in the one case and of behavior in the other. But does this mean the same as saying that I have real toothache and the other person has not? No, for the word "I" has now vanished from the language. We can only now say "There is toothache," give its locality and describe its nature.
>
> In doing this we are keeping the ordinary language and beside it I am putting another. Everything said in the one can, of course, be said in the other. But the two draw different boundaries; arrange the facts differently. What is queer about an ordinary notation is that it draws a boundary round a rather heterogeneous set of experiences. This fact tempts people to make another notation, in which there is no such thing as the proprietor of a toothache. But without the people realizing it, or even realizing that there are two, the two notations clash.
>
> Put it another way. To the person who says, "Only I can have real toothache," the reply should be, "If only you can have real toothache there is no sense in saying, 'Only I can have real toothache.' Either you don't need 'I' or you don't need 'real.' Your notation makes too many specifications. You had much better say, 'There is toothache,' and then give the locality and the description. This is what you are trying to say and it is much clearer without too many specifications." "Only I have real toothache" either has a common sense meaning, or, if it is a grammatical (philosophical) proposition, it is meant to be a statement of a rule; it wishes to say, "I should like to put, instead of the notation, 'I have real toothache,' 'There is real toothache,' or 'I have toothache,'" Thus the rule does not allow "Only I have real toothache" to be said. But the philosopher is apt to say the thing which his own rule has just forbidden him to say, by using the same words as those in which he has just stated the rule.
>
> "I can't know whether another person has toothache" seems to indicate a barrier between me and the other person. I want to point out to you that this is a pseudo-problem. It is our language which makes it seem as though there were a barrier.
>
> I talked before of the differences which our language stresses, and the differences it hushes up. Here is a wonderful example of a difference hushed up, for of course all the notations must have the same multiplicity. Nothing can be said in the one which can't also be said in the others. But a notation can stress, or it can minimize; and in this case it minimizes.[26]

Even a cursory reading of these words exposes a number of different tendencies in Wittgenstein's thinking about philosophy. Thus, he describes the question as to whether it is possible to know that another person has a pain as a "pseudo-question." There is also the hint that a philosophical problem is some sort of mix-up, the linguistic symptom of a mental cramp. There is further the notion that philosophical theories, or at least some of them, introduce alternative forms of expression that translate into expressions in ordinary use: i.e., keeping the ordinary language and beside it . . . putting another, the difference between the two being that they 'arrange the facts differently.'" To bring into connection what Wittgenstein says here with other things he says about philosophy, it may be pointed out that it is hard to see how an alternative notation could in any way be an attack on common sense, to be cured by bringing philosophers back to ordinary language. It is equally hard to see how a notation using "the words 'flux' and 'vagueness' wrongly, in a typically metaphysical way, namely, without an antithesis" could translate into ordinary language where "in their correct and everyday use, vagueness is opposed to clearness, flux to stability. . . ." Indeed, it is not hard to see that a notation which translates into the language of common sense cannot be an attack on common sense; and it is not hard to see that a notation in which ordinary words occur without their antitheses cannot translate into—have "the same multiplicity" as—a language in which they occur with their antitheses. All this only goes to show that on different occasions and in somewhat different connections Wittgenstein tried out various ideas to explain the enigma that is philosophy.

If we do not let ourselves be diverted by the different ideas in the above passage (concerning what a philosopher does and how he gets himself into difficulties), we are led to the notion, not that the philosopher fails to "command a clear view of our use of words," but that the perception he has into the uses of words makes him wish to modify or in some way alter those uses. It is evident that the alterations he institutes do not have any of the functions that alternative forms of expression usually have, e.g., to say the same thing with greater economy or with improved efficiency for calculating, or with greater vividness, or just to avoid monotony of expression. The picture of the philosopher that begins to come into focus is of someone who scans the intricate map of language and, unlike the grammarian and the thesaurus compiler, is not satisfied merely to report rules embedded in the language, but in various ways changes the rules. Differences in the uses of expressions that ordinary language does not perspicuously display (i.e., differences that it "hushes up"), the philosopher is sometimes impelled to try to bring out in sharp relief; and he is sometimes inclined to mute those differences in the uses of expressions that ordinary language "stresses." The reasons that he gives, in the form of arguments, for the changes he introduces quite obviously make negligible connection, or no connection at all, with the everyday kinds of work language does for us. The conclusion, which is at least latent in a good many things Wittgenstein said, is that a philosopher alters ordinary language, or "puts another language beside it," for the remarkable effects created by doing so. In the above passage, ordinary language is represented as responsible for the idea that a barrier exists between people, which prevents one person from knowing that another has a pain. But it should be realized at once that the sentence "I cannot know whether another person has a toothache"—i.e., the sentence creating the idea of a barrier—is *not* an ordinary sentence. Wittgenstein was, of course, aware that ordinary language does not put this idea in the mind of "the man in the street": in his words, "we don't feel these difficulties in ordinary life." The sentence is a philosophical production whose job is not at all like that of a sentence such as "I cannot know whether Socrates has a toothache; he endures pain with stoicism." To describe what is happening in the way Wittgenstein would state it, a philosopher who says, "I cannot know whether another has a pain" is objecting to the conventional use of "has a pain" but is not aware that he is objecting to a convention. His sentence announces the academic deletion from language of such phrases as "knows that another person has a pain," "knows that another person sees red," and in this way he brings out the great difference between the use of "has a pain" and the use of "has a tooth." But he introduces his re-editing of language conventions in such a way as to create the idea that there is some sort of barrier between people. It is not everyday language but the manner in which the philosopher announces changes in everyday language that is responsible for the inappropriate idea.

When Wittgenstein said, "What we are destroying is nothing but houses of cards and we are clearing up the ground of language on which they stand," quite possibly what he intended to convey was that, like the pretense use of cards as building materials for a house, a philosophical theory rests upon a pretense use of language. Quite possibly he wanted to convey that to give utterance to a philosophical theory is not to use language to express a theory but is only to use language to create the false idea that a theory is being expressed. And when he observed that "we may be irresistibly attracted by a notation," he may have been referring to deeper things in our minds that philosophical utterances link up with. It is not easy to know where one is reading too much or too little into the mind of an extraordinary original thinker.

M.L.

NOTES

1. Correspondence between John Wisdom and Morris Lazerowitz, February 1966.

2. *Philosophical Studies* (London: Routledge and Kegan Paul, 1922), p. 217.

3. *Philosophical Investigations,* p. 47.

4. Ibid., p. 49.

5. Ibid.

6. *Preliminary Studies for the "Philosophical Investigat.ons," Generally Known as The Blue and Brown Books* (New York: Harper and Row; Oxford: Basil Blackwell, 1958), p. 48.

7. Ibid., pp. 45–46.

8. *Philosophical Investigations,* p. 19.

9. Ibid., p. 51.

10. In this connection Mr. Steven L. Mitchell has contributed the following observation: "Wittgenstein's use of the metaphor of a ladder to describe the value of his analysis is much like Buddha's statement that his teachings are like a raft. Once one has crossed the river one has no more need of the raft."

11. From notes taken by Margaret Masterman and Alice Ambrose in the intervals between dictation of *The Blue Book.* These notes will henceforth be referred to as *The Yellow Book.*

12. "Meaning and Verification," *The Philosophical Review* XLV (July 1936), p. 341.

13. Edmund Husserl, *Ideas: General Introduction to Pure Phenomenology,* trans. by W. R. Boyce (New York: Macmillan Co., 1931), p. 11.

14. W. D. Ross, *Aristotle* (London: Methuen and Co., 1930), p. 20.

15. *Philosophical Investigations,* p. 48.

16. Ibid., p. 33.

17. *The Blue Book,* pp. 58–59. (See note 6 above.)

18. *Philosophical Investigations,* p. 43.

19. Ibid., p. 48.

20. *The Blue Book,* p. 41.

21. Ibid., p. 46.

22. Ibid., p. 56.

23. *Philosophical Investigations,* p. 48.

24. *The Blue Book,* p. 57.

25. *Wittgenstein's Lectures, Cambridge 1932–1935,* p. 69.

26. *The Yellow Book.*

II

Necessity and Philosophy

It has always been thought that technical, reasoned philosophy is the comprehensive science of reality and brings under its special scrutiny such fundamental concepts as *space, time, contingency, mind, causation, language.* It has been said that the task of philosophy is to delineate "the generic traits" of reality; and even if its scope were less than this, the value placed on philosophy would fade away if it were thought incapable of yielding ontological information. The process of value-deflation has in fact set in, for the classical notion of philosophy has begun to wear thin. The philosophical tree of knowledge has so far borne only phantom fruit and has created intractable disputation. A closer look at philosophy can no longer be dismissed or thought unnecessary. In the last fifty years, the work of G. E. Moore, the logical positivists, and Ludwig Wittgenstein has made it uncertain *what* a philosopher is talking about when he says that motion does not exist or that no two terms are really synonymous, although it is still natural to think that the first statement is about the occurrence of motion and the second is about the existence of synonymy in a language.

I

Wittgenstein has said, with the air of giving utterance to a commonly recognized fact: "Philosophical problems are, of course, not empirical."[1] To my knowledge, he made hardly any concrete attempt to show the correctness of this metaphilosophical thesis; but if correct, it would help us understand why a time-honored investigation that professedly wishes to discover truth about what there is employs none of the methods of the natural sciences. It is hardly necessary to point out the fact that there are no philosophical laboratories; philosophy has no recourse to special observations of its own, as against those made in the sciences and in ordinary life. The implication would seem to be that philosophy is neither observational nor experimental. Wittgenstein's remark underscores the inappropriateness of saying that observation or an experiment shows that motion does not occur or that synonymy does not exist.

Some of Wittgenstein's remarks were based upon deep perceptions into philosophy, and his claim that philosophical problems are not empirical is a result of insight. However, it is by no means true that philosophers in general agree with this claim. He was speaking for himself and in disregard of contrary opinions implied or expressed in philosophical writings; and at least some of these opinions need to be examined. What was obvious to him is certainly not obvious to all philosophers, many of whom explicitly deny his proposition about the character of philosophical problems. Bertrand Russell, for instance, has asserted that the longstanding controversy over the existence of a causal tie amongst occurrences reduces to one of "empirical fact."[2] According to him, the question is, "Do we or do we not sometimes perceive a relation which can be called causal?"[3] It is not necessary to look long in the literature to find accounts of philosophical investigations that any normal reader would understand to be describing empirical procedures.

I shall limit my discussion to descriptions of three philosophical procedures: one, a procedure that seems to have recourse to an experiment; another, that appears to fall back on observation; and a third, that seems to resort to a search. The basic proposition of F. H. Bradley's famous essay, *Appearance and Reality,* is that "Sentient experience . . . is reality, and what is not this is not real. We may say, in other words, that there is no being or fact outside of that which is commonly called psychical existence. Feeling, thought, and volition . . . are all the material of existence, and there is no other material, actual or even possible."[4] Parmenides, it will be remembered, maintained that what is thinkable coincides with what there is, and Bradley, we might say, maintained that psychical phenomena coincide with what there is. Parmenides appears to have tried to establish his thesis by means of a thought experiment, one that consists of attempting to grasp in conception *non-being,* or what does not exist. Bradley, in seemingly plain words, invites us to make the experiment of removing from any designated object all feeling and perception and attempting to conceive the remainder. He writes: "When the experiment is made strictly, I can myself conceive of nothing else than the experienced. . . . And as I cannot try to think of it without realizing either that I am not thinking at all, or that I am thinking of it against my will as being experienced, I am driven to the conclusion that for me experience is the same as reality."[5] C. H. Langford makes a similar experiment in the laboratory of his mind: "When we try to envisage the unitary meaning of a statement of this kind ["Men exist and men do not exist"], we find that this is quite impossible, and that therefore it has no single meaning, but rather one meaning corresponding to one part of the verbal expression, and another to another."[6] Wittgenstein also invites us to make a mental experiment, the experiment of trying to think of the meaning of an expression without thinking of the expression. In his own words:

> Make the following experiment: say and mean a sentence, e.g., "It will probably rain tomorrow." Now think the same thought again, mean what you just meant, without saying anything (either aloud or to yourself). If thinking that it will rain tomorrow accompanied saying it will rain tomorrow, then just do the first activity and leave out the second. — If thinking and speaking stood in the relation of the words and the melody of a song, we could leave out the speaking and do the thinking just as we can sing the tune without the words.[7]

The outcome of his experiment, as is well known, is the anti-Platonic thesis that the meaning of an expression is not an "accompaniment," but the use it has in the language.

If we can put aside for a moment the idea suggested by the words of these philosophers, and reflect on the words themselves, it can easily be realized that these words are not actually being used to describe an empirical procedure, the experimental attempt to conceive or think or envisage an idea or a proposition. It is necessary to keep in mind the difference between conceptual impossibility and what might be called "natural" impossibility, i.e., between impossibility built into concepts and impossibility built into phenomena, psychological as well as physical. It is important to be clear about the difference, for example, between the impossibility of physically being in one place while being in another place a mile away and the impossibility of dashing from the one place to the other in a minute, and the difference between the impossibility of carrying out in one's mind the decimal expansion of π to the thousandth place and the impossibility of conceiving a six-sided pentagon. What is logically impossible to conceive is not something that transcends anyone's powers of conception; instead, it is by its very nature not subject to being conceived. This means that an expression whose meaning is a logically impossible concept or proposition has no descriptive function in the language. The expression does not thereby lack meaning, but the meaning it has is such as to prevent it from functioning descriptively. It is readily seen that the likeness between the following sentences tends to conceal an important difference between them:

(α) It is impossible to carry out in one's head the decimal expansion of π to the thousandth place.
(β) It is impossible to conceive of the completed expansion of π.

Sentence (α) tells us what is being declared impossible: the phrase "carries out in one's head the decimal expansion of π to the thousandth place" describes a mental feat that is beyond the powers of ordinary mortals. In this respect (β) differs radically from (α). The phrase "conceives the completed expansion of π" does not refer to a theoretical act of conceiving something, the reason for this being that "completed expansion of π" has no use to refer to an expansion. It makes *no descriptive sense* to say, "Mount Everest has been climbed, and to match this feat the completed expansion of π has been conceived."

Paralleling this difference is the difference between experimentally attempting to carry out in one's head the expansion of π to the thousandth place and experimentally attempting to grasp in thought the completed expansion. The implication of the fact that the completed expansion of π is *logically* inconceivable, and not that it is psychologically impossible to conceive, is that it is logically impossible to *try* to conceive it. To put this more explicitly in terms of the language involved, the fact that it makes no sense to speak of thinking of the completed expansion of π implies that it makes no sense to speak of trying to think of the completed expansion — any more than it makes sense to speak of trying to bring to a stop a stationary object. The correlated linguistic fact is that the expression "conceives the completed expansion of π" has no descriptive use in the language; and this implies that the expression "tries to conceive the completed expansion" lacks descriptive use also. Trying to think of a completed expansion of which one has no idea is no more possible than trying to milk a goat that does not exist or trying to remember a face that has never been seen. A sentence of the form "experimentally tried to think so-and-so" refers to no experiment if "so-and-so" describes nothing.

These remarks apply directly to the philosophical experiments made by Bradley, Langford, and Wittgenstein. And this fact confirms Wittgenstein's general observation about the nature of philosophical problems: a philosophical experiment is not an empirical experiment, whatever else it may be. The general maxim may be stated in the following way: if the outcome of an investigation is that something is logically impossible, then the investigation is not empirical.

Consider, now, the putative Gedanken experiment reported by Langford. His attempt, and failure, to envisage the unitary meaning of the sentence "Men exist and men do not exist" is an attempt and a failure in semantic appearance only. Parenthetically, it is worth noting that there can be no attempting anything without the possibility, in principle, of succeeding; and there can be no failure to achieve something without the possibility, in principle, of achieving it. When Langford tells us that he found it "quite impossible" to envisage the proposition expressed by "Men exist and men do not exist," as against the propositions expressed by the two parts of the conjunctive sentence, he implies that the impossibility is one of logic, that it is conceptual, and not an impossibility in nature. It is a correct use of descriptive English to say, "The king's men tried to put Humpty Dumpty together again, but failed"; but it is only a semantic joke to say, "Langford tried to combine the two propositions 'Men exist' and 'Men do not exist' into a single proposition and found that his mind was not up to the task." It would not be a correct use of language, as he employs it, for him to go on and say, imitating Hume: "If anyone upon serious and unprejudiced reflection thinks he has envisaged the unitary meaning which I have failed to envisage, I must allow him that he may be in the right as well as I." The reason that the language he used to refer to his putative experiment describes no empirical procedure is that since the sentence "Men exist and men do not exist" expresses what is logically impossible, in his use of the word "proposition" it does not express a single proposition. That is, Langford is so using the word "proposition" that it does not apply to what is normally referred to as a logically impossible proposition: an indicative sentence having a self-contradictory meaning no more expresses a proposition than "greatest prime number" describes a number. The consequence of his contracted use of the word "proposition" is that the phrase "unitary meaning of a self-contradictory sentence"[8] could not have been used by him to refer to the subject of a thought-experiment, something the achievement of which he found "quite impossible."

It is a simple matter to see that this line of reasoning applies also to Bradley's experiment regarding the possibility of there being anything that is not an experience, and to Wittgenstein's invitation to try to think of the meaning of an expression in separation from the expression. Their investigations, like that of Langford, are empirical only in delusive linguistic appearance: the words are the words of science, but the substance of science is absent. Bradley was so using the words "experience is the same as reality" that they express a logical necessity, with the consequence that the phrase "a reality that is not an experience" denotes what is logically impossible. That is to say, for *him,* in his philosophical lexicon, "exists but is neither feeling, thought, nor volition" has no use to describe what exists. He clearly tells us this when he says, "I can myself conceive of nothing else than the experienced"; for he certainly does not mean to imply that someone else just might succeed where he had failed. He can be certain that no one will succeed, because the expression "something other than the experienced," in his use of language, is made to stand for a logical impossibility; it is an expression from which application has been withheld. In Bradley's way of speaking, the phrase "not sentient experience" describes nothing and thus describes nothing that might be investigated empirically, by observation or by an experiment. Bradley's account of his procedure misrepresents what he was actually doing; it conjures up an inappropriate, if intriguing, picture of the philosopher at work.

Consider now the reason Wittgenstein adduces against the Platonic theory that the literal meaning of an expression is an entity that accompanies the expression and can exist apart from it. It is presented, verbally, in the form of an experimental attempt to think of the meaning by itself, an attempt comparable to trying to think of a person's mirror image actively continuing by itself, in the absence of the person. The supposed outcome, unlike that of the mirror image, is the impossibility of thinking of the meaning apart from its expression. As in the preceding cases, the impossibility has to be taken as logical. For Wittgenstein did not mean to leave it an open possibility that Platonic philosophers might have succeeded where he had failed. This possibility could be excluded with complete assurance only by *making* the word "impossible" in the sentence "It is impossible to think of the meaning of an expression apart from the expression" denote the impossibility of logic.

Philosophical investigations are in some cases presented as falling under an empirical procedure employing observation and induction. To all appearances, instances of a certain class are inspected and generalizations are constructed on the basis of the findings. But if Wittgenstein's dictum is correct, the appearance that natural science is being practiced is a bogus facade behind which a different kind of work is being done. It needs to be said immediately that if it turns out that philosophers misrepresent their investigations, as in the preceding cases, there is no hint of conscious deception to be found in their writings. They are more like magicians who, because of deep inner needs, believe in their own tricks rather than like the rascally tailors in the fairy tale who were aware of their hoax. Berkeley observed that "could men but forbear to amuse themselves with words"9 they would soon agree with him that matter does not exist. And if Wittgenstein's dictum turns out to be correct, it will lend plausibility to the suspicion that philosophers choose to amuse themselves with words rather than to work with things. Indeed, a number of Wittgenstein's later thoughts have already given substance to the uneasy notion that the dwelling philosophers have built for themselves with so much pride and in which they find their pleasure and security is an insubstantial shadow cast by the invisible manipulation of words.

Berkeley is an example of an important philosopher who seeks knowledge of things by "leaving concepts"10 and going to the things themselves for answers, which is presumably why he counts as an empiricist. This is the way his quest looks at first glance. Berkeley undertakes to determine whether causation exists amongst phenomena, and he seemingly does this with the help of observation. The reader of the following passage might well note the imagery it conjures up:

All our ideas, sensations, notions, or the things which we perceive, by whatsoever names they may be distinguished, are visibly inactive: there is nothing of power or agency included in them. So that one idea or object of thought cannot produce or make any alteration in another. To be satisfied of the truth of this, there is nothing else requisite but a bare observation of our ideas. For, since they and every part in them exist only in the mind, it follows that there is nothing in them but what is perceived; but whoever shall attend to his ideas, whether of sense or reflexion, will not perceive in them power or activity; there is, therefore, no such thing contained in them.[11]

Berkeley's assertion that *all* ideas are causally inactive goes beyond the statement that his ideas are without exception causally inactive, and it is to be supposed that the generalization is arrived at inductively from his experience.

When Berkeley reports that inspection discloses no agency in his ideas and that they are all visibly inactive, the picture we get is that of someone who looks at the people in a room and reports that all of them have upturned noses. In advance of looking at the people there is no telling what the shapes of their noses are, and in advance of attending to his ideas Berkeley could only speculate about their inactivity. In the case of the people's noses observation shows a rather surprising thing, and it is clear that observation *might* show a different and less surprising group of people: looking *could* reveal the opposite of what it in fact happens to reveal. In Berkeley's case also, if looking is relevant to and required for the determination of the facts, looking could, possibly, have shown the opposite of what Berkeley reported. The mark of an empirical investigation is that the opposite of what it discovers remains conceivable and could, therefore, have been discovered instead. The outcome of an investigation that employs observation cannot imply the *logical* impossibility of the opposite.

A second reading of Berkeley's statement will bring to our attention an omission that it is natural to overlook. It contains no hint of what it would be like for an idea to be active. It turns out that the term "inactive idea," which at first glance appears to have descriptive content, i.e., to function the way "indolent adolescent" functions, is not linked to "active idea," and this omission is not an oversight. It tells us that the term "active idea," in Berkeley's way of speaking, has been given no descriptive assignment. The following sentence, which continues the above quoted passage, makes this evident: "A little attention will discover to us that the very being of an idea implies passiveness and inertness." To say that the *very being* of an idea implies inertness is just another way of saying that being an idea *entails* being inert. Hence, in Berkeley's use of the word "idea" the phrase "idea that is not inert," or the term "active idea," denotes a logically impossible concept. The term does not refer to anything that observation could, in principle, reveal. Looking is not relevant to determining whether ideas are inactive. For if observation could discover for us that ideas are inactive, it *could*, in principle, discover the opposite, which is ruled out as being logically impossible. The sentence "Ideas are visibly inactive" has been given no use to refer to anything that is or could become visible to an observer. If Berkeley had given it such a use, the phrase "visibly active idea" would make descriptive sense. But this he prevents by his declaration that "the very being of an idea" implies inertness.

A. J. Ayer is another philosopher who sometimes appears to make use of observation in the practice of philosophy. He has written that when anyone perceives a physical object ". . . all that his senses reveal to him is the presence of sense-data."[12] It is natural to take these words to be stating a conclusion about what seeing and feeling a shilling, tasting an avocado, or smelling a melon comes to, a conclusion that is based on an inspection of what our senses reveal to us. It appears to be an inductive generalization from instances such as these. Ayer goes on to append the following comment: "This does not mean that [a person's] sensory experiences must be of the same sort we are all familiar with: they might be very queer; but however queer they were they would still be experiences of sense."[13] The point of this comment is not immediately clear; but it seems to be that nonstandard or distorting conditions under which things may be experienced have been included in the investigation, and in such cases it has also turned out that our senses are confined to revealing sense-data.

This is the import of his words on a first reading, and it is not to be supposed that the idea of scientific activity they put into our minds is wholly unintentional. If, now, we look at his words a second time and attend to the language that surrounds them, a different reading emerges. In his use of the term "sense-datum" the following sentence gives expression to a logical entailment: "If anyone is perceiving a physical object it *follows* that he is sensing a sense-datum: and not only that, but that all that his senses reveal to him is the presence of sense-data."[14] In his special way of speaking, it is correct to say that it is logically impossible for anyone to perceive an object and to be presented with something that is *not* a sense-datum. It turns out that in Ayer's phenomenalistic language the sentence "All that our senses reveal to us are sense-data" does not express an experiential proposition, one that an inspection of our sense-contents would tend to establish or upset. No empirical investigation is relevant to Ayer's proposition, any more than an empirical investigation would be relevant to the proposition that all blue things are colored. It is of some interest to notice that Ayer himself gives oblique recognition to this fact when he remarks that the sense-datum notation enables one to learn facts about the nature of physical objects, "but not in the way that doing science does."[15] Freud has remarked that we cannot get elsewhere what we get from science, and we may well be puzzled to know what Ayer learns about the *nature* of stars, mountains, and the water he drinks, from the adoption of a notation. What seems to come through is that semantic inventiveness is at work.

It should be pointed out that we may reach the same understanding of Ayer's claim about what our senses reveal to us by noticing that it is not linked with a description of anything that could, theoretically, go against it. For we are not told what in addition to, and other than, sense-data our senses might bring to us. Ayer does not say what would falsify the proposition that all they reveal to us are sense-data; it is clear from his omission that he has ruled out the possibility of providing such a description, which means that the proposition is in principle not open to falsification. Thus, it is the kind of statement that is by its nature not open to empirical testing, any more than is the proposition that all blue things are colored. As Ayer is using language, it is just as inappropriate to speak of inspecting our sense-contents in order to determine what our senses reveal to us as it would be to speak of examining blue things in order to determine whether they are all colored.

There remains to be considered the third kind of case in which a seemingly empirical investigation is conducted to determine the truth-value of a philosophical claim. Essential to this kind of investigation is a search, or something that is represented as a search. Nonphilosophical explorations readily come to mind. In astronomy the existence and location of Pluto were predicted by E. C. Pickering, and some years later Pluto was found by C. W. Tombaugh. In anatomy the quest for the eternity bone had, regrettably, a different outcome. In philosophy Hume has recorded the three most famous searches in the literature of the subject: for a continued and independent physical object, for a simple and continued psychological entity, and for agency, or the "tie" of causation, in the external world. With regard to the continuing disagreements revolving around the idea of causation since Hume, Russell has said that they come down to disagreement over whether we sometimes perceive agency in the world. He sums up the situation, from Hume to the present, in the following words: "Hume says no, his adversaries say yes, and it is not easy to see how evidence can be produced by either side."[16] Causation in the world seems to be as elusive as the Loch Ness monster in Scotland, attested to by some and denied by others. Nevertheless, Russell makes the comment that Hume's conclusion is in agreement with scientific practice: "So far as the physical sciences are concerned, Hume is *wholly* in the right: such propositions as 'A causes B' are never to be accepted, and our inclination to accept them is to be explained by the laws of habit and association."[17]

Hume describes his search for agency, or natural necessity, in the following well-known passage: ". . . I consider in what objects necessity is commonly supposed to lie; and, finding that it is always ascribed to causes and effects, I turn my eyes to two objects supposed to be placed in the relation, and examine them in all the situations of which they are susceptible. I immediately perceive that they are *contiguous* in time and place, and that the object we call cause *precedes* the other we call effect. In no one instance can I go further, nor is it possible for me to discover any third relation between them."[18] Hume seems to be reporting the negative outcome of an empirical search, and to the assertion that agency does not exist he joins a challenge: "If anyone thinks proper to refute this assertion, he need not put himself to the trouble of inventing any long chain of reasoning, but may at once show us an instance of cause where we discover the power or operating principle."[19] He stands ready to be convinced if others can exhibit to him what he himself has not been able to find; and this seems a scientifically correct attitude to take.

If we re-examine Hume's account of his quest and its outcome, we see that it issues in two negative results, not just one; and they are not compatible with each other. One is that agency does not exist in the physical world. The other is that we have no *idea* of agency: "All ideas derive from and represent impressions. We never have any impression that contains any power or efficacy. We never, therefore, have any idea of power."[20] The idea of agency is both "impossible and imaginary."[21] And it cannot be both. For if, like the idea of a winged horse, it is imaginary or fictitious, there could in principle be a corresponding reality; and if, like the idea of a cube with eleven edges, it is impossible, there could be no corresponding reality: if it were both imaginary and impossible, it would be such that there both could be and could not be something answering to it. It is now easy to see that Hume's report of his procedure, instead of detailing an empirical search, describes one in verbal appearance only. An inquiry cannot even commence, much less be carried on, if its outcome is that there is no idea of what is being sought. One can no more search for something answering to an idea that does not exist than one can open a window that does not exist. There is no such thing as finding something that answers to a nonexistent idea.

The cases considered, all of which appear to involve either an experiment, a careful observation, or a search, have turned out to be in agreement with Wittgenstein's claim about the nature of philosophical problems; they are not as first represented. We may be puzzled to know what Hume's philosophical investigation, Berkeley's examination of ideas, and Bradley's experiment are, but it is certain that they are not the empirical inquiries one naturally takes them to be. We might say that Wittgenstein is in Hume's position of being able to present philosophers with a challenge: "If anyone think proper to refute the statement that philosophical demonstrations are never empirical, he need not put himself to the trouble of inventing any long chain of reasoning, but may at once show us an instance to the contrary." Hume's demand to be shown an instance of causation over and above what are normally regarded as instances of causation, such as the action of one billiard ball on another, may be a semantic deception of a piece with the method he described. The demand, however, to be shown a nonspurious empirical investigation in philosophy is a genuine request, for we know what an empirical investigation is like.

Wittgenstein's claim about the logical character of philosophical problems implies not only that philosophical investigations are not empirical but also that philosophical theories are not empirical. Without arguing the matter, it would seem clear that a factual proposition cannot be a proper answer to a nonfactual question. If, for example, the question raised by Zeno regarding the existence of motion is not empirical, the statement that Diogenes supported by standing up and walking in view of everyone would not be a relevant answer to the question. And we could understand why the problem was not thought solved, and also why we tend not to treat Diogenes' demonstration seriously, and even to take it as a joke. It is interesting in this connection to note that Wittgenstein has remarked that philosophy could be written as a series of jokes.[22]

A relevant answer to a philosophical question will have to share its logical character with that of the question; and if a philosophical question is not a request for empirical information, a philosophical theory does not supply empirical information. Immanuel Kant argued for the view, still held by many philosophers, that a proposition could be both *a priori* and about things, which implies that it could be informative of what there is and also be nonempirical. There is no question that philosophical theories appear to be about the world, and it is widely taken for granted that they are. The possibility that suggests itself is that philosophical questions are requests for *a priori* information about things, and philosophical theories are logically necessary statements about things but do not require empirical testing.

II

Wittgenstein once stated, "The great problem around which everything I write turns is: 'Is there an order in the world *a priori,* and if so what does it consist in?'"[23] His answer in the *Tractatus* (5.634) was that "There is no *a priori* order of things." Both the philosophical question and the philosophical answer appear to be about the world; and if they are, the one is a request for *a priori* information which the other provides. In a number of places in his later writings he asserts, either explicitly or by implication, that when the words "can," "must," and "cannot" occur in philosophical sentences, they are used in their logical sense: logical possibility, logical necessity, and logical impossibility.[24] Ayer's sentence, "It is logically impossible for a sense-experience to belong to the sense-history of more than a single self,"[25] is an illustration. What it says is equivalently and perhaps more naturally said by the sentence, "A sense-experience *cannot* belong to the sense-history of more than one self."

The importance of determining whether philosophical propositions are *a priori* in character, and whether they make declarations about what is logically possible, impossible, or necessary, goes without saying. Before taking up this matter, the possible relationships between empirical propositions and logically necessary ones must be investigated. The question as to whether an *a priori* proposition can, in principle, tell us anything about the world also requires examination. It is important to do this without making use of *philosophical* theories about the nature of necessity, such as conventionalism and Platonism.

A logically necessary proposition, one having its truth-value by inner necessity,[26] is such that its actual truth-value is its only theoretically possible truth-value. Using C. I. Lewis's symbol for logical possibility, "*p* is necessarily true" becomes " $\sim \Diamond \sim p$," and the point about the truth-value of an *a priori* proposition is made perspicuous in the following identities: $\sim \Diamond \sim p = \sim \Diamond (\sim p)$, $\sim \Diamond \sim (\sim p) = \sim \Diamond p$. By contrast, an empirical proposition is such that the truth-value it happens to have does not crowd out the possibility of its having the opposite truth-value. The fact that p is true does not eliminate $\Diamond \sim p$, and the fact that p is false does not eliminate $\Diamond p$; that is, $p . \Diamond \sim p$ and $\sim p . \Diamond p$ are consistent conjunctions. An empirical statement is one whose actual truth-value is not its only theoretically possible truth-value, and this is also the case with regard to contingent statements. This fact makes it natural to identify them. However, there is a special class of propositions whose actual truth-values are not their only possible truth-values, but to which some philosophers prefer not to apply the term "empirical." These are so-called "basic propositions," such as *I am in pain* and *There looks to me to be a lake in the distance,* which, although they could be false, are not open to verification procedures by the persons asserting them. I can say with sense, "Perhaps my pain is caused by an abscessed tooth," but I cannot with sense say, "Perhaps I am in pain." Allowing the difference between basic propositions (which count as contingent) and non-basic empirical propositions, the important thing for the present investigation is the property of possibly having a truth-value other than the actual one. In order to avoid a monotonous vocabulary, the words "empirical" and "contingent" will be used interchangeably.

The problem of determining how an *a priori* proposition might be related to an empirical proposition comes down, for the present purpose, to finding the answers to the following two questions:

(1) Can an *a priori* proposition entail an empirical proposition? That is, can a proposition having only one possible truth-value entail a proposition having two possible truth-values?

(2) Can an *a priori* proposition be entailed by, or be deducible from, an empirical proposition? That is, can a proposition having two possible truth-values entail a proposition having only one possible truth-value?

And there is a connected question, concerning the relation of an *a priori* proposition to reality:

(3) Can a proposition having only one possible truth-value present a claim about things?

To make a parenthetical remark about (3), if philosophical propositions are *a priori,* such that their truth-values are discoverable "without leaving concepts," and if logically necessary propositions are capable of conveying information about the world, then we can understand why philosophers have not found it necessary to make use of laboratories or scientific aids to the senses, such as microscopes or sonar devices.

The first of the three questions would seem hardly to stand in need of investigation. Hume stated that nothing contingent can follow from what is necessary. This would seem obvious, and it could pass without discussion except for the frequently asserted statement that a necessarily true proposition is also true as a matter of fact. The normal reading of the phrase "true as a matter of fact" is the reading it has in a sentence like "It is as a matter of fact true that Brutus stabbed Caesar." What is in fact true could in fact be false: it could, in principle, be true that Brutus did not stab Caesar. The implication of the claim that what is necessarily true is also in fact true is that logically necessary propositions have empirical consequences. This thesis underlies much of the reasoning of theologically oriented metaphysicians like Descartes, Leibniz, and Spinoza, who profess to demonstrate truths about the world from the necessary existence of a supreme being.

Looked at by itself, uncolored by philosophical theories in which it might be embedded, the claim that what is necessarily true is also factually true can readily be seen to be false and Hume's thesis to be correct. A proposition with only one possible truth-value cannot imply a proposition with more than one possible truth-value, for the reason that a necessarily true antecedent precludes any other than the implied truth-value from being a possible truth-value of the consequent. In other words, the truth-value imposed on what is implied by a necessary statement will be its only possible truth-value, which means that the statement is not empirical.

The second question, regarding whether it is possible for an empirical proposition to have *a priori* consequences, or whether a proposition with two theoretically possible truth-values can entail a proposition having only one possible truth-value, has been answered in the affirmative by philosophers and logicians. Wittgenstein, for example, has said, "A tautology follows from all propositions,"[27] his reason perhaps being that a tautology "says nothing." Putting aside his special view about what a tautology says, a tautology has only one possible truth-value, and if it follows from all propositions, it follows from empirical propositions. An apparently plain case of a tautology being a consequence of a contingent proposition is a statement such as, *If poltergeists exist, then either poltergeists exist or poltergeists do not exist.* To many logicians the statement that a tautology, and in general any logically necessary truth, is deducible from a contingent proposition, presents itself as intuitively evident. C. I. Lewis has attempted to fortify this intuition with the following well-known demonstration (given here in somewhat abbreviated form):

(1) If p is true, then either p is true and q false or p and q are both true:

$$p. \, \prec \, :p. \sim q. \vee .p.q.$$

The consequent of (1) is equivalent to and replaceable by

$$p. \sim q \vee q.$$

Since we have

(3) $\qquad\qquad\qquad p. \prec .p. \sim q \vee q,$

we may infer $\qquad\qquad p. \prec .q \vee \sim q.$

Lewis goes on to say, "Thus tautologies in general are deducible from any premise we please: the theorem

$$\sim \diamondsuit \sim q. \prec .p \prec q$$

states a fact about deducibility."[28]

Despite protestations to the contrary, maintaining that a necessary truth is deducible from any proposition, for example, that *A mouse is an animal* is deducible from, or can be "figured out,"[29] or calculated from, *There is a mouse in Westminster Abbey,* would be to introduce a paradox as violent as any encountered in philosophy. A logician who announces it is able to do so with no show of embarrassment only because it is tacitly understood to be a piece of *Alice Through the Looking Glass* logic, a game played with the term "deducible from," and is understood as such by those who debate it. There is no question that *A mouse is an animal* is strictly implied by *There is a mouse in Westminster Abbey* and that $(a+b)^2 = a^2 + 2ab + b^2$ is strictly implied by *Brutus stabbed Caesar.* But these implications are not paradoxical. They only produce an air of paradox when they are described as cases of deducibility, or entailment. How a logician can with complete assurance say, "...strict implication, $p < q$, coincides in its properties with the relation 'q is deducible from p' "[30] very likely has the following explanation: to his explicit definition of "$p < q$" he has added an invisible Pickwickian redefinition of "deducible," which permits him to replace "$p < q$" by "q is deducible from p." Hidden redefinition is the recipe making the properties of strict implication coincide with those of deducibility.

Without attempting to give a full account of deducibility, which would require seeing how it works in various contexts, one general condition that a pair of propositions must satisfy in order for one of them to be deducible from the other needs to be highlighted. The condition is that the denial of the putative implication between them, i.e., asserting the antecedent and denying the consequent, gives rise to an inconsistency *between* them. Letting "ϕ" denote inconsistency, a conditional statement, If p, then q, will be a case of q following from, or being deducible from, p only if $p. \sim q$ implies $p \phi \sim q$. If there is no inconsistency between p *and* $\sim q$, regardless of any inconsistency within $\sim q$ itself, there is no entailment between p and q, and there is no deducing q from p. There is no inference-bridge *from p to q* unless p is inconsistent with $\sim q$. Where the inconsistency is absent, q will be logically idle, and plays no role in the deduction of q.

Consider again Lewis's demonstration of the theorem, $\sim \Diamond \sim q . < . p < q$, which, according to him, shows that strict implication is the same as entailment. It is readily seen that his proof is reversible. Beginning with $p < p : p . < . q \vee \sim q$, from which $p . < . q \vee \sim q$ is detached, we arrive at the first line, $p . < : p . q . \vee . p . \sim q$:

$$
\begin{array}{ll}
(1) & p < p : p . < . q \vee \sim q \\
(2) & p . < . p . q \vee \sim q \\
(3) & p . < : p . q . \vee . p . \sim q .
\end{array}
$$

Read in reverse order, we can see what has happened. An implication not resting on an inconsistency between antecedent and denied consequent, viz., $p . < . q \vee \sim q$, rides in on an implication, i.e., $p < p$, which does rest on an inconsistency between antecedent and denied consequent. An implication holding simply because the negation of its consequent embodies an inconsistency is carried to the conclusion, $p . < . q \vee \sim q$, by an implication-statement in the negation of whose consequent the antecedent is involved. A hitch-hiker is represented as a paying passenger by the use of a distributive rule of logic.

Whatever else may be involved, if there is a relation of deducibility *between* two propositions, there will be an inconsistency between the antecedent and the negated consequent and not only an inconsistency in the negated consequent. When both antecedent and consequent of a statement of the form *if p, then q* are empirical, the impossibility of its denial, $\sim \Diamond (p . \sim q)$, will rest on p being inconsistent with $\sim q$; and the inconsistency, and also the logical impossibility, will vanish with the suppression of p. When p is contingent and q necessary, suppressing p clearly will not remove the inconsistency in $\sim q$.

There is a special class of cases in which a necessary proposition appears to be entailed by a contingent one, for example, *if p, then p $\vee \sim p$*. Here the antecedent is a component of the consequent. The denial of this implication gives rise to an inconsistency that obtains between antecedent and negated consequent, between p and $\sim p . p$. It needs no second glance to see that the inconsistency between them simply iterates the inconsistency within the negated consequent. We have $\sim \Diamond (p . \sim p . p)$, which may be rewritten $\sim \Diamond (\sim p . p . p)$, which is nothing more than $\sim \Diamond (\sim p . p)$. There are not *two* inconsistencies, one inconsistency between $\sim p$ and p and a second within $\sim p . p$; there is only one. The claim that $p \vee \sim p$ (or *if p, then p*) is deducible from p is only an apparent instance of a logically necessary proposition being entailed by a contingent proposition; for *if p, then p $\vee \sim p$* is only an artificially expanded version of $p \lor \sim p$, and deflates into it. As for the general proposition, *if p, then q* $\lor \sim q$, where *p* is not a component of the consequent, there is no inconsistency between antecedent and negated consequent, and the implication is not an entailment.

An implication-claim the denial of which results in an inconsistency between antecedent and negated consequent, where the inconsistency is duplicated within the negated consequent, fails to satisfy a condition for one proposition to be *deducible* from another, and is not a correct entailment-claim. Thus, the statement,

If there is a mouse in Westminster, then a mouse is an animal

or the statement,

If there are four goats in the barn, then 2 goats + 2 goats = 4 goats,

cannot correctly be restated as an entailment, such that its consequent follows from its antecedent, although it is correctly restatable as a strict implication. To make an immediate application of the principle that an *a priori* proposition cannot be deduced from one that is contingent, or that a proposition having only one possible truth-value cannot be calculated from a proposition having two possible truth-values, the metaphysical claim that the contingent is grounded in the necessary can be seen to be in obvious violation of this logical principle. All arguments professing to demonstrate the existence of a necessary Being from the existence of a contingent thing can be known to be invalid without examining them.

The third question requiring investigation is whether it is possible for an *a priori* truth, e.g., the proposition that a material thing can be in one place only at any given time, to provide information about things, i.e., to inform us of what there is in the world. Bertrand Russell has said that $2 + 2$ equals 4 even far out in space, and the suggestion of his words is that the arithmetical truth states a fact about things in at least some regions of space in addition to our own region. It is not to be questioned that many philosophers have thought that at least some logically necessary propositions are about things and supply us with knowledge of them. Leibniz, for instance, distinguished between truths of fact and truths of reason, and held that the latter were true for all possible worlds. He also held that there was no real difference between the two kinds of truths, that a truth of fact was an infinitely complex analytic proposition—which would seem to imply that there is only one possible world. This idea perhaps underlies all philosophical thinking, empirical as well as rationalistic thinking, and any other kind of thought that counts as philosophical. For the dream of the philosopher is to be able to learn what is in the Book of Knowledge, not by studying its pages, but by consulting his mind. Kant gave expression to this dream with his conception of synthetic *a priori* propositions, which, like analytic propositions, are truths of reason, but unlike them supposedly augment our knowledge of the things referred to by their subject-terms. They thus provide ontological information.

Tautological propositions seem clearly to be one class of necessarily true propositions that make no declaration about the contents of any possible world. Wittgenstein maintained that tautologies "say nothing," and hence say nothing about the world. If we hold that they are true for all possible worlds, then we shall have to go on to hold that this is so because they are not falsifiable by any possible world. It requires neither subtle reasoning nor acute perception to see that saying unicorns either exist or do not exist, or that if there are no unicorns, then there are no unicorns, is to say nothing whatever about the existence of unicorns. It does not serve as a possible answer to the question, "Do unicorns exist?" The same thing is seen to hold for tautologies of any degree of complexity. Consider for a moment the slightly more complex tautology, *If q, then either p or q*. To say, for example, that if pelicans exist, then either storks or pelicans exist, is to say nothing about the existence of either pelicans or storks, and hence is to say nothing about what there is in any possible world. It is the same with tautologies the components of which refer to properties of things, i.e., to the nature of what there is. The statement that Jones's necktie is lavender or not lavender says nothing about the color of Jones's necktie, and the statement that what Jones is wearing around his neck is a scarf or is not a scarf says nothing about the nature of what Jones is wearing around his neck.

Wittgenstein has said that tautologies are not pictures of reality,[31] that "They do not represent any possible situations,"[32] and this fits in with the idea that tautological propositions say nothing about what there is. The question now is whether any proposition that is characterized by logical necessity can be a "picture," or a description, of things, i.e., whether a proposition whose actual truth-value is its only possible truth-value is prevented from saying anything about things by the way it possesses its truth-value. To put the question in another way: Do propositions that share with tautologies the attribute of being necessarily true, and therefore like them have no truth-conditions, also share with them the property of standing in no "representational relation to reality"?[33]

One reason for thinking that a proposition which is unconditionally true makes no declaration about any possible world is that it cannot, in principle, be falsified by any conceivable reality, nor can it be made true by any conceivable reality. For being unconditionally true, no condition of things and no state of affairs could *make* it true; and being necessarily true, no conceivable reality could upset it. The truth-value of a logically necessary proposition is not subject to change; hence, no imaginable change in the world could affect it. The conclusion to draw with regard to *a priori* true propositions would seem to be that they are ontologically mute. Their truth-value is not determined by what the world is like, and therefore they say nothing about what the world is like: they do not "stand in any representational relation to reality." The consequence of this line of reasoning is that such an assertion as "A shilling cannot be in two different pockets at the same time" says nothing about where a shilling cannot be; it says nothing about shillings. And the assertion that a mouse is an animal says nothing about what a mouse is; it says nothing about mice. Russell's remark that 2 plus 2 equals 4 even far out in space makes no factual claim about the relationship between the arithmetical equation $2 + 2 = 4$ and its range of operation in space.

Some philosophers contend that a distinction should be made amongst the properties of things, which, if correct, implies that a proposition can be both about things and *a priori* true. It is easily seen that Kant's conception of synthetic *a priori* propositions implies the Aristotelian view that some of the properties of a thing are logically essential to it, without which the thing cannot exist. Consider the following statements:

> Every effect has a cause.
> Every change has a cause.
> Every change is abrupt.

The first statement is analytic and only iterates a component of the subject-term. The second, according to Kant, makes an attribution; it ascribes a logically necessary property to what is referred to by the subject-term. The third makes a contingent attribution; it ascribes a property to occurrences that they could fail to have. The first is unfalsifiable in every possible world, because it, like the tautology that if there are goats, then there are goats, says nothing about any possible world. The second says what holds good for all possible worlds: it gives expression to an informative cosmic invariant. The third is a truth for only some possible worlds.

C. I. Lewis takes the proposition, *A cat is an animal,* to be analytic, but he apparently construes it to be a proposition that attributes a property to a thing. *A cat is an animal* is represented as being a subject-predicate proposition on a footing with *A cat is a mouser,* the difference between them being that the first ascribes an essential property and the second a nonessential, or "accidental," property to the subject. Lewis's idea is that the claim made by the proposition, *A cat is an animal,* "can be assured by reference to the meanings of 'cat' and 'animal' without recourse to further and empirical evidence. But it also might be established—as well established as most laws of science—by generalization from observed instances of cats."[34] It is not easy to see how the truth-value of a proposition could be determined *both* by an examination of the meanings of the words used to express the proposition and also by an examination of things to which the subject-term refers. Putting this aside for the moment, what is clear is that some philosophers have the idea that certain properties of a thing are entailed by it, as against other properties which characterize it but are not logically essential to it.

A feature that is entailed by a thing will have to be essential to the *nature* of the thing, such that to suppose something is of that nature but lacks the feature is to entertain an inconsistent concept. It is like supposing that there is a cat that is not an animal or that there is a cat that is in more than one place at a time. The expression "the nature of a thing" carries with it the possibility of endless philosophical obfuscation. Here it means nothing more esoteric than the concept under which a thing falls or to which it answers. Talk about concepts under which things fall is a nonverbal, substitutive way of talking about words that apply to the things. It is a linguistically oblique way of talking about words which are general names of things, words like "cat" and "shoe." And a feature or a property that is essential to a thing, or is entailed by the concept to which the thing answers, is a criterion for the application of the word that is the generic name of the thing. In general, the rules for the use of a term determine the *meaning* of the term, which is nothing in addition to them. It is this linguistic fact that made it possible for Wittgenstein to give us the formula for avoiding a part of metaphysics: Don't ask for the meaning of a word, ask for its use.

It will be clear that an essential or an entailed property of a thing of a given kind is a criterion for the application of a general word to things of that kind, which is to say that its presence makes it correct to apply the word to them. A term which denotes an entailed property, e.g., "animal," unlike a term denoting a nonessential property, e.g., "mouser," does not have a use to describe or characterize what answers to a general name such as "cat." Talk about essential properties is an ontologically formulated way of talking about verbal matters, a way that makes it look as though attributes of things are being referred to. The fact that the sentence "A cat is an animal" expresses a logically necessary proposition is equivalent to the fact that the sentence "'Animal' applies to whatever 'cat' applies to" expresses a true verbal proposition. The verbal sentence makes it plain that the nonverbal equivalent does not attribute a property to a thing. The fact that talk about essential properties comes down to talk about the application of terms makes it an impropriety of language to say, "*This* cat is an animal and *that* one is an animal, too," as against saying, "*This* cat is a mouser and *that* one is a mouser, too."

We can now see what is at work behind Lewis's contention that the proposition, *A cat is an animal,* is open to verification by observing cats. Whether by mistake or by unconscious intent, Lewis has taken a word denoting a feature whose presence determines the correctness of applying a term to a thing to be a word for a characterizing property of what is referred to by the term. Lewis's conventionalist claim that the truth-value of the proposition expressed by "A cat is an animal" can be ascertained by reference to the meanings of "cat" and "animal" comes nearer the truth: "animal" gives expression to a feature whose presence is required for the correct application of "cat." This is the reason why the phrase "cat but not an animal," unlike "cat but not a mouser," has no descriptive function in the language.

The view that amongst the properties of an object, such as a cat or a tree, there are some that are logically necessary to it is the result of either a semantic misrepresentation or a grammatical alteration of some sort. The philosophical view about the essential nature of things fades away when words denoting essential properties are seen in a correct linguistic light, i.e., when their actual use in the language is made perspicuous. What we are left with, after the philosophical impediment has been removed, is the idea that a logically necessary proposition has no ontological import and therefore says nothing true or false about things. Regardless of appearances, a proposition whose actual truth-value is its sole possible truth-value makes no reality claim, either directly or by implication. It neither entails nor is entailed by any proposition making a factual assertion about the world. The outcome of this for philosophical statements, construed as *a priori,* is as disconcerting as it is perplexing: they say nothing whatever about the reality to which they appear to refer. With respect to things, actual or possible, existent or nonexistent, all necessary statements share with tautologies the feature of being ontologically uninformative.

It may be useful to review briefly several well-known philosophical propositions, which, whether accepted as true or rejected as false, have been naturally taken to be about the world. Consider the proposition that the contingent is grounded in the necessary, a proposition underlying all cosmological arguments for the existence of a supreme being. John Locke's variant, it will be remembered, is that since he, a contingent thing, exists, "from eternity there has been something." Expressed in propositional terms, the claim that the contingent is grounded in the necessary implies that a logically necessary proposition is entailed by, and is thus deducible from, a contingent proposition. Read literally, this, as has been argued, rests on an error of logic. Consider now the ontological argument, which Kant said lies hidden in the cosmological argument. This proof makes no use of any contingent proposition, and arrives at its conclusion "without leaving concepts": the concept of a being "without defect" entails the existence of such a being. In his well-known paper, "Anselm's Ontological Arguments,"[35] Norman Malcolm distinguishes between two Anselmic arguments, one of which he thinks is valid, the other invalid. One professes to demonstrate the existence of a perfect being; this one he thinks contains a mistake. The other, which he thinks valid, has as its conclusion the proposition that a perfect being has necessary existence, or, what would seem to be the same thing, the proposition that it is necessary that a perfect being exists: $\Box(\exists x)Px$. Theologians and others go on to say that God *exists,* in the same sense in which we say that the sun exists or the Great Pyramid exists; and philosophical logicians such as von Wright would justify their claim with the inference-formula that what is necessarily true is also true as a matter of fact, i.e., $\Box p \rightarrow p$.

In accordance with this formula we are logically entitled to infer *God exists* from God *necessarily exists*. But the formula does not stand up to scrutiny. No matter of fact claim can be deduced from an *a priori* claim. The proposition asserting God's actual existence cannot be deduced from the claim that He exists by *a priori* necessity.

Let us go on to several other philosophical statements that are naturally taken to be declarations about things. Russell has said that ". . . there are no such things as 'illusions of sense.' Objects of sense, even when they occur in dreams, are the most indubitably real objects known to us."[36] He has also said: "We cannot point to a time itself, but only to some event occurring at that time."[37] These two utterances seem unmistakably to be about things: the first, about the existence of sense objects, the second, about the impossibility of pointing to a time itself. But if they are to be understood as expressing *a priori* propositions, then the first sentence says nothing about the existence or nonexistence of what are called "illusions of sense," and the second sentence says nothing whatever about what we cannot do. This holds true generally, for all philosophical statements. It holds for the pair of statements, "We do not know that material things exist," and "We do know that material things such as tables and shoes exist." It holds equally for a large number of other statements.

It is hard not to think that the goal of philosophy is knowledge of reality. But if that is its true goal, philosophers can only gain knowledge of reality by recourse to empirical investigations of things. And if neither the methods nor the theories of philosophy are empirical, then philosophers live in a dream. Spinoza's conception of a systematic *a priori* science of what there is will have to be discarded as an intellectual chimera. If, however, philosophy is an empirical discipline, it is strange and mystifying that it has developed no experimental nor observational techniques, especially since in our own time the natural sciences have made such remarkable advances in techniques of investigation.

III

It will be useful to review what has been done in the first two parts. Philosophical methods of investigation and philosophical theories have been shown not to be what it is natural to take them to be. The empirical pictures they bring to mind do not portray what actually takes place when we do philosophy. It has also been shown that if philosophical theories are *a priori,* they cannot impart information about things. One piece of evidence against the view that represents philosophical activity as being like that in mathematics is that philosophical theories and their supporting arguments have remained the subject of debate for so long. If philosophy is an *a priori* discipline, then one is confronted with a fact which stands out in stereoptican relief: that it is a riot of entailment-claims. This by itself is a sufficient reason for rejecting the view that philosophical utterances are *a priori*. The utterly strange fact that philosophers show no discernible anxiety about the chaotic condition of their subject and, moreover, have no realistic expectation that it will ever be anything more than an expanding conglomerate of *sic et nons*, fortifies the evidence against the *a priori* view.

We can now say what a philosophical theory is not, but we are not yet in a position to say what it is. One thing is certain: a philosophical utterance is somehow able to create the appearance of stating a fact about the world, an appearance so convincing that it has the power permanently to bewitch the mind. What stands in need of explanation is the mechanics of this beguiling appearance, i.e., the semantic work that goes into its production.

Wittgenstein has expressed one idea about the nature of philosophical statements which has influenced a number of philosophers, particularly so-called ordinary language philosophers. He has said: "Philosophy may in no way interfere with the actual use of language; it can in the end only describe it. . . . It leaves everything as it is."[38] Accordingly, a paradoxical theory such as *motion is impossible* or *illusions of sense do not exist* misrepresents actual usage, and can be known to be mistaken without showing the mistake in the argument adduced in its support. Just as a false philosophical theory misdescribes usage, a true one correctly describes usage. The view is that ordinary language, i.e., the actual use of terminology, determines the truth-value of a philosophical theory.

This view about the nature of philosophical utterances is not the only one to which Wittgenstein has given expression. An alternative theory, which so far has not won the attention of philosophers, is also to be found in his later work. It states that a philosophical question, rather than being a request for factual information about the use of language, is an academic request for a redecision about expressions in current usage, and that a philosophical theory presents a piece of edited terminology. Although from a reading of the literature on his post-*Tractatus* work one would form the impression that Wittgenstein expressed only one metaphilosophical hypothesis about the nature of philosophical problems and theories, it needs to be emphasized that he tries out two different hypotheses. The first represents a philosophical theory as describing usage, mistakenly or not, without interfering with it. The second hypothesis represents a philosophical theory as introducing revised usage, which, because it is not meant for actual incorporation into the language, also does not interfere with usage. Wittgenstein has remarked that philosophy is an idleness in mathematics,[39] and it might be said quite generally that it is an idleness in the normal use of language. For a statement that presents academically revised terminology, i.e., terminology not meant for practical adoption, "leaves everything as it is."

One explanatory advantage that the second hypothesis has as against the first needs to be pointed out immediately. The hypothesis according to which a philosophical view describes actual usage does not explain the infinite durability of philosophical disputation, whereas the hypothesis that represents a philosophical view as presenting a concealed piece of academically revised language does. For the truth-value of a statement about conventional verbal usage, and thus made either true or false by facts of usage, is determinable by recourse to existing speech practices. And the fact that a philosophical statement remains in permanent suspension and a philosophical problem continues indefinitely to elude solution shows, not that philosophers are remiss in their investigations, but that their problems and theories are not about usage. The problems are not resolvable by recourse to usage and the theories are not accepted or rejected because of facts of usage.

The reason why answers to philosophical questions are open to indefinitely prolonged debate, and also why philosophical problems permanently resist solution, is that philosophical assertions have no truth-values and the problems they are bound up with are not the kind that have truth-value solutions, or are solved by finding *correct* answers. Like aesthetic and moral utterances, which give expression to emotional preferences, philosophical statements give expression to verbal preferences. The form of words in which aesthetic and moral utterances are couched, their indicative grammar, which makes them outwardly different from exclamations and ejaculations, makes it possible to represent them as fact-claiming statements.[40] It undoubtedly was a perception of the underlying likeness between philosophical and aesthetic statements that elicited from Hume the comment: " 'Tis not solely in poetry and music we must follow our taste, but likewise in philosophy."[41]

Wittgenstein's second hypothesis has kindled no interest in philosophers, but I have tried in a number of places to clarify, develop, and apply it to basic problems.[42] In explication of the second hypothesis, Wittgenstein has observed that philosophers suffer from the confusion of thinking themselves to be upsetting a fact-claiming proposition when what they are actually doing is "rejecting a form of symbolism."[43] They imagine that a philosophical problem "concerns a fact of the world instead of a matter of expression."

Philosophy is the kind of field that lends itself to interesting and penetrating observations, which on a second reading become merely perplexing until they are linguistically unmasked. It is a well-known fact that wishes and thoughts previously rejected for powerful emotional reasons can, nevertheless, return and win acceptance if they are made unrecognizable by disguise. The disguised return of unacceptable thoughts regularly occurs in dreams. And it sometimes happens that a theory which would otherwise be rejected if expressed in straightforward language, i.e., language that makes the theory easy to recognize, may be made acceptable by being expressed in opaque language. By way of illustration, consider these puzzling remarks about metaphysics: "Metaphysics has a long and distinguished history, and it is consequently unlikely that there are new truths to be discovered in descriptive metaphysics. But this does not mean that the task of descriptive metaphysics has been, or can be, done once and for all. It has constantly to be done over again. If there are no new truths to be discovered, there are old truths to be rediscovered."[44] These words obviously do not apply to mathematics and the natural sciences. It would be the height of absurdity to say that mathematical and scientific truths are constantly being lost and in need of being rediscovered. It does not, however, seem absurd to say this about metaphysics, although on second thought it is equally absurd. It would seem to be a safe maxim that a falsehood can be advanced as if it were a truth when its purpose is to gloss over an unwelcome fact. The fact is that metaphysical and, quite generally, philosophical theories are introduced over and over again in new words and presented as new theories. What is happening in modern advertising has been happening in philosophy for centuries. One way to renew excitement and sustain interest in a discipline that is basically stationary is to repeat the old in new ways. A change of clothes can be very important, and in philosophy it would seem to be of first importance.

Let us turn our attention now to Wittgenstein's disturbing idea that a philosopher presents an altered piece of ordinary terminology under the guise of advancing a theory about the world; for example, that when he declares knowledge of other minds to be impossible all that the philosopher is doing is rejecting the phrase "knows that there are others who think, feel, etc." It is to be expected that Wittgenstein's idea would encounter strong resistance in philosophers;[45] and coming to terms with it may, as a preliminary, require adopting a disguised version of it. Consider the following remarks taken from Professor Elmer Sprague's recent book, *Metaphysical Thinking*:

> When we treat the topics of metaphysics as notions, we are saying that the things that interest metaphysicians are to be found only by learning how to talk about them. . . . I am prepared to say that *self* or *person, world* and *God* may name entities. They will, however, be entities of a distinctive kind; and we must be very careful to understand what we are doing when we speak of metaphysical entities. They are entities that are brought into being by someone's wielding these notions in discourse; and we shall learn to find them only by learning what to say.[46]

These are strange and arresting words. They plainly hark back to earlier times and to earlier stages in our own mental development, and they belong to the past rather than the present. Reading the words literally, they express a primitive superstition which it is hard to think anyone might consciously harbor. Learning how to talk about poltergeists in haunted houses or leprechauns in Galway cannot be a way of finding them. More is necessary than learning a particular way of talking, except in the land of make-believe.

In everyday life, where fantasy plays only a restricted and contained part, none of us imagines that the things we handle and see are brought into being by "wielding notions." Things like books, the sun, and the Parthenon resist being summoned into existence by words, except when the God of

Genesis utters them. Sprague does not mean to refer to such things when he speaks of entities that can be made to exist by someone wielding notions. The "distinctive" entities that are susceptible to this kind of control are metaphysical, and it is not hard to guess what their nature is. Entities found by learning how to talk in certain ways and which are stirred into existence by doing things with notions can be nothing more substantial than mirages. In metaphysics, and in all of philosophy, learning how to talk in ways that appear to discover entities is to learn to alter usage in ways that give rise to intellectual illusions. Concealed semantic maneuvering is the efficacious technique used to produce metaphysical entities and cosmic philosophical theories. It is interesting to find Wittgenstein's neglected view about the nature of philosophical theories buried in the words of a philosopher who undoubtedly would not consciously associate himself with the view. This concealed acceptance may perhaps even count as evidence for the view.

The hypothesis that a philosophical theory is only the appearance of a theory, brought to life by an academic alteration in the use of terminology, gives us an explanation of what it is in the nature of a philosophical theory that makes it susceptible to continuous disagreement. William James's question as to whether the man who goes around the tree also goes around the squirrel that goes around the tree while constantly facing him is capable of indefinite debate because it is neither about what occurred nor about the actual use of the term "goes around." The question is a request for an academic decision as to whether a known expression should be applied to an unusual case, one that differs in a certain respect from a normal case. Depending on whether a person feels the difference to be important or unimportant, he will decide one way or the other; he will say that the man did or did not go around the squirrel. Taste, to use Hume's word, and not fact determine one's answer to the question. It is the same with a philosophical answer. A philosopher who asserts "No one really perceives things, really smells a lemon or tastes a lozenge" has made the decision to banish from the language, in what Moore calls a "philosophic moment," the phrase "perceives things." His view gives expression to a semantic preference, and opposing views give expression to opposing preferences, all this being part of a language game. It is understandable that such a game can go on endlessly.

One thing that needs to be explained is the linguistic mechanics by means of which the deceptive appearance of a theory is brought about. Wittgenstein has pointed out that a form of words used to express a philosophical theory may also have a use in everyday speech to refer to a matter of fact: ". . . an assertion which the metaphysician makes . . . can also be used to state a fact of experience."[47] A philosophically edited term is different in its range of application from the range it has in its usual employment, but this difference is made invisible by the way a philosopher introduces the edited term. It is presented in a sentence formulated in the nonverbal, fact-stating idiom, i.e., in the mode of speech in which words are used, not mentioned, and in this way creates the erroneous idea that he is using the term in a statement about the world. For another thing, the redistricted application of the term is not introduced for practical adoption; it is not intended to supplant ordinary usage. Everyday language is left as it is and beside it the philosopher places another,[48] or rather, he superimposes the one on the other. He projects a semantic fantasy onto linguistic reality. A philosopher speaks with two tongues, but he gives the impression of speaking with only one, and of revealing important truths about things. When a Parmenidean states, "Everything remains the same, nothing changes," and a Heraclitean states, "Everything is constantly changing, nothing remains the same," they appear to be making opposite factual claims about reality. The truth of the matter is that they are presenting academic changes in the application of terminology, while the language in actual use remains unaltered. The first utterance introduces an expanded application of "remains the same," in which it applies to everything, and a contracted application of "changes," in which it applies to nothing. The second utterance introduces an expanded use of "changes," in which it has universal application, and a contracted use of "remains the same," in which it has no application. The utterances can create their illusion by being presented in the fact-stating idiom, which makes it look as if the terms are being used instead of mentioned. Undoubtedly this account is not complete. It does not explain the continued acceptance of illusions, an acceptance that might be expected to wear thin after so many centuries. Anxiety perhaps more than anything else was responsible for the quick interment of Aristarchus's astronomical speculation, and it delayed for a long period of time the erosion of the comfortable belief that the earth was the center of the universe. We may guess the presence of powerful, if hidden, determinants that prevent erosion of the illusion that philosophy, equally with the sciences, investigates the world.

As an illustration of the notion that the work of philosophy is to fabricate sham theories, consider Russell's assertion that there are no illusions of sense. To go back to his own words, he wrote: "The first thing to realize is that there are no such things as 'illusions of sense.' Objects of sense, even when they occur in dreams, are the most indubitably real objects known to us."[49] If we read these words literally, and take the expression "illusion of sense" to have its familiar use, their implication is that nothing in fact occurs to which the expression "illusion of sense" applies. Plainly, it *could,* as a theoretical possibility, be the case that sense-illusions do not occur, that no one dreams, that sticks partly immersed in water never look bent, and that magicians actually, and not just in appearance, saw ladies in half. But it is not to be thought for a moment that Russell wishes to imply anything of the sort. We cannot construe his words, viz., "The first thing to realize . . . ," as being intended to call our attention to a fact that we might have overlooked and that we might wish to check. He is not using the phrase "illusion of sense" in the normal way or maintaining that we are mistaken about the nature of the cases to which we apply it. When he tells us that the sense objects occurring in our dreams are "real" we cannot rightly understand him to be saying that the people and things we dream about are present in our dreams, that images in our dreams are the things they represent. Russell has written that only a philosopher could fail to distinguish a post from the idea of a post,"[50] and although Russell himself was a philosopher we cannot think that on this point he suffered confusion.

He is not using the expression "illusion of sense" in the accepted way, which he knows as well as anyone else, nor is he misdescribing the use it has. Instead, he is keeping ordinary language and putting another beside it. He academically redistricts the phrase "illusion of sense," reducing its range of application to zero; and he does this in the form of speech in which nomenclature is not mentioned. Keeping ordinary language and adding his contrived expression to it are sufficient to fashion a semantic trap,[51] which has held philosophers captive from Protagoras to the present.

With the term "object of sense" Russell does a comparable thing: he subjects it to semantic manipulation. The expression normally is used to refer to objects like shoes, trees, and automobiles—to things we are said to perceive. Russell stretches its use to cover mental images, dream contents, afterimages, and the like. This stretches the application of the word "object" or "thing" to cover what in everyday language do not count as objects or things. When Hume says that "every perception is a substance, and every distinct part of a perception a distinct substance,"[52] he makes the same maneuver with the word "substance." Instead of advancing a theory about the nature of images, tastes, smells, and the like, he presents a rigged use of the word "substance." He places his semantic contrivance alongside of everyday speech, and in this way creates an erroneous but powerful idea in the minds of his audience and in his own mind as well. By means of unwitting linguistic duplicity Hume generates the intellectual illusion that he is revealing a discovery about the inner nature of substance.

Next, consider Russell's statement, "We cannot point to a time itself, but only to some event occurring at that time," from which he infers that "there is no reason in experience to suppose that there are times as opposed to events. . . ."[53] It is not clear from these remarks whether Russell wishes to say that we are unable to point to "a time itself" because there are no "times as opposed to events," or urges this for another reason. One cannot point to a goat that does not exist and nor can one point to a goat that is hidden from view. The first *cannot* is the *cannot* of logic: it is logically impossible to point to a nonexistent thing. The second *cannot* is the physical *cannot*: it is physically impossible to point to something if one's hands are tied or if a high wall hides the thing from view. But what we are physically prevented from doing, we *could* in principle do.

To leave this point for a moment, it will be evident that the nonexistence of *a time itself* is not a correct inference from our inability to point to it, any more than the nonexistence of a goat can be a correct inference from the fact that we are prevented from pointing to it by its being hidden. In general, if it is argued that it *follows* from our not being able to point to something that it does not exist, then the reason for our not being able to point to it is that it does not exist. Russell has turned the argument around, putting the cart before the horse: what he offers as the premise of his argument should be the conclusion and what he sets forth as the conclusion should be the premise. His reason for maintaining that we cannot point to *a time itself,* as opposed to an occurrence or an object, is that it does not exist.

But what could be meant by saying that a time itself does not exist and that for this reason we cannot point to it? Russell would not say that it might exist and that if indeed it did exist it could be pointed to — just as a centaur could be pointed to if it did exist. We must suppose that he wishes to convey that a time, as opposed to something existing or occurring at that time, is such that by its nature it cannot be pointed to. Some metaphysicians have argued that time is self-contradictory, which would seem to imply that time, or a particular time, can no more be pointed to than one can point to a seven-faced cube. But Russell has something else in mind, which is indicated by his assertion that we can point to an "event occurring at that time." The implication is plain: we can point to things and events, but not to time. And this is so not because time, or a time interval, does not exist, but because time cannot, by its very nature, be pointed to.

The explanation of why we cannot point to time, or to a time interval, is not hard to discover. Time is not a thing nor is it an occurrence or a process, which is an ontological way of saying that the word "time" is not the name of a thing or of an occurrence. Wittgenstein has observed that when we come upon a substantive we tend to look for a substance, and poets and mystics attest to the substantial correctness of this observation when they speak in various ways of time as an occult cosmic river. It is logically impossible to point to what is denoted by the word "time" and by related temporal nouns, because temporal terms are not object-denoting terms like "brick" or "explosion." The reason for stating that we cannot point to a time itself, as opposed to an occurrence at that time, is to highlight this fact: as temporal nouns are used in the language it makes no literal sense to speak of pointing to what they denote.

One philosophical way of marking the difference between what might be called substantival nouns and grammatical nouns is to suppress grammatical nouns, academically exorcising them from the language. Maintaining that time or that a time by itself does not exist is an ontological way of expressing the decision to eliminate temporal nouns. Again, to express it in Wittgenstein's way, Russell puts his linguistic innovation alongside unaltered everyday language, in which temporal terminology functions in the usual ways; and doing this creates the idea that the nonexistence of time is being declared.

A few remarks should be made about the statement that the contingent is grounded in the necessary, that, concretely, the existence of a humming-bird entails the necessary existence of some being. The term "necessary being," or "necessarily existent substance," appears to have a characterizing use, a use to describe the nature of a thing. Hume stated that "the idea of existence is nothing different from the idea of any object," and went on to remark, "When I think of God, when I think of him as existent, and when I believe him to be existent, my idea of him neither increases nor diminishes."[54] Hume's remarks make clear the use "exists" has in relation to terms that denote things, occurrences, and the like, i.e., its use outside of mathematics: to say that an object *a* exists is to say something about *a* but not to describe or characterize it.

The term "necessary existence" appears to be of a different kind. Some able philosophers think that, unlike "exists," "necessarily exists" and "has necessary existence" do have a use to characterize things, a use to say *what* they are and not merely a use to say *that* they are. Norman Malcolm, for example, maintains that the words "necessary existence is a perfection"[55] express a truth and thus by implication holds that the term "necessary existence" functions descriptively to say what a thing is. As was stated earlier, he distinguishes between two Anselmic arguments and thinks one of them to be correct, namely, the argument professing to demonstrate the necessary existence of a supremely perfect being, than which a greater is inconceivable. Here we are only interested in the term "necessary existence" as it occurs in cosmological formulations, particularly in the sentence "The contingent is grounded in that which has necessary existence," and in separation from its occurrence in the expression of ontological arguments. The latter proceed from an examination of the *concept* denoted by the phrase "a being which lacks no possible perfection, than which a greater is inconceivable," and do not proceed from the existence of an ordinary thing, whether minute or astronomically massive.

The problem here is to determine whether the phrase "necessary existence" has a use to characterize a thing or a substance, apart from any characterizing use it may have in mathematical disciplines. To determine this, one device that might be used is to pass in review things that come to mind when we think of the term "necessary existent," and decide in each case whether the term correctly applies. It turns out that nothing which comes to mind, from atomic particles to planets and the stars, answers to the supposed description. Furthermore, if we attempt to identify something that might in theory fall under the term, we draw a conceptual blank. This means that the term "necessary existent," or "necessary being," has no *actual* use to characterize or describe a thing or object. Kant appears to give recognition to this linguistic fact in the following words: ". . . if I take the concept of anything, *no matter what,* I find that the existence of this thing can never be represented to me as absolutely necessary, and that, whatever it may be that exists, nothing prevents me from thinking its nonexistence. . . . If I am constrained to think something necessary as a condition of existing things, but am unable to think any particular thing as in itself necessary, it inevitably follows that necessity and contingency do not concern the things themselves; otherwise there would be a contradiction."[56] It is not entirely clear what Kant means by the words "contingency does not concern the things themselves," but he has made plain what construction is to be placed on the words "necessity does not concern things." This is that the expression "necessarily existing thing" has no application to anything, "no matter what." The noun term "necessary being" has been given no descriptive or characterizing use, and its function in the sentence, "The contingent is grounded in the necessary," or in the sentence, "The fact that I exist implies the existence of a necessary being," is wholly grammatical: the term functions as a grammatical, not as a semantic, noun-expression. To use Kant's word, in a different connection, it is a flimflam noun. What gives this pretence implication support and life undoubtedly is a subjective need to which it gives indirect expression. The term "contingent thing" is easily and naturally identified with *dependent thing,* specifically, *dependent child*; and the term "necessary being" is tailor-made to stand for *protective parent,* a being who has the power to protect the child against all dangers.[57] The sentence, "The contingent is grounded in the necessary," lends itself to the interpretation that the child owes its existence to its parents, and also to the interpretation that the parent is necessary to the defenseless child's welfare. With this philosophical formula, the grown man gives comfort to the child still within him.

Let us return to the semantics of the philosophical formula. Kant's remark that contingency does not concern things is puzzling, since he states that "whatever it may be that exists, nothing prevents me from thinking its nonexistence."[58] The claim that the nonexistence of any conceivable thing is itself conceivable implies that being a thing *entails* being such that it could fail to exist. The claim thus implies the impossibility of the concept denoted by "necessarily existing thing"; it indirectly implies the verbal fact that "necessarily exists" has no application to things. Now, if one of a pair of antithetical terms is denied a use, the other loses its use. Kant seems to give recognition to this fact by maintaining that neither "necessary" nor "contingent" has a use to characterize things, that since "necessary" has no such use, "contingent" has none. This enables us to understand better how terminology is being used in the sentence, "The contingent is grounded in, or implies, the necessary." Metaphysicians have stretched the ordinary use of "contingent" (which normally implies being dependent on or determined by something) so that it applies to things that entail the *logical* possibility of their nonexistence. Being a shoe or the moon entails the *logical* possibility of ceasing to exist or of being nonexistent, quite apart from any actual condition on which the existence of the thing is *causally* dependent. Hence a shoe and the moon fall under the stretched use of "contingent": in the language of metaphysics, shoes and the moon are said to be "contingent things."[59] This stretched application of the word "contingent" is used to justify the introduction of the antithetical expression "noncontingent thing," or "necessary being," without assigning a meaning to them or giving them an actual application to anything. The statement that the contingent is grounded in or implies the necessary is to be understood as asserting, roughly, that if the term "contingent thing" is given a use, then the term "necessary thing" should also be given a use, even if only in semantic appearance. A philosopher like Heraclitus creates a "theory," i.e., the semantic imitation of a theory, by academically suppressing one of a pair of antithetical terms. Some metaphysical theologians create a world view by doing the opposite thing: they introduce a manufactured antithetical term, one which is descriptively idle. The work of the term "necessary thing" is to create the semblance of talk about the structure of the world.

M.L.

NOTES

1. *Philosophical Investigations,* p. 47.
2. Bertrand Russell, *A History of Western Philosophy* (New York: Simon and Schuster, 1945), p. 669.
3. Ibid.
4. F. H. Bradley, *Appearance and Reality* (London: George Allen & Unwin, Ltd., Seventh Impression, 1920), p. 144.
5. Ibid.
6. C. I. Lewis and C. H. Langford, *Symbolic Logic* (New York and London: The Century Co., 1932), p. 447.
7. *The Blue Book,* p. 42.
8. C. I. Lewis and C. H. Langford, op. cit., p. 477. In Langford's way of speaking, "unitary meaning of sentence S" = "proposition expressed by S."
9. George Berkeley, *The Principles of Human Knowledge,* Part First, Section 24, in *Works,* edited by A. C. Fraser (Oxford: The Clarendon Press, 1901).
10. Kant's expression.
11. Ibid., Section 25.
12. A. J. Ayer, *Philosophical Essays* (London: Macmillan; New York: St. Martin's Press, 1954), p. 141.
13. Ibid.
14. Ibid.
15. Ibid.
16. Russell, *A History of Western Philosophy,* op. cit.
17. Ibid.

18. David Hume, *A Treatise of Human Nature* (Oxford: The Clarendon Press, 1888), Book I, Part III, Section XIV (edited by L. A. Selby-Bigge), p. 155.

19. Ibid., p. 159.

20. Ibid., p. 161.

21. Ibid., p. 158.

22. For an independent development of this idea, see "Moore's Paradox," in *The Structure of Metaphysics* (London: Routledge and Kegan Paul, Ltd., 1955).

23. *Notebooks 1914–1916* (Oxford: Basil Blackwell, 1969), p. 53e.

24. *The Blue Book,* pp. 55–56.

25. A. J. Ayer, *Language, Truth and Logic,* second edition (London: Victor Gollancz, Ltd., 1948), p. 125.

26. Kant's phrase.

27. *Tractatus Logico-Philosophicus* (5.143) (New York: Harcourt, Brace & Company; London: Kegan Paul, Trench, Trubner & Co., Ltd., 1922). Trans. by C. K. Ogden.

28. C. I. Lewis and C. H. Langford, *Symbolic Logic,* op. cit., p. 251.

29. One child's expression for obtaining a conclusion from premises.

30. C. I. Lewis and C. H. Langford, op. cit., p. 251.

31. *Tractatus* (4.462).

32. Ibid.

33. Ibid.

34. C. I. Lewis, *An Analysis of Knowledge and Valuation* (LaSalle, Ill.: The Open Court Publishing Co., 1946), p. 91.

35. *The Philosophical Review* LXIX (January 1960).

36. Bertrand Russell, *Our Knowledge of the External World as a Field for Scientific Method in Philosophy* (New York: W. W. Norton & Co., 1929), p. 90.

37. Ibid., p. 125.

38. *Philosophical Investigations,* p. 49.

39. *Remarks on the Foundations of Mathematics,* p. 157.

40. See "The Nature of Value," in my *Studies in Metaphilosophy* (London: Routledge and Kegan Paul, Ltd., 1964).

41. Hume, *A Treatise of Human Nature,* Book I, Part III, Section VIII, p. 103.

42. See, for example, *The Language of Philosophy, Freud and Wittgenstein* (Dordrecht, Holland; Boston, Mass.: D. Reidel Publishing Co., 1977).

43. *Wittgenstein's Lectures, Cambridge 1932–1935,* p. 69.

44. P. F. Strawson, *Individuals, an Essay in Descriptive Metaphysics* (London: Methuen, 1959). Introduction, p. 10.

45. See especially Donald C. Williams's "Philosophy and Psychoanalysis," where he characterizes the hypothesis as "repulsive and cumbersome," *Psychoanalysis, Scientific Method and Philosophy* (New York: New York University Press, 1959), a symposium edited by Sidney Hook, p. 178.

46. Elmer Sprague, *Metaphysical Thinking* (New York: Oxford University Press, 1978), p. 4.

47. *The Blue Book,* pp. 56–57.

48. Wittgenstein's expression in *The Yellow Book.*

49. Russell, *A History of Western Philosophy,* op. cit., p. 90.

50. Bertrand Russell, *The Principles of Mathematics* (New York: W. W. Norton & Co., 1938), second edition, p. 451.

51. Wittgenstein's "fly-bottle."

52. Hume, *A Treatise of Human Nature,* Book I, Part III, Section V, p. 244.

53. Russell, *Our Knowledge of the External World,* op. cit., p. 125.

54. Hume, *A Treatise of Human Nature,* Book I, Part III, Section VII, p. 94.

55. Norman Malcolm, *Knowledge and Certainty* (Englewood Cliffs, N.J.: Prentice-Hall, Inc., 1963), p. 146.

56. Immanuel Kant, *The Critique of Pure Reason,* trans. by Norman Kemp-Smith (London: Macmillan & Co., Ltd., 1950), p. 515. [Italics mine.]

57. Sigmund Freud, *The Future of an Illusion* (London: The Hogarth Press & The Institute of Psycho-Analysis, 1943), especially ch. 3.

58. For an illustration of this see Malcolm's discussion of necessary existence and dependent, or contingent, existence, *Knowledge and Certainty,* pp. 146–147.

59. Ibid.

III

Commanding a Clear View of Philosophy

Wittgenstein said that "a philosophical problem has the form: 'I don't know my way about'"[1] and that "a main source of our failure to understand is that we do not *command a clear view* of the use of our words."[2] Ordinary language is the labyrinth in which the philosophical fly has lost its way. The implication of Wittgenstein's words is that the way out of a philosophical problem is to obtain a clear view of the workings of our language, that the nature of a philosophical view is hidden from us, and can only be rightly understood when we become clearly aware of how the words which express it are being used. Wittgenstein frequently commented in his lectures that what he said was not something new, something we do not already know, and that his remarks should be construed as reminders. What I shall have to say in this study may also be thought of as reminders, which will bring us to a realization of what it is we are doing when we philosophize.

A first step is the recognition of a fact we tend to forget, a fact deplored by Descartes and cited by Kant, that "despite of all the zeal with which other sciences of every kind are prosecuted,"[3] "in all ages one Metaphysics has contradicted another, either in its assertions or their proofs."[4] This fact has been minimized or ignored altogether, and the need to explain *why* anarchy reigns disappears from the central place it should have in our professional attention. I shall start from the perplexing fact that philosophical theories are in unending debate, and devote myself to developing an explanation of this state of affairs, an explanation which has its source in a number of neglected observations of Wittgenstein.

Part of the task of accounting for the condition of philosophy, which professes to be a reasoned discipline, will be to determine whether philosophical

---

From *Proceedings of the American Philosophical Association* XLIX (1975–76), pp. 5–21, Copyright © 1976 by the American Philosophical Association. Reprinted by permission of the publisher.

propositions are what they so obviously appear to be, and whether disputes centering on them are what they appear to be. A description of arithmetic given by Bertrand Russell in *The Principles of Mathematics* provides an analogue to the description many philosophers give of their own subject. "Arithmetic," he said, "must be discovered in just the same sense in which Columbus discovered the West Indies. The number 2 . . . is an entity which can be thought of. Whatever can be thought of has being, and its being is a precondition, not a result, of its being thought of."[5] An analogous account of philosophy represents its subject matter as being, in part, the concrete things of the world, and its results as reports of their essential features. Like a geographer, the philosopher is thought of as exploring the world, except that his work is presented as disclosing the "inner" nature of things, rather than the superficial features investigated by science. It should be noted that the philosopher, unlike the geographer, has no need to leave his study. He carries on without the help of either observation or experiment. This fact makes understandable Wittgenstein's assurance when he said that philosophical problems "are, of course, not empirical,"[6] which implies that he took philosophical propositions also not to be empirical.

The construction he placed on philosophical propositions can be seen best by comparing them with the way he viewed the propositions of mathematics. Both sorts of propositions he at various times called "grammatical," but this is not to imply that there is no difference between types of "grammatical" propositions. For although he was explicit on the point that both mathematical and philosophical propositions are grammatical, he did not go on to assert that philosophical propositions are *a priori*. Once I have brought out certain features of the *a priori* propositions of mathematics, my object will be to examine the character of several philosophical positions which resemble them. I shall hope to show that philosophers misconceive what they are doing when they announce, and argue for, a position. To say precisely what they are doing will carry us beyond anything Wittgenstein made explicit. It has been made explicit in some of my own work, but especially in the work of Morris Lazerowitz.

Mathematical propositions differ among themselves in an important way which it is useful to take note of, inasmuch as one of the two classes of mathematical propositions has a close affinity with the propositions of philosophy. The difference is evidence in the language by which the two kinds of proposition are expressed. Some propositions are deductions, in accordance with rules of inference, from *a priori* premises. The sentences expressing them make use of no terms other than those in the vocabulary provided by the discipline. With regard to these the mathematician is like a chess player who operates within a set of rules, and his deductions are like calculations. Other mathematical propositions, however, occur within proofs whose expression involves an extension of language. The emergence of a new branch of mathematics brings with it an enlargement of mathematical language. For example, the theory of complex numbers introduces the new expression $a + bi$, where $i = \sqrt{-1}$. Group theory uses the symbol $\times$, but the fact that the expression $a \times b \neq b \times a$ can state an *a priori* truth shows that $\times$ has been given a new use. A similar comment applies to the term "surface" occurring within the expression "Moebius surface," and to E. E. Kummer's designation "ideal numbers."

Regardless of whether a proof makes a move in an existent game, or introduces a new rule of the game[7] (which augments language), talk about the propositions deduced always suggests that they have a subject matter, sometimes discovered, sometimes invented. G. H. Hardy describes the mathematician as a Platonic explorer of a realm of abstract entities, and this description is especially appealing when theorems are demonstrated within an already fixed body of mathematics, that is, where proving a theorem is like playing a game under a set of stated rules. The path to the goal already exists, and the only problem is to find the path. The description of mathematics as creation, or invention, is the more natural one when there is an extension of the boundaries of language—where the existing rules do not govern the steps to be taken. Carl Friedrich Gauss was said to have "introduced" the number $a + bi$; Kummer was said to have created a new species of number. Yet even where invention plays such an important role, we find talk of "investigating" an area, e.g., the algebraic number field generated by a root of $i^2 + 1 = 0$. It is as if an invented term is thought of as a name that is coined for what already exists. Mathematical language often imitates the language of empirical exploration, where what is found may outstrip the available vocabulary, and is identified by being given a name. Humankind in its primitive stages had a language too limited to describe many things that were seen and heard, and gradually a vocabulary was built up. But the case is different with mathematics: description and what is described are in tandem. The subject matter does not outrun language; instead, it is created along with language, or better, it is created by language. Nevertheless, Russell's description of arithmetic is a tempting one, in suggesting that the field of arithmetic, like some unknown terrain, awaits scientific investigation, the findings of which are to be recorded in language.

This Russell-Hardy conception of mathematics has been dwelt on here because philosophers seem to have the same idea about their own subject. Many, and perhaps all, philosophers take their views to have factual content, although they make no attempt to support them by empirical evidence. It was possibly an awareness of this that made C. D. Broad remark that "philosophy has no use for experiment."[8] One scholar has complained that Parmenides had an argument but no evidence for his view about Being, to which Broad could well have replied that only an argument would be relevant. In philosophy a position is advanced with the air that what is being asserted makes an *a priori*, not an empirical, claim about things. Thus, when Zeno said that motion is impossible, and A. J. Ayer said that "it is logically impossible for a sense-experience to belong to the sense-history of more than a single self,"[9] they thought themselves to be stating logically assured truths. In these respects, then, the propositions of philosophy are like those of mathematics. In some places Wittgenstein indicated that he thought them similar to those propositions of mathematics which exhibit some extension of mathematical language. But of course the similarity comes to an end at some point inasmuch as the propositions of mathematics are not in chronic debate, whereas those of philosophy are. A clue to the difference is given by two important features in Wittgenstein's thinking on the subject, one an omission and the other the charge that philosophers misconceive the nature of their subject. First, it is significant that although Wittgenstein said the problems of philosophy are not empirical, he did not go on to say that they are *a priori*. The other is something he is reported to have said while dictating *The Blue Book*. In a set of notes taken by Margaret Masterman and myself, the so-called *Yellow Book*, we report him as saying that a confusion pervades all of philosophy, namely, that of supposing a proposition has been rejected as false when what has been rejected is a notation. Inasmuch as philosophers conduct their investigations in the material mode of speech and do not usually mention terminology, this remark of Wittgenstein's appears to be false. But if it is true it is of fundamental importance. In what follows I shall elaborate and illustrate this thesis and its implications. Among the things implied by his charge is that not only are philosophical propositions not empirical, they are not statements of the kind that have truth-values, and, in disagreement with what many philosophers think, they are not synthetic *a priori*.

Kant, and a number of philosophers after him, thought that the introduction into philosophy of the category of synthetic *a priori* propositions allowed for the possibility of a proposition having the logical necessity of a tautology while having factual content. It was thought to make room for statements that are not empirical but provide information about things. The classification has appealed to many philosophers, who have even thought that it saved philosophy from disaster. In *Zettel* Wittgenstein said of metaphysics what could also be said of philosophy in general: that it "obliterates the distinction between factual and conceptual investigations."[10] By "conceptual investigations" I take it is meant the analysis of concepts, which when successful results in necessary truths. Kant's idea that propositions of philosophy could have both inner necessity and factual content encourages the idea that factual and conceptual investigations can come to the same end-result. Inasmuch as verification procedures are irrelevant to philosophical propositions,[11] I shall, without adducing further considerations, proceed on the idea that they are not empirical and hence do not possess their factual content in virtue of being empirical. The question is whether they can at the same time have factual content and be necessary, i.e., can be synthetic *a priori.* If they cannot, and should it turn out that they are neither synthetic nor *a priori,* then it would appear that no truth-value attaches to them.[12]

The iconoclastic thesis that philosophical utterances have no truth-value has its source in ideas to be found in Wittgenstein's later work, and in places other than the *Yellow Book* notes. It has been applied in a detailed way by Morris Lazerowitz to a number of outstanding problems, e.g., to questions about the validity of inductive procedures and about the nature of value predicates. The thesis is not a welcome one, since if correct, it destroys the picture of the philosopher as the investigator, in depth, of what there is. Indeed, as Wittgenstein said in his *Philosophical Investigations,* "it seems to destroy all that is great and important, . . . leaving behind only bits of stone and rubble."[13] What compensates, however, for the negative, destructive consequences of this thesis is that, if correct, it improves our understanding of the nature of philosophical propositions, and thus, on its positive side, gives us insight into the mystery of the ever-recurring disputation about them that has distressed and embarrassed the greatest minds.

To many philosophers some statements present the appearance of being factual and at the same time necessary. Despite such appearances, I wish to argue that a proposition cannot be factually informative and *a priori* true. This can be done without subscribing to the conventionalist thesis that necessary propositions, instead of being about things, are about words. As is well known, it has been held that all necessary propositions record facts of verbal usage. Wittgenstein characterized them as "rules of grammar," which implies that they are about verbal rather than nonverbal facts. To see how it can be held, independently of the conventionalist thesis, that necessary propositions "say nothing about things,"[14] consider an elementary tautology of the form $p \vee \sim p$. The fact that no experiential evidence is required for knowing that it is true does not seem to some philosophers to warrant concluding it is not about things. Thus, W. H. B. Joseph has held that it is about things. If $p \vee \sim p$ is expressed in its conditional form, *If p, then p,* the temptation to say it is about things is reduced.

The difference between *If p, then p* and an empirical proposition, which makes a declaration about things, can best be seen when it is restated in the form $\sim (p . \sim p)$. Consider the sentence, "It is not the case that *a* is both red and not red." This does not say what *a* is not. If the denial that a certain predicate characterizes *a* does in fact, and not merely in verbal appearance, say what *a* is not, the predicate must have a characterizing use in the language. But the predicate expression "both red and not red" has no use in the language to describe anything: There is no knowing what it would be like for a thing to be both red and not red, which is a nonverbal way of saying that the phrase "both red and not red" is not descriptive. Hence the denial that *a* is both red and not red, unlike the denial that it is red, does not state what *a* is not or cannot be. In the case of an empirical proposition about a thing, we know what it would be like for it to be what it cannot in fact be. Thus, in knowing that water cannot flow uphill we know what it would be like for it to flow uphill. But when we do not even know what it would be like for things to be so-and-so, e.g., for *a* to be both red and not red, or for water to flow uphill while flowing downhill, or for 17 oranges to be exactly 2 more than 14, we *have no idea* of the attribute so-and-so. And if a form of words expresses what in principle there is no conceiving, this is because the words have no descriptive use. Wittgenstein's frequently quoted last statement in the *Tractatus* is that whereof we cannot speak we must remain silent,[15] and we might add that what neither we, nor angels, nor God can think about we must attribute to the descriptive muteness of an expression. Any phrase that expresses what there is no conceiving must be relegated to the limbo of expressions which fail in that language to have descriptive use.

To sum up, the negation of a sentence which expresses a necessary proposition is a sentence whose descriptive part is a phrase having no descriptive use in the language. Negating "Tigers are animals," for example, yields "There are tigers which are not animals," whose descriptive part, "tigers but not animals," in contrast to "tigers but not carnivores," describes no theoretically possible creature. To put it somewhat differently, the negation of a necessary proposition of the form $(x)fx \supset gx$, namely, $(\exists x)fx. \sim gx$, says nothing about things. But if $(\exists x)fx. \sim gx$ does not assert the existence of something, then $\sim (\exists x)fx. \sim gx$ does not deny the existence of something answering to $fx. \sim gx$. Thus, neither "All tigers are animals" nor "Something is a tiger and not an animal" say anything about what there is. This point holds also for propositions Kant classified as synthetic *a priori*. Regardless of any special feature ascribed to a logically necessary proposition, what prevents it from having factual content is just the fact that it is logically necessary.

If this is in essentials a correct account of sentences that express logically necessary propositions, then philosophers who put forward theories that purport to convey information about the essential or "inner" nature of things or about what there is do no more than pantomime science. The illusion they labor under is difficult not to succumb to. It is the kind of illusion from which, in Kant's words, "even the wisest of men cannot free himself."[16] When Russell put his confidence in logic as an instrument enabling philosophers to establish secure results, what he did seems to be analogous to what physicists do who use mathematics to help them discover new facts, e.g., the existence of Uranus. But the application of logic to philosophical problems has borne no fruit: the disagreements have remained. Other philosophers have turned to the investigation of language to solve philosophical problems, a development that was deplored by Broad as a bizarre delusion.[17] J. L. Austin, to mention one philosopher, turned his attention to language with the idea that an examination of verbal usage will in some way improve our understanding of things. He wrote: "When we examine . . . what words we should use in what situations, we are looking again not *merely* at words . . . but also at the realities we use the words to talk about: we are using a sharpened awareness of words to sharpen our perception of phenomena."[18] It is unclear how examining words, not things, can improve or increase our knowledge of things. Underlying the supposition that it can is perhaps the notion that analyzing the meanings of words reveals the nature of objects denoted by the words — that necessary propositions can have factual content. And it may be that a perception of the hidden verbal import of necessary propositions coupled with their appearance of being about things made it seem reasonable to think that examination of words would lead to knowledge of what the words stand for.

Although necessary propositions, which make no mention of the words used in expressing them, are not about words, their necessity is connected with some fact about the conventional use of these words. Specifying this connection will enable us to understand Wittgenstein's claim that where a philosopher advances a theory with the air of asserting a necessary truth, he is merely giving vent to a dissatisfaction with a linguistic convention. We can state in a general way the connection between necessity and language as follows: The fact that a sentence expresses a necessary proposition is equivalent to a fact about the conventional use of words in the sentence. Consider a sentence expressing a simple necessary proposition: "A square is four-sided." To know that this sentence says what is true, all that is required is to know that in point of usage "four-sided" applies to whatever "square" applies to. That is, to know the empirical verbal fact that this sentence expresses a necessary truth is to know the empirical verbal fact that in English "four-sided" applies to what "square" applies to. Nothing more. This account of sentences for necessary truths, which derives from Morris Lazerowitz, can be carried over to sentences stating philosophical theories, for these at least *purport* to express *a priori* necessities. It may be that they only appear to do so, and that there is no fact of usage to support the idea that they do.

We cannot conclude that the philosopher is making a mistake about usage from the fact that there is no convention in the language to back the idea that his sentence asserts a necessary truth. Views are held in the face of actual conventions, which philosophers could not fail to know run counter to them; for example, Bradley's view that space is a self-contradictory appearance. If this view were true, then space-denoting words would all be self-contradictory. Ordinary spatial terminology is, of course, not in this plight: it would be absurd to say or imply that, for example, the sentence "Moore sat next to Russell" is a self-contradictory expression and says nothing conceivable about Moore and Russell. It might be urged that Bradley speaks with the vulgar and thinks with the learned. But it would be mere fantasy to suppose that he is pretending to think with the vulgar when he speaks their vernacular, or that for practical purposes he finds a self-contradictory way of speaking to be the more convenient. Unquestionably he thinks as he speaks. Yet, just as unquestionably Bradley thought himself to be stating a truth about space. At the same time, he could not fail to know that the verbal sentence connected with his statement made a false claim, namely, that the word "space" is self-contradictory and hence lacking in descriptive use. How is this situation to be explained? I think it is because "Space is not real" has the form of a sentence having factual content and therefore creates the impression of being factual. If a sentence professing to express a necessary proposition is not linked with a sentence that makes a true statement about usage, then the correct inference is that the sentence, construed in terms of the normal use of the words occurring in it, does not do what it professes. The conclusion about the sentence "Space is unreal" is that it neither expresses a necessary proposition nor one that is empirical. It does not make a claim to which a truth-value attaches.

What construction, then, is to be placed on the utterance? As Bradley is using the sentence, "Space is unreal" neither says something about a phenomenon nor does it convey information about the actual use of the word "space." To sum up the matter in John Wisdom's way, Bradley's sentence presents a *linguistic decision*: in a nonverbal mode of speech it puts before us, as *a fait accompli,* the result of his deleting space-referring terminology from our vocabulary, a decision which is clearly not introduced for the practical purpose of reforming language. The sentence "Space is unreal" illustrates what Wittgenstein described as the rejection of a notation under the guise of rejecting a proposition as false. When a mathematician introduces a language change a new use becomes part of an enlarged language which is continuous with the old one. But in the present case the philosopher does no more than academically banish the use of the word from the language, which, independently of his decision, works as before. The banishment is idle. But what is gained is considerable: the generation of the illusion that a fact about space is being revealed. Producing this intellectual illusion seems to be its *raison d'être.*

We now have a vantage point from which to apply to a number of philosophical views the idea that a philosopher rejects a notation rather than refutes a theory. What is being done with language will not in all cases be the same; the problem in each case will be to see precisely what is being done. In view of the fact that a number of influential philosophers maintain that Wittgenstein's thought from the *Tractatus* on is a continuous philosophical development, with no metaphilosophical[19] interludes, it will be of interest to see how the earlier Wittgenstein thought about causation and logical necessity. In the *Tractatus,* he makes the following assertion: "There are no grounds for believing that the simplest course of events will really happen. That the sun will rise tomorrow is an hypothesis; and that means that we do not *know* whether it will rise."[20] And in *Zettel* he said, "It should be possible for us to know future events if causality were an inner necessity—like, say, that of logical inference." Again, in the *Tractatus* he stated: "A necessity for one thing to happen because another has happened does not exist. There is only *logical* necessity." Two things are evident from these quotations: one, that one cannot know that regularities in nature exist; two, that there can be no such thing as causal necessity. The language Wittgenstein uses is the language of empirical discourse; what he says is like saying that only Clydesdales exist and that there are no grounds for believing that any other horses exist. The belief in causation, he says, is a superstition.[23] Of course any superstitious belief could theoretically be true.

Nevertheless, when Wittgenstein denies that there is any necessity other than logical necessity he is not making a denial on a footing with "Winged horses do not exist." It is more like denying that prime numbers that are composite exist. In a different connection, he remarked that "we could not say of an 'unlogical' world how it would look."[24] We know how a world with winged horses would look, but not what a world would look like that contained a prime number of pebbles consisting of equal subsets. It might seem now that his philosophical view about necessity is not to the effect that no necessity other than a logical one in fact exists, but rather that we have no idea of necessity other than that of logical necessity. Restated in linguistic terms, the view would seem to amount to holding that the phrase "physical necessity" (and more concrete expressions falling under it) has no application, either in fact or in theory. The implication is that a whole class of expressions in everyday use has no function in the language. It implies that such sentences as "Bodies heavier than air if unsupported must fall," "Water freezes at 32°," and all statements referring to what Galileo called "immutabilities of nature," are literally senseless. Only the spell of an illusion could make anyone hold a view having such consequences. The later work of Wittgenstein sheds light on what has happened. The idea that a philosopher rejects a form of words under the illusion that he is upsetting a factual proposition enables us to understand what makes it possible for him to hold his supposed view. He rejects a *notation,* but he does it in the fact-stating mode of speech, which both conceals what is being done and also creates the agreeable illusion of a discovery having been made. The philosophical debate centering on his view is presented as being a divergence of opinion as to the facts of the case, but contrary to the appearances and hidden from the debaters is a contest over linguistic taste. The debate, to put it in Lazerowitz's way, is constituted of nothing more substantial than the expression of rival notational preferences. This is not to say that philosophical disputes are emotionally aseptic, to use John Wisdom's word; it is evident, rather, that they are invested with strong feeling. Wittgenstein has remarked on "how much a notation . . . may mean to us,"[25] and his words suggest that the disputes go much deeper than the academic contest over terminology that we can now discern.

Examples of notational alterations such as Wittgenstein's abound in philosophy, alterations confined to philosophical discussion where disagreements remain, so to speak, in animated suspension. Consider the assertion that time is irreversible. One thing it implies is that time has a direction, from past to future. The past, we say, cannot be changed; what is past and done cannot be undone. A philosopher might say that this means that nothing can be erased from the ledger of the past or be added to it. It would seem that this idea is in the background of philosophical thinking about time. Now, eradicating an event that has already happened or making a past event occur that did not occur is logically impossible; it is not a factual impossibility, the contrary of which, as Hume put it, is "perfectly conceivable." To change the past by causing what happened not to have happened, or by causing something to have happened that did not happen would amount to bringing about a self-contradictory state of affairs. For to undo a past occurrence implies both that it had happened, and in consequence of having been removed from the past, that it had not happened. Spinoza said that not even God could bring it about that from a certain cause no effect shall follow. Nor could He bring it about that past occurrence did not occur. What might be called "metaphysical regret" over the impossibility of changing the past is pseudo regret, a verbal imitation of the real thing: it is regret over something we cannot conceive.

But when the ordinary person says, regretfully, that the past cannot be undone he is not regretting what he cannot conceive—for example, causing the social blunder previously committed not to have been committed. His regret is over not being able to make amends. And certainly it is conceivable for amends to be made. Some things cannot in fact be undone. The slain, unlike the Valhalla warriors, cannot be brought back to life; Humpty Dumpty cannot be put back together again; the ageing process is physically irreversible. But what is physically out of the question is in principle possible. It is theoretically possible for a Lazarus to be raised from the dead, and for Humpty Dumpty to be put back together again. The fountain of youth that Ponce de Leon looked for, could in theory have existed and have been found by him. What is contrary to the order of things can be imagined as being the order of things. In everyday language the phrase "undoing what has been done" describes what *could,* imaginably, be done. Scrooge's later behavior was an undoing of his earlier behavior.

In *The Blue Book,* Wittgenstein remarked that a metaphysical sentence "can also be used to state a fact of experience."[26] I am suggesting that this is the case with the sentences "Time is irreversible" and "The past cannot be changed." Time with a capital "T," to use G. E. Moore's description, cannot conceivably be turned back. What has happened cannot be made not to have happened. The river of Time cannot be made to reverse its course. But a Hercules could make a physical river reverse its course. And an ordinary person can, at least conceivably, undo a past action: he can, in his imagination if not in fact, make restitution. And this does not imply rendering a past action nonexistent. To use the words "undoing what was done" to imply reaching into the past and removing something from it is to turn into a contradiction an expression which in ordinary language is free from contradiction. The statement "The past cannot be undone" creates the impression of making a cosmic statement about Time which, moreover, has the security of a necessary truth. But to present it as though it expressed an *a priori* fact when it does not is to present in the ontological mode of speech a linguistic innovation. It represents, in Wittgenstein's words, a "discontentment with our grammar."[27] In the present case this takes the form of an innovation that goes counter to present usage.

It is not always the case that the truth-value form of speech conceals an alteration in language. An alteration either extends or goes against common usage. But many of Moore's statements, especially those in his "Defense of Common Sense," are associated with no innovation, but have as a consequence the defense of ordinary language. Consider his rejection of Bradley's claim that material things are unreal. If the Bradleian sentence "Material things are unreal" made an *a priori* claim, then ordinary expressions referring to physical objects such as "statues in the square," "the round church in Cambridge," or "the antique desk I bought" would be self-contradictory. Moore's procedure was to confront Bradley's view with particular statements which are its translations into the concrete, that is, with statements such as "I do not possess shoes," which he took to be implied by "Material objects do not exist." Since it is a *fact* that I do have shoes the view was declared false. It comes seriously in question, however, whether the view does have empirical translations into the concrete. There is also the question how Moore's view that material things are real is to be construed if it is to counter Bradley's view. The sentence "Material things are real," which seems to mean the same as "There are material things," unlike the sentence "Material things are not real," would appear to bear only an empirical construction. And its possible translations into the concrete, e.g., "There are bronze lions in Trafalgar Square," would normally be taken to be empirical statements. But if so, then we are required to suppose that this empirical statement could be used to upset a statement that is not empirical. To suppose that this is possible is to suppose that "necessary p" is logically *inconsistent with* "empirical q," in which case "necessary p" would entail $\sim q$. The proposition $\sim q$ qill be empirical if and only if q is empirical. This goes against the principle Hume expressed in the words: "from something necessary nothing contingent follows."

I have said that if the sentence "Material things are unreal" did express a logically necessary proposition, then it would be the case that words ordinarily used to refer to things are self-contradictory. This interpretation of "Material things are unreal" carries with it implications for Moore's counter-claim, "Material things are real." If it and its possible specifications into the concrete, are to go against "Material things are unreal," then they likewise will have to be interpreted as verbal. A verbal proposition can only be countered by a verbal proposition, and a claim about the use of a term can only be countered by a rival claim about the use of that term. We shall have to construe "Material things are real" and sentences into which it might specify as also representing claims about usage. The sentence "Material things are real," if it is to count against the verbal import of "Material things are not real" (assuming the latter to express a necessity), will have to be taken to state that such sentences as "There are bronze lions in Trafalgar Square" have a use in our language, to convey factual information.

What is unsatisfactory about placing this linguistic construction on Bradley's view, however, is that no one could think that such a sentence as "There are bronze lions in Trafalgar Square" did not refer to sculptures. This includes Bradley, who used object-words as naturally as the rest of humankind. I think, therefore, that the arguments, which look as though they are directed to showing that "Material things are unreal" is an *a priori* truth, and hence that words normally thought to refer to things are self-contradictory, must have a different interpretation. The statement that the sentence "Material things do not exist" expresses a logical necessity is to be understood as introducing a linguistic innovation not as stating a fact of our language. Correspondingly, the assertion "Material things are real" is to be differently understood — as opposing the verbal change. It represents a decision to retain ordinary usage, to keep in the language sentences like "There are lions in Trafalgar Square." Moore's positive aim in making his translations into the concrete is, as Lazerowitz has put it, to defend the linguistic *status quo*.

I turn now to a final illustration of the view that philosophical pronouncements are not truth-value statements. In this example I think something different is being done with language than introducing or resisting a linguistic change. The view is that space is an infinite magnitude. It is instructive to note several remarks Kant made at the beginning of his examination of the concept of space. "What then are space and time?," he asked. "Are they real beings?"[28] "It is impossible to imagine that there should be no space," he stated, "though one might well imagine there should be space without objects to fill it."[29] Another of his remarks is: "We can imagine one space only, and if we speak of many spaces, we mean parts only of one and the same space. . . . Space is essentially one."[30] And finally, "Space is represented as an infinite quantity.[31] Like words such as "container," "box," etc., the word "space" is a substantive. Philosophers who have written about space as if it were a receptacle (it has been described as a box without sides) gives the impression of having the idea that "space" is the name of a kind of thing, something in which all physical existents are housed and which they cannot vacate. But it misrepresents the nature of space to say or imply that it is a cosmic container with no exits: the word "space" is not the name of a container. Wittgenstein helps us understand philosophers' talk about space by citing what he calls "one of the great sources of philosophical bewilderment,"[32] namely, that when we encounter a substantive we look for a thing that corresponds to it. The word "unicorn" brings to mind a creature, and the noun "space" makes us think of a container.

Philosophers who, to all appearances, hold directly or by implication that the noun "space" is the name of a container put forward their view that space is a magnitude with the air of revealing an *a priori* fact about the structure of reality. They do not give the impression of making an insecure empirical speculation about the universe, nor yet do they seem to be saying anything verbal. Nevertheless, the associated verbal claim is close to the semantic reality that is hidden behind the appearance of a cosmological pronouncement. It will be remembered that Carnap gave a like explanation of the statement that a rose is a thing. His well-known claim was that it comes to saying the word "rose" is a thing-word. The parallel interpretation of "space is a magnitude" is that the word "space" is a thing-word. This states the position without the refinements required to avoid conventionalism, but the point can be made without committing ourselves to conventionalism, in the following way: To say that the sentence "Space is a magnitude" expresses an *a priori* fact is equivalent to saying that " 'Space' is in point of usage the name of a kind of thing." But the matter does not end there. The philosopher is not making a declaration about the actual use in the language of the word "space." Instead, he is legislating a classification of the term "space" with nouns which, like "box," are names of things. Kant held that we legislate the laws that we discover in nature, and we may say that the philosopher of the cosmic receptacle is legislating a piece of grammar. What he does is in a certain respect similar to what a mathematician does who describes a point as a circle with zero radius. His description represents the word "point," which is not the name of a geometrical figure, as being the name of a circle. But unlike the philosopher's supposed view, his linguistic innovation has a practical motive. It is to introduce uniformity into a notation.

Wittgenstein's assertion that when we encounter a substantive we tend to look for a subtance suggests a distinction between substantives which are names of things and those which are not. Now the word "space" is not, as a matter of linguistic fact, the name of a kind of thing. To say that one can enter and leave a room but cannot enter and leave space is not to point out a physical difference between two sorts of chambers. Rather, it is to mark a difference in the use of the noun "space" and the substantive "room." It is an oblique way of saying that "room" is the name of a kind of thing, as "pitcher" is the name of a kind of container, but that "space" is not. The philosopher, to be sure, is as aware of this as is anyone else. If in thinking of the word "space" the image of a room comes to mind, he knows that the image is no sort of picture of what the word is used to refer to. When a philosopher thinks of the word "space" he does not look for a substance any more than does a person who encounters the word "tomorrow" embark on a search for tomorrow. To give a better idea of what the philosopher does on encountering the noun "space," Wittgenstein's maxim might be amended in the following way: the philosopher *creates* a substance to correspond to the noun. But to say this is only a metaphorical way of describing what he does linguistically. His creation is not physical, like that of a builder; it is semantic. What he creates is a piece of grammar, and an academic one at that. A substantive that is not used in the language as the name of a thing is changed by grammatical fiat into one that is.[33] The same is done with the noun "time," which the philosopher, in common with the poet, turns in semantic appearance into the name of a ghostly river.

What the philosopher says of space he takes as citing an essential property of it. But in this case we cannot go on to say that what he supposes himself to be doing cloaks the *rejection* of a notation. The change he introduces into grammar—a change constituted by artificially enlarging a grammatical category without a corresponding change being introduced into the actual use of the word—neither goes against present grammar nor is it part of present grammar. Our grammar does not stipulate two different noun categories, those which name things and those which do not. In contrast to views having as their verbal import changes that either go against usage or defend its retention, the view that space is an infinite quantity goes beyond anything on which present grammatical usage makes a decision. Dissatisfied with a notation that does not appeal to him, the philosopher transforms a noun, which is not the name of a thing, into a cosmic thing-name.

A.A.

NOTES

1. *Philosophical Investigations,* p. 49.
2. Ibid.
3. Immanuel Kant, *Prolegomena to Any Future Metaphysics* (Chicago: The Open Court Publishing Co., 1929), edited in English by Dr. Paul Carus, p. 141.
4. Ibid., p. 20.
5. Bertrand Russell, *The Principles of Mathematics,* p. 451.
6. *Philosophical Investigations,* p. 47.
7. See *Zettel,* trans. by G. E. M. Anscombe (Oxford: Basil Blackwell, 1967), edited by G. E. M. Anscombe & G. H. von Wright, p. 82.
8. C. D. Broad, *Scientific Thought* (New York: Harcourt, Brace & Co., Inc.; London: Kegan Paul, Trench, Trubner & Co., Ltd.), p. 19.
9. A. J. Ayer, *Language, Truth and Logic,* second edition, p. 125.
10. *Zettel,* p. 82.
11. Some philosophers, notably Hume, create the impression that there are relevant verification procedures.

12. On this point see J. W. N. Watkins's "Word Magic and the Trivialization of Philosophy," *Ratio* 7 (December 1965), pp. 206–218, and Morris Lazerowitz's criticism of the falsifiability thesis in "Moore's Ontological Program," *Ratio* 14 (June 1972), pp. 45–58.

13. *Philosophical Investigations,* p. 48.

14. *Tractatus* (see 4.461, 5.43, 6.11).

15. Ibid., 7.

16. Immanuel Kant, *The Critique of Pure Reason,* pp. 327–338.

17. See *G. E. Moore: Essays in Retrospective,* edited by Alice Ambrose and Morris Lazerowitz (London: George Allen & Unwin, Ltd.; New York: Humanities Press, 1970), p. 203.

18. J. L. Austin, *Philosophical Papers* (Oxford: Clarendon Press, 1961) edited by J. O. Urmson and G. J. Warnock, p. 130.

19. This term was coined by Morris Lazerowitz for the specific purpose of referring to the kind of investigation Wittgenstein has called "the heir of philosophy." See his note in *Metaphilosophy* 1 (January 1970), p. 91.

20. *Tractatus* (6.3631–6.36311).

21. *Zettel,* p. 432.

22. *Tractatus* (6.37).

23. Ibid. (5.1361).

24. Ibid. (3.63).

25. *The Blue Book,* p. 57.

26. Ibid.

27. Ibid.

28. Immanuel Kant, *The Critique of Pure Reason,* trans. by F. Max Müller, second edition, revised (New York: The Macmillan Co.; London: Macmillan & Co., Ltd., 1927), p. 18.

29. Ibid., p. 19.

30. Ibid., p. 20.

31. Ibid.

32. *The Blue Book,* p. 1.

33. For a more extended discussion see "The Metaphysical Concept of Space," in Morris Lazerowitz's *Studies in Metaphilosophy.*

IV

Bouwsma's Paradox

O. K. Bouwsma has given expression to a paradox which so far has hardly been discussed by philosophers. It consists of two connected parts which I shall develop and try to explain in the following pages. Bouwsma has remarked on an important and perplexing difference between the investigation of the world by philosophers and its investigation by ordinary, non-philosophical observers. Unlike the natural scientist, the philosopher, regardless of whether he is an empiricist, a rationalist, or a logical positivist, makes no use of experimental techniques. Indeed, we should think a technical, academic philosopher to be under the influence of a strange delusion if he told us that he had set up a special laboratory for testing philosophical ideas, such ideas, for example, as that nothing really changes, we do not really see things, and motion does not occur. Unlike the explorer and the traveler he makes no use of observation.[1] A philosopher who wishes to know what there is and how things work satisfies his craving for knowledge without using his eyes, or any of his other senses. Both the philosopher and the voyager learn facts about the world, but the philosopher learns them without observing it. Bouwsma has written:

> The traveler goes far away. He visits, and he tells about what others have not seen. He tells us about what is covered by great distances, about what is hidden from eyes that stay at home. Let us say then that the traveler describes the hidden, and that this is also what the philosopher does. But the hidden is now obviously of a different sort; for whereas sailors sail the seas, the philosopher stays at home.[2]

What Bouwsma points out is puzzling and stands in serious need of explanation, but what he points out can be no surprise to a philosopher. For no philosopher can fail to be aware of the fact that his researches do not require him to leave his study. In this respect the hidden which the philosopher

78

discovers is more like that which the pure mathematician discovers than like the hidden which the natural scientist unearths. The mathematician who applies mathematics to things in order to obtain new information about them makes investigations that require him to leave his study, or else uses the findings of others who do leave their study; but like Spinoza, a pure mathematician can remain withdrawn from the world in his inner sanctum.

Consider a further statement made by Bouwsma:

> They, [Robinson Crusoe and Gulliver] too, described, mentioning all sorts of most important kinds of things which they had seen. This helped me to see both how what Moore did was like what they did, and also how what he did was different from what they did. They were all discoverers, and they all wrote home about what they discovered. There were 'melons and grapes' and 'sense-data', and 'material objects' and a 'huge creature' and 'pleasant savannahs and meadows' and 'universals.' The difference between these different sorts of things immediately suggests different means of discovery. Robinson Crusoe and Gulliver sailed, landed, and looked. But Moore stayed at home.[3]

What is the difference between the *things* discovered by an observer of the world and those discovered by a philosopher, between melons and sense-data and between meadows and Platonic universals? And what is the difference between the means of discovering them? Parenthetically, it should be noted that Bertrand Russell and C. D. Broad thought it necessary to explain how it is that universals and sense-data came to be overlooked and needed to be discovered by philosophers. That they thought it necessary is understandable, since both universals and sense-data are held to be objects of which we are directly aware. Thus, Broad has written: ". . . we are not as a rule interested in sensa, as such, but only in what we think they can tell us about physical objects, which alone can help or hurt us. We therefore pass automatically from the sensum and its properties to judgments about the physical object and its properties."[4] And according to Russell: "We do not naturally dwell upon those words in a sentence which do not stand for particulars; and if we are forced to dwell upon a word which stands for a universal, we naturally think of it as standing for some one of the particulars that come under the universal."[5]

Not only is there a strange difference between the ways things are discovered by the traveler or the scientist and by the philosopher, but there is also a mystifying difference between the things themselves, i.e., between what might be called *philosophical* objects like sense-data and universals, and ordinary nonphilosophical objects like exotic melons and bacteria. Bouwsma has remarked that "it sometimes happens that if one philosopher announces that he has discovered a new and 'important kind of thing,' some other may announce that there has been only a new and important kind of mistake."[6] Bouwsma says that this may *sometimes* happen. The fact is, however, that this *always* happens. As the history of philosophy shows, it is a *regular* feature of objects discovered in philosophy that their existence comes into question and remains so. We may say that it *sometimes* happens, and even that it often happens, that the announced discovery of a scientist is contested and the announced discovery of an explorer is mistaken or even fraudulent; but this does not always happen. In philosophy it is always the case that what is an indisputable discovery to one philosopher, or group of philosophers, is a plain mistake to others. We cannot think that divisions of opinion about the existence of such objects as universals and sense-data are due to the intellectual incompetence or waywardness of philosophers. The disagreements have lasted too long for this sort of explanation to be acceptable. Instead, we have to think that it is something in the *nature* of the objects which makes possible intractable disagreements about their existence. Philosophical entities become strange indeed; and it goes without saying that they stand in need of special and careful scrutiny, which so far they have not received.

One paradoxical and unexplained difference that Bouwsma has pointed out between things discovered by philosophers and those discovered by others is that philosophical objects, such as sense-data and universals, and even "material objects," remain hidden while yet seen. Unlike Edgar Allan Poe's purloined letter, which went unnoticed although it was in plain view, or like a lens which we see through without seeing it, we cannot help but see them while nevertheless they are hidden and their existence is debated by philosophers. Russell, for example, has remarked that with few exceptions only students of philosophy realize that in addition to concrete, particular objects there are such things as universals.[7] But his explanation of how it is that universals come to be overlooked, whether by ordinary folk or by philosophers who deny their existence, won't do. Universals are not like the purloined letter; they are objects of immediate awareness, and are "represented as what one cannot help but see."[8] The paradox that Bouwsma highlights is that the objects discovered by philosophers, such as abstract entities, sense-data, and material objects, are of such a kind that they are hidden but nevertheless seen.

Broad's explanation of our myopia for sense-data also won't do. Even if it were the case that we are not ordinarily interested in sense-data "as such" because "they cut no ice,"[9] it would hardly be the case that we fail to notice them. It is only by noticing them, whether or not we dwell on them, that we could pass automatically from sense-data to judgments about physical things and their properties. Ordinarily we do not fail to see an object that is pointed out to us, but this is not the case with regard to objects referred to in philosophy: they remain hidden from the sight of at least some philosophers who see them. Consider the well-known example of a straight stick which appears bent when partly immersed in water. Many philosophers report seeing a bent sense-datum, i.e., the sensible appearance presented by a stick which is in fact straight. Other philosophers who see everything that a sense-datum philosopher sees will, nevertheless, deny seeing the sense-datum which is 'of' the partly immersed stick. Thus, J. L. Austin has said that when we see a stick which looks bent we do *"not* see" an immaterial bent stick; what we do in fact see is a stick that is partly immersed in water. There can be no doubt that Austin sees everything a sense-datum philosopher sees; they both have the same visual experience. They both see the same, but nevertheless one fails to see what the other sees. Bouwsma's paradox reappears: an object discovered by a philosopher is capable of being seen and of being at the same time hidden.

As is well known, many philosophers deny that there are such objects as material things. F. H. Bradley has stated that all that exists is "sentient experience," that there is nothing in addition to volitions, thoughts, and feelings, none of which are material things.[10] And Berkeley has written that "if you stick to the notion of an unthinking substance or support of extension, motion, and other sensible qualities, then to me it is most evidently impossible there should be any such thing: since it is a plain repugnancy that those qualities should exist in, or be supported by, an unperceiving substance."[11] Samuel Johnson professed to refute this claim by kicking a stone; and G. E. Moore professed to prove the existence of physical things by holding up his hands and calling attention to them with the words, "Here is one hand, and here is another."[12] Moore's proof by no means convinced all philosophers who denied the existence of material things, things characterized by "extension, motion, and other sensible qualities." There can be no question that all philosophers see the same; there is no difference in their everyday experience of things. But there is a strange difference in their experience with regard to objects to which attention is called by philosophers. Again, Bouwsma's paradox presents itself in connection with physical things, which gives rise to the idea that being referred to in philosophy turns a thing into an enigma: a physical thing becomes capable of being seen while it remains unseen.

The objects of special concern to philosophers are not only strangely different from those met with in everyday life; they also require a "definite technique for their discernment,"[13] a technique or method of investigation not employed in any of the natural sciences. A clue that directs our attention to unknown objects which yet are known is different in kind from a clue that merely leads to the discovery of an unknown object. Thus, a clue leading to the discovery of a universal is entirely different from one that leads to the discovery of a new planet; and a clue leading to the philosophical discovery of sense-data is altogether different from one that leads to the scientific discovery of the cause of a disease. A clue followed by a philosopher enables him to bring to light what we are already aware of, e.g., the hidden material objects, which, parenthetically, "are not to be confused with the material objects almost everybody knows."[14] About philosophical clues, Bouwsma has written: "Anything is a clue, of course, only when taken in a certain way, and this is the conception I want to use. It is something which, taken in a certain way, leads to the discovery of sense-data, to the discovery of 'material objects,' or to the discovery of universals. It is especially the nature of these clues which I want to explore."[15] It turns out that it is language that contains the required clues and provides the "knotholes"[16] through which we can see the philosophical entities and examine their nature.

One clue which, according to Bouwsma, leads to the discovery of sense-data lies in the difference between the use of sentences like "The envelope is rectangular" and the use of sentences like "The envelope looks like a rhombus," i.e., the difference between uses of sentences that say what a thing is and sentences that state how a thing looks. The latter sentences bear a likeness to still other sorts of looks-sentences, e.g., "There looks to be a lake in the distance," and noticing facts like these "will lead straight to the conception of the sense-datum as a 'thing' which intervenes in perception."[17] A man who dons a policeman's uniform *looks* like a policeman, a church may be camouflaged to *look* like a barn,[18] and a man who dresses like a woman will *look* like a woman. Bouwsma goes on to say: ". . . if in interpreting the sentence 'The envelope looks like a rhombus' you follow the pattern of 'He looks like a policeman,' then the analogy will require a mask for the envelope. And how then could an envelope look like a rhombus? Naturally, by wearing the suitable mask. And this then is what it must do since it does look like a rhombus."[19] It is clear that the clue which ends in the discovery of sense-data consists of similarities and differences between various types of sentences. The clue, in other words, is linguistic, as is also the 'knothole' through which sense-data are seen as *things*. It is understandable why the philosopher, unlike the sailor and the natural scientist, does not find it necessary to leave his study in order to make his discoveries of what there is: he arrives at the kind of knowledge that he is interested in by looking into language.

As in the case of sense-data, the clue which leads to the discovery of material objects—i.e., the 'material objects' which are of special interest to philosophers—consists in "a peculiarity of sentences of a certain kind,"[20] sentences like "The envelope is rectangular" and "The church spire is 150 feet tall." Attending to the functioning of such sentences in the language, which is "intertwined"[21] with the functioning of the corresponding "looks like" sentences, leads to the philosophical discovery of things "in the dark which have no looks at all."[22] When sentences such as "The envelope is rectangular" and "The spire is 150 feet tall" are "taken in a certain way," they serve as "chinks"[23] through which the inner nature of physical things may be seen. Whatever the view of things seen through the chink comes down to, it is plain again that the chink is linguistic, i.e., the function certain kinds of sentences have in a language. The question that arises is whether any sort of examination of language, such as noticing how expressions function with respect to each other, can yield knowledge of things. It may be that philosophers are deceiving themselves about what they see through the chinks offered by language.

The last case that Bouwsma considers is that of universals, or abstract entities. He has the following to say: "Most people have never heard of them. And many people who are told about them and who are directed to discover them, never do discover them. Those, relatively few, who have discovered them have, however, established a definite technique for their discernment, and it is to this technique that we must attend in order to understand this discovery. In this case we begin, however, not with sentences, but with certain individual words. Words are the clue, and what, of course, is involved here is that they, words, have meaning."[24] Words like "two," "justice," and "elephant," as against such syllables as "brund" and "wabe," have meaning, and the Platonic claim is that the meaning of a general word is a *thing*. It is easily seen that, taken as a thing, the meaning of a general word will have the familiar properties attributed to it by Platonic philosophers, such as being intangible to the senses. Again, as in the preceding cases, it is noticing features of linguistic usage, whether of sentences or of words, which leads to the discovery of a new galaxy of objects. Unlike Robinson Crusoe who has to leave his home in order to find the pleasant savannahs he describes, the philosophical voyager of the sixth and seventh books of the *Republic* has no need to leave his study in making his journey and his discovery: his voyage takes place in his mind. We need to recall, however, the disconcerting thing that Bouwsma has pointed out: among philosophers it sometimes happens that what one philosopher announces as a discovery another philosopher will declare to be a mistake. Bouwsma says that this *sometimes* happens, but, as has already been pointed out, the fact is that it *invariably* happens. This cannot be emphasized enough, for it is constantly being ignored. There is no such thing as an uncontested claim in philosophy and no such thing as a secure finding. Austin speaks of some words as being "substantive-hungry,"[25] and we may say that *all* philosophical questions, no matter how old and time-honored, are without exception "answer-hungry." The fact that a high value is placed on philosophy requires that this be called to the attention of philosophers again and again.

To return to Bouwsma's talk about knotholes and chinks, it is quite plain that he is not using the words "knothole" and "chink" in their literal senses to refer to openings through which what is on the other side of a barrier can be seen. A language is not a wall or a fence or a curtain with peepholes in it, and he was, clearly, using the words metaphorically. Verbal usage as well as likenesses and differences between the functioning of sentences and words are capable of providing clues but not "chinks" and "knotholes." It would seem that he is using them as colorful and vivid ways of referring to philosophical *inferences* which are made from the clues provided by language. To say, for example, that the difference between a meaningful general word and a nonsense word affords us an aperture through which we can see that a universal, or the meaning of a general word, is a thing, would seem to be another and more colorful way of saying that the difference justifies the philosophical inference about universals. There is the well-known case in astronomy in which the existence of an unknown planet, Neptune, was inferred from the perturbations of the planet Uranus from its orbit. The new planet was later sighted through a telescope. But the philosophical inference that universals are things, or the inference that sense-data are things, is entirely unlike the astronomical inference. In the philosophical case there are only the clue and the inference from it; there is no independent confirmation of the inferred object. It makes sense to say, "The existence of Neptune was first made probable and was subsequently rendered certain by being seen"; it makes no literal sense to say, "The claim that universals are things was first made probable and was later rendered certain by their being apprehended."

The statements about sense-data, material objects, and universals appear to make factual claims about objects the nature or existence of which eludes most people. The idea, suggested by the word "appear," that they may not be about objects, is in the eyes of philosophers so patently false as to deserve nothing better than impatient dismissal. It is well, however, to keep in mind Bouwsma's observation that what one philosopher calls a discovery an equally competent philosopher may call a mistake. It is important to realize also that there is no difference between philosophers with respect to any possible information that would be relevant to removing their disagreement. Regardless of whether the claimed findings about sense-data, universals, and material objects are about what there is in the world, philosophers *think* that their claims are about the world. And it is plain that they are led to their results by an examination of language. The working idea behind Bouwsma's metaphors is that facts about things can be inferred from facts about verbal usage. Some philosophers have given explicit expression to this idea, which has caused C. D. Broad to say: ". . . many able men, who might have contributed to solving the real problems of the philosophy of sense-perception [have been led] to waste time and labor and ingenuity in semi-linguistic studies of the usages of ordinary speech in the language with which they happen to be familiar. To imagine that a careful study of the usages, the implications, the suggestions, and the *nuances* of the ordinary speech of contemporary Englishmen could be a substitute for, or a valuable contribution towards, the solutions of the philosophical problems of sense-perception, seems to me one of the strangest delusions which has ever flourished in academic circles."[26] Broad's comment applies not only to philosophical problems of sense-perception; it applies to all problems revolving around inferences that proceed from language to things. If this indeed is what philosophers are doing, then they suffer from a strange delusion which requires the support of magical thinking. But it is hard to believe that philosophical thought could be so regressive. There must be an explanation of what the philosopher is doing, an explanation which will also explain Bouwsma's paradox. And it cannot be the hypothesis that philosophers attempt to learn facts about the behavior of things from facts about the conventional behavior of words in a language.

It is not to be doubted that the statements about universals, sense-data, and material objects appear to be about what there is, i.e., about items in the world. But if they are inferred from the workings of "phrases and sentences,"[27] the statements cannot have the nonverbal factual content they appear to have. Bouwsma states that the difference between melons and sense-data, material objects and a huge creature, and pleasant savannahs and universals "suggests different means of discovery," and we may say that the different means of discovery suggest a difference in what is discovered, a difference in the content of the philosophical claims. To be sure, careful scrutiny of the claims shows that they do not have the kind of factual content they are naturally taken to have. The statement "A sense-datum is a thing" is utterly unlike the statement "A diamond is the hardest substance known to man"; and the question "Is a sense-datum a thing?" makes a request that is different in kind from the request made by "Is a diamond a harder substance than say, cobalt?" A verification procedure involving the use of the senses is relevant to determining the truth-value of the statement about the hardness of a diamond, and also the truth-value of the further statement that a diamond has a crystalline structure. But no empirical procedure is relevant to determining that a sense-datum is a *thing,* or that it is not a thing. No experiment and no observation, however refined, could *in principle* give support to the discovery which is expressed by the sentence "Sense-data are things," and this implies that the philosophical sentence does not express an *empirical* proposition. The same consideration can readily be seen to apply to the sentences referring to universals and material objects. No theoretical observation could either prove or disprove the proposition expressed by the sentences "The meaning of the word 'two' is a thing" and "A material object has 'no looks in the dark.' "

The implication with regard to the three philosophical sentences, about matter, sense-data, and universals, is that the propositions they express are not empirical, which is to say, not open to confirmation or refutation by experience. Thus, it is not intelligible English to say, "Experience shows that universals are things" or "Experience shows that a material object, as against the appearances it presents, is itself not an object of perception." The two sentences, "Universals are things" and "A material object is itself not an object of perception," are not, however, literally unintelligible; they only require an interpretation. They do say *something* about material things, sensible appearances, and the meanings of general words, whatever the something they are saying may turn out to be. They appear to express nonverbal propositions which refer to objects, whether apprehended by the senses or by thought, but which cannot be established or upset by experience. In other words, the sentences are used, apparently, to state logically necessary propositions about what they refer to. The sentence (1) "A gazelle is an animal" would be interpreted by many philosophers as referring to gazelles and stating something that is necessarily true of them. It makes an *a priori* claim about them, as against (2) "A gazelle is a swift runner," which states a contingent fact about gazelles, to the verification of which observation is relevant. But both are the same in respect of the object to which they refer, and they differ in respect of what they assert about it. The interpretation of the three sentences, "Sense-data are things," "A material object is not one among its sensible appearances," and "Universals are things," seems to be that they state *a priori* facts about what the sentences refer to: sense-data, universals, and material objects. Viewed in this way, the sentences are to be construed as expressing entailment claims: *"Being a universal entails being a thing,"* etc. If this is their correct interpretation, if from the function of expressions the philosopher infers putative entailments, it is easy to understand why he has no need to travel in order to make his discoveries. Through the chinks and knotholes to which he is led by linguistic clues he is able to see entailments which escape others. The explanation of how it is possible to be aware of something which is yet hidden from us is that we are aware of it without knowing what it implies—something we are not unfamiliar with in mathematics.

One thing, however, which is not explained by the present interpretation of the nature of the discoveries a philosopher is able to make from his special scrutiny of language, is the continued disagreements that gather around the claimed discoveries. No philosophical proposition has been able to free itself from debate and no philosophical question has been able to free itself from disagreement. It can no longer be thought that they are the kind of statements and questions that *can* free themselves from disagreement; and the idea that they are different kind from the proposition that a gazelle is an animal needs to be looked into. What needs to be explained is the peculiar nature of a statement such as *A universal is a thing,* which permits what might be called open-ended disagreement, and makes it unlike the statement, *A gazelle is an animal.*

The statement *A gazelle is fleet-footed* makes a contingent attribution, and the statement *A gazelle is an animal,* a noncontingent attribution. Denial of the first does not yield a logical impossibility, whereas denial of the second does: the words "gazelle but not an animal," unlike the words "gazelle but not fleet-footed," express a logically impossible concept, one to which nothing could, in principle, answer. The sentence "A gazelle is an animal" expresses an entailment, i.e., that *being a gazelle* entails *being an animal*; and it would seem now that the philosophical sentence "A universal is a thing" also expresses an entailment, such that the phrase "universal but not a thing" denotes a logically impossible concept. Both sentences express equally elementary entailments. It requires no subtle or complex chain of reasoning to see that *being a gazelle* entails *being an animal.* And if *being a universal* does entail *being a thing,* it is equally elementary and requires no reasoning to see it. The perplexing thing, however, is that the claim that the second is an entailment is subject to unending disputation, while no disagreement attaches to the first. The explanation of this mystifying difference can best be arrived at by an examination of the *sentence* "A gazelle is an animal."

The sentence "A gazelle is an animal" expresses a nonverbal proposition, and in this respect it is like the sentence "A gazelle is fleet-footed." But each sentence has a verbal correlate, i.e., a statement about the use in the English language of the terms occurring in the corresponding sentence. The verbal correlate of "A gazelle is fleet-footed" is the statement (1) that the term "fleet-footed" applies to whatever "gazelle" applies to; and to the sentence "A gazelle is an animal" there corresponds the verbal statement (2) that the word "animal" applies to whatever "gazelle" applies to. An important difference between the two verbal statements is immediately evident: the truth-value of (2) is determined by a fact of English usage, the truth-value of (1) by a fact of nature. It is the behavior of gazelles which makes true what the sentence "A gazelle is fleet-footed" says, and therefore makes true the statement that "fleet-footed" applies to whatever the term "gazelle" applies to; and observation of nature, not a study of English language usage, is required to verify it. By contrast, the truth-value of the statement that the word "animal" applies to whatever "gazelle" applies to is determined by English usage and is verified, not by observing the behavior of what "gazelle" denotes, but by a study of the speech habits of those who use the English language. It is hardly necessary to point out that the sentence "A gazelle is an animal" does not *say,* or express the verbal fact, that the word "animal" applies to what "gazelle" correctly applies to. Some philosophers have indeed held the view that necessary propositions are verbal; but taken at face value this is to embrace a glaring contradiction which can be accepted only in the bewitchment of what Moore has called a "philosophic moment." As an aside, it might be observed that philosophy is the final sanctuary of contradictions, where they can thrive and multiply.

Although the sentence "A gazelle is an animal" does not express the verbal proposition that "animal" applies to what "gazelle" applies to, it is clear that *all* we are required to know in order to know that the sentence expresses a necessary proposition is *usage,* i.e., that the use "animal" has in the language, dictates its application to what "gazelle" correctly applies to. The equation that emerges is:

The fact that the sentence "A gazelle is an animal"
expresses a logically necessary proposition

entails and is entailed by

> The fact that in point of usage the term "animal" applies
> to what the term "gazelle" correctly applies to.

We may say that a sentence which expresses an *a priori* truth *mentions* no words, although in understanding its meaning we know *only* facts about the use of words. It is easy to see now why talk about essential, or necessary attributes of things, e.g., saying that *animal* is an essential attribute of a gazelle, is a picturesque, if bogus, way of talking about the use of nomenclature in a language.

The theorem of arithmetic, e.g., $x > y . \supset . x + 1 > y + 1$ and $(a + b)^2 = a^2 + 2ab + b^2$, alike with the assertions of philosophy, e.g., a universal is a thing, are nonverbal ways of referring to the use of terms and to connections between them. Like the sentence "A gazelle is fleet-footed" they mention no words, but, unlike it, they have only verbal import. The implicit claim they make is verbal, and this is made invisible by the nonverbal form of speech in which they are framed. One difference between the sentences "A gazelle is an animal" and "The word 'animal' applies as a matter of usage to whatever the word 'gazelle' correctly applies to" is that the negation of the second sentence expresses a factually false proposition, whereas the negation of the first expresses a logically impossible proposition. And it can be seen that the fact that the sentence "There is a gazelle which is not an animal" expresses a logically impossible proposition implies that the use "gazelle" and "animal" have in the language makes the expression "gazelle which is not animal" inapplicable to anything. "Gazelle which is not an animal" no more refers to a creature than "circle whose circumference is shorter than its radius" refers to a geometrical figure. It is the fact that usage dictates the application of "animal" to what "gazelle" correctly applies to which *prevents* "gazelle but not an animal" from having a use to describe anything, actual or conceivable. To be sure, the phrase "gazelle but not an animal" could arbitrarily be given an application, but then its use would no longer be determined by the use which the component terms have in the language.

It becomes plain now that what the verbal sentence says about the words it mentions is the hidden import of the sentence referring to the logical impossibility, although the latter makes no explicit mention of words. The same holds for the entailment sentence and its verbal correlate. The difference in the form of speech between the ontologically phrased sentences and their verbal correlates determines whether a verbal claim or a logical claim is being made. The entailment sentence "*Being a gazelle* entails *being an animal*" does not *say* what is said by the verbal sentence "The word 'animal' applies, as a matter of usage, to what 'gazelle' applies to," but is nevertheless the *message* it conveys. The two sentences are semantically inseparable twins. If the first sentence failed to express a logical necessity, the second would not be a true statement about usage; and if the second sentence did not state a truth about usage, the first would fail to express a logical necessity.

Whether a sentence makes a verbal claim about conventional usage in a language or makes an entailment claim is determined by its mode of expression. We might say that if there were no nonverbal way of calling attention to verbal usage, there would be no logical necessitation. The same consideration applies to the following pair of sentences:

> It is logically impossible for there to be a gazelle
> which is not an animal,

and

> The phrase "gazelle which is not an animal" is prevented
> by the use of "gazelle" and "animal" from having a
> descriptive function in the language.

If the claim of the second sentence were not the *unexpressed* content of the first sentence, the first sentence would not refer to what is logically impossible.

We are now in a position to see what the difference between the two entailment claims is, namely between

> *Being a gazelle* entails *being an animal,*

and

> *Being a universal* entails *being a thing.*

What it is that makes the first entailment secure and the second permanently controversial comes into view. How it is possible, to put it in Bouwsma's way, for one philosopher to announce a philosophical discovery when he makes the second entailment claim and for another philosopher to declare the discovery to be a mistake, can now be explained.

If the philosophical entailment statement that *being a universal* entails *being a thing* is of a kind with the entailment statement that *being a gazelle* entails *being an animal,* the first would be as uncontroversial as the second. For if it is an entailment statement, which is to say, a statement asserting the deducibility of *being a thing* from *being a universal,* it involves no chain of reasoning and is as direct and immediate as is the deducibility of *being an animal* from *being a gazelle.* The difference between the two cases, and the reason why one is controversial and the other secure, becomes clear when we consider the verbal counterparts of the two entailment statements: (1) the statement that "animal" applies to whatever "gazelle" applies to, and (2) the statement that "thing" applies to whatever "universal" applies to. No one who knows English usage would argue about (1), and anyone who was ignorant of the actual use of the terms mentioned in (1) would accept instruction.

But people who disagree about the philosophical entailment claim and thus, by implication, disagree over (2), know usage in the language and continue to disagree in the face of their knowledge. Neither side asks for instruction nor would they accept it from the opposing side, or for that matter from anyone else. No semantic Solomon could break the deadlock between the disagreeing philosophers. Wittgenstein has expressed the opinion, which has won acceptance in certain circles, that a philosopher who states a false or a paradoxical view, such as the view that we never do perceive things, or the view that we never act voluntarily, is misdescribing the actual use of language. In accordance with this notion, a philosophical theory comes down to a description, true or false, of usage.

Let us consider in more detail the metaphysical view that universals are things, which gives rise to the idea that a fact about the nature of individuals is being revealed. Unlike the insubstantial shadows cast by things, universals are things. If we replace the term "universal" by "meaning of a general word" in "Universals are things," we have "The meanings of general words are things." Wittgenstein apparently took the philosophical claim made by this utterance to be false, and to avoid being entrapped by Platonism he recommended talking about the use of an expression instead of talking about its meaning.[28] It would seem that he thought that the ontologically expressed philosophical theory, and therefore its verbal counterpart— namely the statement that "thing," in point of usage, applies to whatever "meaning of a general word" applies to—was a misdescription of language. He appeared to think that this error could be prevented by avoiding the word "meaning" and, instead, talking about the use of words. The point of this recommendation was that no one would be tempted to call the *use* of a word, any more than the use of a hammer, a thing or object. But this sort of avoidance technique, even if it worked, would hardly improve our understanding of the tendency to embrace philosophical mistakes with such tenacity.

This notion of Wittgenstein's, that a philosophical theory describes usage, truly or falsely, demystifies Platonism. The latter is, so to speak, brought down to linguistic earth. But it holds out no possibility of explaining the persistence and incorrectability of philosophically mistaken descriptions. Viewed as mistakes, their persistence requires us to fall back on a Kantian explanation. About some errors Kant wrote: "There exists, then, a natural and unavoidable dialectic of pure reason—not one in which a bungler might entangle himself through lack of knowledge, or one which some sophist has artificially invented to confuse thinking people, but one inseparable from human reason, and which, even after its deceptiveness has been exposed, will not cease to play tricks with reason and continually entrap it into momentary aberrations ever and again calling for correction."[29] Kant's explanation, which is comparable to Moore falling back on what he calls a philosophic moment, serves only to deflect our attention away from something that eludes our present understanding, and holds off the investigation it needs.

Another idea to be found in the later work of Wittgenstein concerning the nature of philosophical theories is that they present pieces of altered usage. In Kant's phrase, philosophers are "metaphysical jugglers,"[30] or, it would be better to say, "semantic jugglers." This notion of Wittgenstein's has not received the attention it deserves, especially since it has great explanatory power. With its help certain things can be explained which remain a psychological enigma under the other idea. It makes the incorrectability of philosophical errors understandable, without resorting to explanations which are themselves mystifying. Philosophical errors are not ineluctable mistakes; they are deep-rooted semantic *preferences*. Moreover, a preferred semantic re-editing of a familiar piece of nomenclature is presented in the form of speech in which no term is mentioned. This creates the gratifying belief that the utterance, which presents the re-edited terms, announces a discovery about the contents of the world, about the existence and inner nature of things.

Wittgenstein's second idea of the nature of philosophical theories is purely explanatory, and is not linked with what has been called therapeutic positivism: it requires no special devices for avoiding "mistakes." On this idea, the philosophical assertion "The meaning of a general word is a thing" introduces in a nonverbal way of speaking, a *stretched,* not a mistaken, application of "thing" to whatever the substantive "meaning" applies to. But the ontologically phrased way of presenting the edited use of "thing" brings to mind imagery appropriate to a discovery. What is to be seen through the "chinks" offered by words and phrases are semantically contrived fictions, illusions which are the semblance of science. Discoveries of this kind about the world do not require scientific apparatus and can be made in the seclusion of the study, without the need to travel. Bouwsma has also pointed out, as part of his paradox, that what a philosopher discovers is already known, that what he discovers is "hidden in full view." Everyone knows the meanings of some general words, no matter how limited his vocabulary may be, but, nevertheless, universals are hidden from many. Thus Bouwsma has said: "Most people have never heard of them. And many people who are told about them and who are directed to discover them, never do discover them." According to Bertrand Russell, ". . . all truths involve universals, and all knowledge of truths involves acquaintance with universals."[31] He went on to remark, "Seeing that nearly all the words to be found in the dictionary stand for universals, it is strange that hardly anybody except students of philosophy ever realizes that there are such entities as universals."[32] This paradoxical state of affairs can be somewhat better understood if in Russell's remark the phrase "stand for universals" is replaced by the expression "have meanings," which brings out the point that the meanings of general words are not hidden but universals are hidden and require a "technique for their discernment." Imitating Bouwsma's language, it would be ridiculous to say: "Most people have never heard of the meanings of words. And many people who are told about them and who are directed to discover them, never do discover them." And it would be absurd to say that hardly anybody except philosophers knows that words have meanings. But it is not absurd to say that universals are unknown and have to be discovered.

In *Le Bourgeois Gentilhomme* Molière's M. Jourdain learned from his instructor that all his life he had been speaking in prose. What he learned was a word, the name of what he had been doing. It is not that he had been doing something of which he was unconscious until someone brought it to his attention. Part of what a person learns who is first instructed in Platonic philosophy is a new word, the word "universal," used to refer to the meaning of a general word like "horse" or "justice." This might possibly explain how what is known could also be unknown: meanings of general words are known by everyone, but not what philosophers call them. It is tempting to think that this explains the known-yet-not-known paradox, but it can easily be seen that an important feature attaching to the Platonic theory remains unexplained. This is the astonishingly long life of the disagreements centering on it—disagreements which have withstood the erosion of time more successfully than has the Egyptian sphinx, and which will certainly withstand future erosion as long as philosophy is a live subject. Wittgenstein's second idea as to the nature of a philosophical theory, according to which it presents redistricted nomenclature, throws light on the time-honored dispute over whether universals exist. If the existence of universals were at issue, the verbal counterpart would be "Does the word 'universal' have a use in the language?," which could hardly be the subject of intractable debate. Screened by the ontologically formulated controversy over the existence of universals, is the disagreement over whether universals are *things*. The question as to whether universals are things, which transforms into the question whether the meanings of general words are entities or objects, is the subject of irresolvable debate, which would continue no matter what term replaced "universal," so long as it had the same definition, i.e., "meaning of a general word."

When the application of a term in a given language becomes the subject of endless disputation, whether carried on explicitly about a mentioned word or implicitly, the only acceptable explanation is that an edited application of the word is at issue. In the present instance, the subject of debate is a redistricted range of application of the terms "entity" and "thing." Wittgenstein's formula for avoiding Platonic talk about universals might possibly work for some people, if the application of "thing" to what "meaning of a general word" is used to refer to were a mistake: his formula would then be a device for avoiding a mistake. The idea that a gerrymandered use of "thing" is being presented makes understandable this "mistake," as well as other philosophical "mistakes" which will not be exorcised out of existence.

It is not a mistake, it is a preferred piece of semantics. For no disagreement constituted by opposing verbal preferences is subject to termination by recourse to any sort of fact. Wittgenstein has observed that "we may be irresistibly attracted or repelled by a notation,"[33] and the attractiveness of a notation may have an explanation. In the present case an explanation is not hard to find.

One of Wittgenstein's useful remarks is to the effect that when we encounter a substantive we tend to look for a corresponding substance.[34] And philosophers know how to "create," by semantic means, the substances that they investigate. A Marco Polo discovers new things, such as coal and paper, by journeying into foreign lands. A philosopher creates the objects he discovers, which is why he has no need to travel. In the case of the Platonic discovery, the fact that "meaning of a general word" is a noun phrase is taken as justification for a semantic act of creation, which consists of stretching the range of application of the word "thing" to include what is referred to by the noun phrase. And it is the illusion created by the semantic maneuver which explains the attractiveness of the philosophical notation. By presenting a stretched use of "thing," in the form of speech in which terms are not mentioned, the Platonic philosopher brings to life a semantically contrived illusion of a realm of objects that is too rarified to be perceived by the senses. These are the things which are to be seen through Bouwsma's linguistic knotholes. As it turns out, what the philosopher sees when he looks out at the world through the apertures Bouwsma talks about are Alice-through-the-looking-glass reflections of hidden maneuvers with terminology. Some philosophers place a high value on the Platonic illusion, while others do not. Those who reject it maintain that there are no such things as universals; and equally with Platonists, the way they express themselves hides the verbal nature of the debate, namely that what is at issue is a redistricted use of the word "thing."

The explanation of Bouwsma's paradox developed here is unorthodox, and it may of course be challenged. But the importance of the paradox cannot be challenged, nor can its investigation by philosophers be put aside. The remaining two philosophical theories, the one regarding sense-data and the other regarding the inner nature of material objects (substratum theory), are of the same kind as the theory of universals. Each of the theories has its own specific difference, but they are all generically the same and lend themselves to like metaphilosophical explanations. Their investigation will be left to others who have, as did Bouwsma, a serious desire to improve their understanding of technical, academic philosophy. Bouwsma brought a passion for understanding to philosophy, and the last question in his essay on Moore is "But are phrases and sentences chinks?" It is a loss to philosophy that he did not pursue this question.

M.L.

NOTES

1. The study of codes of ethics and their relations to various professions is an obvious exception.

2. *Philosophical Essays* (Lincoln, Neb.: University of Nebraska Press, 1965), p. 134.

3. Ibid., pp. 147–148.

4. *Scientific Thought,* p. 247.

5. *The Problems of Philosophy* (1943), pp. 146–147.

6. *Philosophical Essays,* op. cit., p. 136.

7. *The Problems of Philosophy,* op. cit., p. 146.

8. *Philosophical Essays,* op. cit., p. 136.

9. *Scientific Thought,* op. cit.

10. *Appearance and Reality,* pp. 144–145.

11. *Principles of Human Knowledge,* Part First, Section 76.

12. *Philosophical Papers,* pp. 145–146.

13. *Philosophical Essays,* op. cit., p. 144.

14. Ibid., p. 134. Bouwsma does not say who fails to know that they are material objects.

15. Ibid., p. 138.

16. Ibid., p. 135.

17. Ibid., p. 139.

18. J. L. Austin's example.

19. *Philosophical Essays,* op. cit., p. 139.

20. Ibid., p. 143.

21. Ibid., p. 142.

22. Ibid.

23. Ibid., p. 144.

24. Ibid.

25. *Sense and Sensibilia* (Oxford: Oxford University Press, 1962), p. 69.

26. "Philosophy and 'Common Sense,'" *G. E. Moore, Essays in Retrospect,* edited by Alice Ambrose and Morris Lazerowitz (London: George Allen & Unwin, Ltd., 1970), p. 203.

27. *Philosophical Essays,* op. cit., p. 148.

28. *The Yellow Book.* (Discussion in the intervals between dictation of *The Blue Book,* 1933–1934. Notes taken by Margaret Masterman and Alice Ambrose.)

29. *The Critique of Pure Reason,* trans. by Norman Kemp Smith (New York: Macmillan & Co., 1950), p. 300.

30. Ibid., p. 100.

31. *The Problems of Philosophy,* op. cit., p. 146.

32. Ibid.

33. *The Blue Book,* p. 57.

34. Ibid., p. 1.

V

The Fly-bottle

A philosophical problem has the form: "I don't know my way about."
                          Ludwig Wittgenstein

In the last half century, analytic philosophy of science, linguistic analysis, and logic have formulated and reformulated again the distinction between science and metaphysics. The outcome was unexpected: metaphysics rather than retreating from the science, shriveling up, dissolving, has instead re-emerged as an acknowledged, even if problematic component of scientific theorizing.
                Robert S. Cohen/Marx W. Wartofsky

. . . concealed lighting can make things look very different from what they are. Why not pull curtains and open the windows? The light will be better, the air will be fresher, and we shall be freer.
                          John Wisdom

It has always been thought that technical, reasoned philosophy is the comprehensive science of reality and brings under its special scrutiny such fundamental concepts as *space, time, contingency, mind, causation, language.* It has been said that the task of philosophy is to delineate "the generic traits"[1] of reality; and even if its scope were less than this, the value placed on philosophy would diminish and eventually fade away if it were thought incapable of yielding ontological information. For that matter, the process of value-deflation has already set in, for the classical notion of philosophy has begun to wear thin. The philosophical tree of knowledge has so far borne only phantom fruit and has succeeded in little more than creating intractable disputes. A closer look at philosophy can no longer be dismissed or thought unnecessary. In the last forty years, the work of G. E. Moore, the logical positivists, and Ludwig Wittgenstein has made it uncertain *what* a philosopher is talking about who says that motion does not exist or that no two terms in a language are really synonymous, although it is still natural to think that the first statement is about the occurrence of motion and the second about the existence of synonymy.

In his post-*Tractatus* writings, Wittgenstein speaks of philosophy as a kind of sickness.[12] He characterizes a philosophical problem, such as the problem regarding the existence of abstract objects, as a mental cramp, and describes the philosopher as being in the condition of a fly that is trapped in a fly-bottle. The philosopher is lost in a linguistic labyrinth and has no Ariadne thread to help him find his way out. Wittgenstein's general notion as to what is required to free the philosopher from his blind and fruitless verbal labor is to obtain a clear view of the language in actual use.[3] The philosopher needs to *see* the ways in which terminology he uses in philosophizing, as well as in his everyday talk, actually functions in the language. It is useful to remind ourselves of St. Augustine's plaintive words: "What, then, is time? If no one asks of me, I know; if I wish to explain to him who asks, I know not." For it would appear that taking Wittgenstein's words to heart and noticing how words are used in discussions and conversations, with occasional recourse to a standard dictionary, is no help whatever. For some mysterious reason, bringing established usage into a *philosophical* dispute, as experience has abundantly shown, has no discernible influence on resolving the dispute. When G. E. Moore soberly observed that it seemed to him that when we talk of "seeing" such things as doors and lampposts we are neither making mistakes of fact nor mistakes of linguistic usage;[4] no philosophical dispute was brought any nearer to a resolution. Instead, what has happened is that new disputes have arisen regarding "ordinary language," what it is, and whether it does the job it is supposed to do. There can be no question that these disputes will remain permanent additions to the growing collection of philosophical disagreements. The first task would seem to be, not to try to *solve* problems, but to lay bare their nature. In lectures Wittgenstein sometimes talked about "dissolving" philosophical problems, and it may be that dissolving a philosophical problem is the same as understanding it rightly.

The notion that a philosophical problem arises from mistakes about the workings of terminology and can be resolved by recourse to actual usage in the language has been widely accepted by philosophers. The implication of this notion of the nature of a philosophical problem is that philosophy is some sort of investigation of language (apparently with the background idea of obtaining basic information about things). As is known, Wittgenstein gave expression to a number of different ideas about the nature of philosophy and philosophical problems. The philosopher is sometimes pictured as being lost in the labyrinth of words, like someone who cannot find his way out of the maze at Hampton Court and needs direction from a guide who commands a clear view of the maze. A second notion about the nature of a philosophical problem Wittgenstein expressed metaphorically, in the following words: "A philosophical problem arises when language goes on holiday."[5] Unlike the first notion, this implies not that a philosopher gets lost in language and puts forward mistaken claims about correct usage, but that he plays semantic games with words, for whatever gain that may bring him. A philosophical theory on this second notion presents a gerrymandered, not an incorrect, use of language. On the first notion, it presents an incorrect use of language, to the correcting of which recourse to ordinary language would seem to be relevant. The second notion has the merit of explaining why calling attention to actual usage does not have the expected effect of detaching a philosopher from his mistake and laying the mistake to rest.

Wittgenstein has said a number of things regarding what needs to be done to remove the problems of the philosopher. What has to be investigated is language, and the required method is, in the words of O. K. Bouwsma, *"the art of clarification, of relief from the toils of confusion."*[6] The confusion is grammatical.[7] As he puts it: "There is strife among these words that will not lie down together and that keep up their turmoil in our heads. And there will be no rest until we put each word into its own bed."[8] Bouwsma describes the result of a successful grammatical clarification in terms of the metaphor of the fly in the fly-bottle in the following words:

> That fly that was let out of the fly-bottle understands how he got in there, since the condition of his being let out is that he should understand that. And now he can fly in and out as he likes. It is no longer a fly-bottle for him. He can now buzz in and out enjoying the structure of the bottle. A fun bottle, then? Yes, until he finds himself in another bottle with a different opening. Eternal vigilance is the price of buzzing freely.[9]

The implication of these words would seem to be that a philosophical problem arises when we fall into a grammatical confusion, and it vanishes, *as a problem,* when the confusion is cleared up and words are put into their proper "beds." The consequence, according to Bouwsma, is that a problem that makes us feel trapped is transformed into a game we can enjoy. As has already been pointed out, Wittgenstein characterized a philosophical problem as involving a holiday use of language, and Bouwsma's words might be restated as follows: clearing up a grammatical confusion turns a philosophical problem into a holiday, or fun, problem. It is something of a puzzle to understand why anyone would take pleasure in being able freely to enter into and leave a confusion, "buzz in and out." There undoubtedly is an explanation, but it does not lie on the surface.

Wittgenstein has said something which it is difficult to think philosophers would be ready to accept. His words are: "The real discovery is the one that makes me capable of stopping doing philosophy when I want to. — The one that gives philosophy peace, so that it is no longer tormented by questions which bring *itself* in question."[10] There may seem to be an inconsistency between Bouwsma's and Wittgenstein's ideas as to the outcome of solving a philosophical problem, or clearing up a grammatical confusion: taking pleasure in freely reviving the problem, without becoming captive to it, and being able to stop doing philosophy. For Wittgenstein a philosophical problem was a mental torment from which he could relieve himself by making the problem "completely disappear."[11] A psychoanalyst could hardly fail to compare this notion of a philosophical problem and its treatment with the stage in the development of psychoanalysis when it was oriented towards the removing of hysterical symptoms as isolated phenomena. Hume, as is known, looked on philosophy as a "delirium" from which he was able to free himself and return to reality by the use of social diversions; and some psychologists resort to comparable reassurance devices. The idea that comes through is that philosophy is a kind of aberration and is to be viewed with some alarm. For Bouwsma a philosophical problem is the kind of problem that presents an intellectual challenge and calls for a solution, not a "dissolution."[12] His idea was to find the right answer, not make the problem disappear, and then to make a game of the problem without danger of being trapped by it, or without the possibility of becoming a problem again. The one wants to be able to stop doing philosophy and make problems disappear; the other wants to solve the problems and turn them into safe games. It is plainly of primary importance for the correct understanding of philosophy to determine what it is about philosophical utterances that makes these attitudes intelligible. To realize how mystifying these attitudes are, one has only to try to imagine mathematicians and scientists taking similar attitudes to their problems.

It has to be kept in mind that philosophy uses chains of reasoning to back its findings, and it takes for granted that its statements have truth-values. Nevertheless, a moment's reflection will tend to throw doubt on the comforting idea that philosophy is a kind of science. Indeed, only emotional resistance prevents our seeing that both Wittgenstein and Bouwsma are indulging in wishful thinking, thinking that pushes aside fact, and blinds us to what is before our very eyes. For no problem in philosophy has been solved or made to disappear. What Bouwsma says about making a game of a 'solved' problem suggests the possibility that in an oblique and disguised way he was describing the nature of philosophical problems. The idea that philosophy consists of playing games with words makes understandable the fact that philosophy can boast no generally accepted findings. It also helps us understand Wittgenstein's wish to be able to stop doing philosophy and to make philosophical problems "disappear." We can express our disturbing perception of the nature of something which has "let us down," like a hero who turns out to have feet of clay or a diamond which scrutiny shows to be paste, by muting it in one way or another, burying it in indefiniteness or in unclarity. What makes it hard to give up something which has suffered deflation and lost our respect, as may have been the case at times with Wittgenstein, must, quite plainly, have a psychological explanation. In my opinion, this cannot be satisfactory without bringing in the Freudian view that part of the mind is unconscious and contains active ideas which are not available to conscious awareness.

As an illustration of the claim that the nature of philosophical utterances is hidden from us, consider the idealistic view, which was once in the ascendancy and continues to have important adherents. In the words of F. H. Bradley, its famous English advocate, it is the view that "our experience, where relational, is not true."[13] The philosophical view that whatever involves relations is unreal leads to the mystical conclusion that the world of space and time is an "impossible illusion"[14] and that ultimate reality is an undifferentiated something which cannot adequately be grasped in thought. In Bradley's words: ". . . a relational way of thought — any one that moves by the machinery of terms and relations — must give appearance and not truth. . . . Our intellect, then, has been condemned to confusion and bankruptcy, and the reality has been left outside uncomprehended."[15] Briefly put, the argument for this view, whose profound appeal can be explained only by supposing that it connects up with active material in the depths of the mind, goes as follows. Where there is a plurality of terms, i.e., a number of things or a thing and its properties or a collection of properties, there are relations between them. Now a relation is *something,* not nothing, and is, therefore, itself a term. Hence a relation, R, between terms is a term which must be related by a new relation, R′, to its terms, etc., without possible end. Thus, a plurality of terms implies relations between the terms, which nevertheless cannot relate them. For a relation to hold, an infinite regress of relations would have to be consummated. This implies a final relation, i.e., a relation that is a term but is not itself related to its terms, which is a contradiction. The idealistic conclusion drawn is that whatever involves relations is unreal.

Different philosophers have reacted differently to this argument. C. D. Broad rejected it with the air of dismissing a mistake too gross and transparent to deserve serious consideration: "Charity bids us avert our eyes from the pitiable spectacle of a great philosopher using an argument which would disgrace a child or a savage."[16] Bradley and his followers were, of course, not stupid, nor incapable of recognizing a mistake once it was pointed out to them. Indeed, Bradley was a subtle and original metaphysical thinker. Anyone who rejects his argument as grossly mistaken has on his hands the task of explaining why the mistake is not, from the beginning, plain to those who accept the argument, and why they cannot be made to see that the "mistake" *is* a mistake. If he does not feel the need to seek for an explanation, or is satisfied with one that is overeasy or frivolous, it only means that he is playing the same kind of game as his opponent, a language game in which a holiday, i.e., a fantasy-creating, use of an expression is at issue. The putative mistake is not transparent to the philosopher who makes it, because it is *not* a mistake. In a number of places I have argued that it is a nonpragmatic re-editing of terminology. The critic, in rejecting the argument as mistake, does nothing more scientific than counter a verbal innovation. And he, like his opponent, effectively conceals the nature of the disagreement by using the language of truth and falsity, i.e., the indicative form of speech.

The philosophical sentence "Relational wholes are self-contradictory and exist only as delusive appearances," unlike the nonphilosophical sentence "The sun does not really revolve around the earth, it only appears to do so," is not used to make a factual statement about what exists and what does not exist. Wittgenstein has said that "we could not *say* of an 'unlogical' world how it would look";[17] and it requires no subtle reasoning to see that there could not be the sensible appearance of a self-contradictory state of affairs. If there could be, we should be able to say how an "unlogical" world would look: *it would look like its appearance.* But there cannot be a self-contradictory appearance any more than there can be a self-contradictory reality. This is particularly easy to see in the present case. If being relational is self-contradictory, then the appearance of there being a relational whole will itself involve differentiation and relations and, hence, be self-contradictory. It will be prevented from existing by what prevents the corresponding reality from existing. But the philosopher who says "Relational states of affairs are self-contradictory and exist only in appearance" cannot be construed as denying the existence of the "appearances."[18] His words are not intended to flout known fact. For his behavior is normal and is consonant with known fact rather than with his philosophical utterances. It is as if he retains ordinary language and beside it puts another, a new language that stands in need of interpretation.[19]

It is also incorrect to take the metaphysician of the undifferentiated One as stating, in an oblique idiom, a proposition about the proper use of relation-terminology. Contrary to the construction that so-called philosophers of ordinary language might place on his declaration, his words cannot with any plausibility be interpreted as implying that such terms as "between," "younger than," and "to the left of" have no use in the language, and that such expressions as "Saturn is between the Earth and Jupiter" and "Bouwsma is younger than Wittgenstein" are devoid of descriptive sense. Bradley uses relation-words correctly in his normal talk and responds with understanding to their use by others. There is no doubt that if he were asked whether the sentence "Bouwsma is younger than Wittgenstein" makes descriptive sense, he would react with surprise that such a question should be put to him and would say that of course it does. This shows that his philosophical utterance is not to be construed as making a factual claim about the actual use of terminology.

If we look with care at the argument for the statement that relations imply infinite regresses and hence are unreal, we can dispel enough of the verbal fog to see what the view comes to. We shall be able to see how a contradiction is *imported* into terminology that is free from contradiction, and how the delusive impression is created that a proposition is being advanced which denies the reality of ubiquitous features of the world. To give the gist of the argument again, the existence of two or more terms implies a relation between them—in Bradley's words, "if there is any difference, then that implies a relation between them"[20]—but a relation is *something* and hence is itself a term which must be related to its terms. Thus an infinite regress is generated. It should be noticed that the ordinary use of the word "related" does not dictate its application to whatever the phrase "different from or other than" applies to. It is intelligible English to say, in some cases, that x and y bear no relation to each other. The statement that difference implies a relation has to be understood as introducing an artificially stretched use of the term "related," a use in which it applies to whatever the term "different from" applies to. The central point of the argument, however, is that relations, since they are not nothing, count as terms, or to put it less ambiguously, they count as *things* or *objects*. The philosophical claim that relations are objects, like the more familiar Platonic theory that properties of things are themselves kinds of things, abstract entities, requires extended explanation.[21] Without going into this, it will be realized that the rules for the use of "object" do not stipulate the application of "object" to whatever "relation" denotes: e.g., the sentence "Betweenness is an object" does not exhibit a correct use of the word "object." The philosophical assertion that relations are things, instead of being the result of a mistaken idea as to the actual use in the language of "thing" or "object," has to be construed as introducing an academically stretched use of the word, a use which stipulates that it apply to what is denoted by relation-terms. To argue that relations are not *nothing* is a way of pointing out a similarity between relation-terms and *substantives,* which is that relation-words can be changed into abstract nouns, "between" into "betweenness," etc. It is this similarity which is used to justify reclassifying relation-terms with substantives. The philosophical statement "Relation-expressions are substantives," when formulated in the nonverbal mode of speech, becomes "Relations are things."

It can now be seen how the regress of relations derives from a stretched use of "relation" and a stretched use of "thing." The expression "stand to each other in a relation" is made, by semantic fiat, to apply to whatever the expression "different things" applies to; and the word "thing," or "term," is made, by semantic fiat, interchangeable with "relation" and relation-expressions. In this way a contradictory regress is manufactured. The ordinary use of "relation" and "term" involves no regress of relations requiring relations in order to relate. The *altered* use of these terms does involve such a contradictory regress; and there is no doubt that the alterations in terminology were made for the purpose of contriving the contradiction. The contradiction, in turn, is used to justify a further retailoring of terminology: the word "appearance" is stretched so that it applies, in a purely formal and empty way, to phenomena to which "relational" applies. The philosophical sentence "Whatever involves relations is unreal and exists only as appearance" gives rise to the idea that it is used to declare the insubstantiality of states of affairs everyone takes for granted, but in fact it presents an academically contracted application of "real" and a stretched use of "appearance." An *ersatz* contradiction is made to justify a non-workaday re-editing of "real" and "appearance."

The philosophical game that is being played with the words "relation," "thing," "appearance," and "real" consists of concealed maneuvering with terminology which, because of the form of speech in which the game is played, creates the vivid illusion that a remarkable claim about phenomena is being argued for. It is hard to think that the game is played solely for the intellectual effect it produces and that it does not link up with deeper material in the mind. Indeed, it would seem reasonable to think that the game with terminology functions for the philosopher in a special way. The overtones of the view and the atmosphere surrounding it make it likely that with his renovated terminology the philosopher expresses his emotional rejection of the world. The sentence "Relational states of affairs are unreal" may well have the underlying meaning: the world for me is unimportant and I wish to detach myself from it. When talk about the unreality of relations is joined with mystifying talk about "unbroken, simple feeling," it is permissible to guess that the words "the relational is mere appearance," "only the nonrelational, i.e., 'unbroken, simple feeling,' is real," express the echo of a wish to return to an early state in our pre-history. The state described so poetically by mystics and metaphysicians has been explained in the following passage in *The Need to Believe, The Psychology of Religion*:

> The state that is attained by a mystic is a state of euphoria or ecstasy in which the outer world seems to vanish and the self to stretch out, lose its boundaries, and engulf everything. This is simultaneously a projection of the self into the whole environment and an introjection of the whole environment into the self. It is a return to what some psychoanalysts call the 'oceanic reunion,' the world of the fed, satisfied baby on the delicious edge of sleep. All one's pleasure impulses are withdrawn from external objects and located inside oneself. And the variegated responses of the mind are narrowed and merged until they approximate the semiconscious, slumbrous, undifferentiated pleasure of the baby immersed in the uniform ocean of his feeling.[22]

It is possible now to reach some sort of understanding of the attitudes to philosophical problems taken by Wittgenstein and Bouwsma. It will be remembered that Wittgenstein looked on philosophy as a sort of mental sickness and on philosophical problems as having dissolutions, rather than solutions, i.e., answers of the kind that provide information about the world or about an existing language. One of his expressed wishes was to be able to stop doing philosophy when he wanted to stop. It is not hard to understand his disenchantment with philosophy and the wish to give up playing tricks with words and foisting them on others as having ontological import. Wittgenstein tried to dissuade some of his students from going into philosophy or from continuing to work in it. The underlying reason may have been that he was put off by his perceptions into the workings of philosophy. What is not so easy to understand is his enduring attachment to philosophy, one might say his addiction to it. Despite characterizing philosophy as language gone "on holiday" and the philosophical use of language as "like an engine idling, not when it is doing work,"[23] Wittgenstein treated it with the greatest seriousness. And despite characterizing philosophical problems as "cramps," his mind was constantly engaged with them. The only reasonable inference is that he had invested philosophy with unconscious content which played an important role in the workings of his mind.

Freud somewhere observes that the small things we tend to pass over can, when looked at with care, open up unexpected vistas. It might be added that sometimes when several of these are put together they give us insight into the thinking of an impressive and original philosopher like Wittgenstein. One philosopher who was a close associate of Wittgenstein reports that he suffered from the fear of going insane: "It is probably true that he lived on the border of mental illness. A fear of being driven across it followed him throughout his life."[24] It is not necessary for the limited purpose here to attempt to determine whether in fact Wittgenstein lived on the border of mental illness, nor is it necessary to go into the matter of deeper determinants of the fear of madness. Only the fact that he was haunted by the fear is pertinent to the present purpose. Otto Fenichel has the following to say about it.

> A simultaneity of punishment and temptation is, as a rule, also the basis of the frequent fear of "going crazy." With regard to this fear, it should be kept in mind that it may be justified. The rule that a person who is afraid of insanity does not become insane is not true; many incipient schizophrenics are aware of their increasing estrangement. However, more frequently this fear is not a warranted judgment but is rather a phobia. Even as a phobia the fear has an objective basis: what the patient senses in his fear of becoming crazy is the interaction of his unconscious strivings, especially the instinctual (sexual or aggressive) impulses operative within him. In this sense, the fear of going crazy is but a special case of the general fear of one's own excitement.[25]

We may well think that Wittgenstein's psychological fly-bottle was his phobia, against which he undoubtedly erected various defenses. A frequently quoted aphoristic remark of his perhaps reveals one of these: "What is your task in philosophy? — to shew the fly the way out of the fly-bottle."[26] It is by no means far-fetched to suppose that Wittgenstein unconsciously used philosophy as a substitute for his psychological problem. It is not out of the question to think that he tried to escape from his psychological fly-bottle, or lessen the severity of his captivity in it, by finding a semantic surrogate for it. He could exercise some measure of control over the philosophical fly-bottle and so keep his anxiety in check. Moreover, in its disguised and intellectualized form, he could make it less personal and share his problem more effectively with others.

The following description, which is not wholly imaginary, is usually passed over as a mere piece of humor, but it strengthens the above interpretation. It shows both that Wittgenstein looked on philosophy as a kind of madness, a semantic aberration, and also as an acceptable madness:

> I am sitting with a philosopher in the garden, he says over and over again, "I know that that's a tree," pointing to a tree that is near us. Someone else arrives and hears them, and I tell him, "This fellow isn't mad; we are just philosophizing."

> Someone says irrelevantly "that's a tree" . . . And now I ask him "How do you mean that?" and he replies, "It was a piece of information directed to you." Shouldn't I be at liberty to answer that he didn't know what he was saying, if he was insane enough to want to give me this information?[27]

Several important gains stand out clearly from converting the neurotic fear of becoming insane into the idea that philosophy is a form of insanity. One of these is that he can think about philosophy constantly without any feeling of embarrassment, which constant brooding on himself might have brought him. Another is that instead of confiding in a small number of his personal friends about his fear he could share it with a large group of people, many of whom became his admirers. And, of course, he did obtain important insights into a highly respected but baffling discipline. There is no question that his insights have contributed to the improvement of our understanding of philosophical questions and philosophical theories, and so has blown away some of the dust from our eyes. Freud has made several illuminating observations on the mental odyssey of the artist from fantasy back again to reality. In some respects they seem to apply to Wittgenstein.

> A true artist . . . understands how to elaborate his day-dreams, so that they lose that personal note which grates upon strange ears and become enjoyable to others; he knows too how to modify them sufficiently so that their origin in prohibited sources is not easily detected. Further, he possesses the mysterious ability to mould his particular material until it expresses the ideas of his phantasy faithfully; and then he knows how to attach to this reflection of his phantasy-

life so strong a stream of pleasure that, for a time at least, the repressions are out-balanced and dispelled by it. When he can do all this, he opens out to others the way back to the comfort and consolation of their own unconscious sources of pleasure, and so reaps their gratitude and admiration. . . .[28]

The construction placed on Wittgenstein's attitude to philosophy and philosophical problems is admittedly highly speculative; and any construction that might be placed on the imaginary game Bouwsma played with philosophical problems will be much more speculative, and will therefore be confined to a bare minimum. Bouwsma was a devoted disciple of Wittgenstein and it is likely that he adopted Wittgenstein's attitude, by and large accepting the latter's ideas about philosophy. As is known, Wittgenstein often, we might say predominantly, talked about philosophical utterances as being true or false (usually false). This left it open for Bouwsma to talk of philosophical problems as having solutions instead of dissolutions and of *remaining* as solved problems instead of disappearing completely. Thus a possible construction to be placed on Bouwsma's game with the fly-bottle is that it is a reassurance game, comparable in certain respects to the game of blind man's buff played by children. It secures him against the inner threat of his mind being made captive to an unconscious wish or to an unconscious fear. It is a fact, for example, that some cured alcoholics test themselves by pouring out a drink which they do not take. The talk about buzzing freely in and out of the fly-bottle, turning it into a "fun bottle," suggests the idea that Bouwsma played with the notion of an unconscious fear against which he could make himself feel secure.

ADDENDUM
by Charles Hanly[29]

The human mind has a natural tendency to reduce the anxiety to which it is subjected by substituting one fear for another or by substituting a worry for a fear. This process occurs in the formation of phobias. For example, Little Hans[30] substituted an animal phobia (fear of horses) for castration anxiety. Once the substitution has been made, anxiety can be reduced by accepting an inhibition (avoidance of horses), something that could not be done with the castration anxiety because of the child's dependent relation to his father. A child who is anxiously ashamed about bed-wetting may substitute this anxiety by a worry about the house being flooded by a defective toilet. It will be easier for a child to talk to her parents about how the toilet works than about how her bladder works because of the guilt associated with bed-wetting. These substitutions, which characterize the struggles of children to master anxiety, also occur in adults. For a fear of death and the pain of mourning, adults who have suffered a loss through death may substitute a worry that the funeral of the deceased may not proceed smoothly and thus become heavily preoccupied with the details of the funeral and wake. Among the religious there are those who substitute the fear of disease for the fear of having displeased God — a substitution which opens out the prospect of being able to rid oneself of the disease by pleasing God.

A student nurse found that she was exhausting herself and the hospital patients in her care because of the excessively zealous way in which she attended to them. She was unable to leave off troubling herself over her patients, even when they would have been better off with quiet and rest. As this symptom gave way in analysis it was replaced, for a period, by a fear of going mad, which eventually dissolved as she became aware of guilty feelings of excitement and triumph deriving from an Oedipal victory over her mother. Feeling guilty about not adequately caring for her patients had substituted for guilt about having taken the place of her mother in the affections of her father.

The instances selected cover a broad spectrum of the phenomenon of self-correcting childhood displacements to neurotic symptoms. In general, whenever the fear of anything becomes intolerable and inescapable in reality, an escape from it will be undertaken psychologically. The prime instigators of psychological escapes from anxiety by means of substitution are anxiety arousing instinctual demands, because they are inescapable in reality.

It has been argued that Wittgenstein may very well have substituted a worry about philosophy being a form of madness needing therapy for a fear of madness. Wittgenstein's fear of madness, attested to by close associates, would itself have replaced anxiety aroused by unconscious libidinal or aggressive impulses, about the precise nature of which one can only speculate, and about which, for the purposes of the present argument, one need not speculate. It is less painful to worry about philosophy being a form of madness, because it is no longer the self that suffers the danger of being mad. Moreover, the self can gain for itself the reassurance involved in being able to diagnose the "disease," design a therapy, and carry out a "cure" for the "madness" of philosophy. Accordingly, it is plausible to suppose that Wittgenstein's mind found solace and refuge in the displacement of the fear of his own madness by concerns about the "madness" of philosophy.

This particular displacement brought with it a particular advantage. The defense involved in the displacement is sublimation. Energy that would otherwise have been entirely bound to narcissistic anxiety was, in this way, devoted to a worthwhile cultural task — that of understanding philosophy. And, whereas Wittgenstein showed no signs of psychological insightfulness, his genius for logical analyses enabled him to make some important contributions to metaphilosophy. Thus Wittgenstein's mind was able to transform anxieties that would otherwise have only been personally debilitating into intellectual work of cultural importance.

M.L.

NOTES

1. John Dewey's phrase.

2. *Philosophical Investigations,* p. 91. *Remarks on the Foundations of Mathematics,* p. 157.

3. *Philosophical Investigations,* op. cit., p. 49.

4. *Philosophical Studies,* p. 226.

5. *Philosophical Investigations,* op. cit., p. 19.

6. *Philosophical Essays,* p. 186.

7. Ibid.

8. Ibid.

9. Ibid.

10. *Philosophical Investigations,* op. cit., p. 51.

11. Ibid.

12. Ibid.

13. *Appearance and Reality,* p. 34.

14. Ibid., p. 30.

15. Ibid., pp. 33–34.

16. *Examination of McTaggart's Philosophy* (London: Cambridge University Press; New York, Toronto: Macmillan, 1933), vol. 1, p. 85.

17. *Tractatus Logico-Philosophicus* (3.031).

18. *Appearance and Reality,* op. cit., p. 132.

19. Wittgenstein's language, but not in the context in which he used it.

20. *Appearance and Reality,* op. cit., p. 29.

21. See "The Existence of Universals" in my *The Structures of Metaphysics.*

22. *Mortimer Ostow and Ben-Ami Scharfstein* (New York: International Universities Press, Inc., 1954), p. 122.

23. *Philosophical Investigations,* op. cit., p. 51.

24. G. H. von Wright, Autobiographical Sketch in *Ludwig Wittgenstein, A Memoir,* by Norman Malcolm, p. 3. Bertrand Russell told Alice Ambrose and me the same thing.

25. *The Psychoanalytic Theory of Neuroses* (New York: W. W. Norton, Inc., 1945), p. 196.

26. *Philosophical Investigations,* op. cit., p. 103.

27. Ludwig Wittgenstein, *On Certainty,* edited by G. E. M. Anscombe and G. H. von Wright, trans. by Denis Paul and G. E. M. Anscombe (Oxford: Basil Blackwell, 1969).

28. *A General Introduction to Psychoanalysis* (New York: Garden City Publishing Co., 1938), Twenty-third lecture.

29. Professor of Philosophy, Toronto University, and practicing psychoanalyst.

30. Sigmund Freud, *A Phobia in a Five-Year-Old Boy, Standard Edition,* vol. 10 (London, 1909, The Hogarth Press, 1955), pp. 5–49.

VI

Sic et Non

Calling this study "Sic et Non" is intended to highlight the quite different approaches Wittgenstein seems to have taken to philosophical problems. The same game of Sic et Non played out by the medieval scholastics, the same swing between advance and retreat experienced by the traditional philosopher when he is tempted by two opposing views seems to be at work in Wittgenstein's own later investigations. Philosophical puzzlement about a specific claim he aptly expressed by "This is *not* how it is!" and also "But this is how it *must be*!"[1] The ambivalence that seemed to beset Wittgenstein was not over the truth of a claim, but about what he set himself to do. It was sufficient to prompt him to ask: "Why should what we do here be called 'philosophy'? Why should it be regarded as the only legitimate heir of the different activities which had this name in former times?"[2] And so we find in the context of a specific problem that what he says can sound indistinguishable from what a traditional philosopher says, but that at the same time he operates under a directive which prevents a traditional answer. I should like to exhibit what appears to be an ambivalence between the traditional and revolutionary in his own thinking which permeates his treatment of the ancient dispute over the existence of universals, or abstract entities.

Before proceeding to the special illustration, conceptions of the nature of philosophical investigation which contrast his earlier and later thought but which also appear *within* his later work, need to be set out in a general way. With the lines clearly drawn between irreconcilable views about the nature of philosophical statements, it will be possible to identify the views as they emerge in the special case. In general, the view current for many centuries about philosophical statements is that they assert something true or false, and, whether empirical or *a priori,* they give information about the world—about what there is and about what its nature is. The resolution of a dispute over these matters would come to determining which proposition is true. Against this is the iconoclastic view that philosophical utterances are

109

the product of linguistic muddles, engendered by obsessions with certain forms of expression, and that only in appearance do they state a theory. In *The Blue Book* Wittgenstein writes: "Philosophers constantly see the method of science before their eyes, and are irresistibly tempted to ask and answer questions in the way science does. This tendency is the real source of metaphysics, and leads the philosopher into complete darkness."[3] His problems "are taken to be scientific problems and are treated perfectly hopelessly, as if they were questions about facts of which we do not yet know enough rather than questions about language."[4] Once we "command a clear view of the use of our words"[5] the temptation to give expression to what purports to be a truth falls away, and what was felt as a problem disappears. "Our investigation," he says, "is a grammatical one."[6] Hence it moves on an entirely different plane from an investigation of what language stands for.

The revolution in Wittgenstein's own thinking can be measured by the gulf between these pronouncements and his statement in the *Notebooks 1914–1916*: "The great problem about which everything I write turns is: Is there an order in the world a priori, and if so what does it consist in?"[7] This concern with delineating the structure, and also the ultimate constituents, of the world found expression in the doctrine of logical atomism set out in the *Tractatus*. Here, admittedly, we do find an examination of certain categories of words—names, predicates, relation-words—but the direction of the inquiry is like the one expressed by Russell: to determine "whether anything, and if so, what, can be inferred from the structure of language as to the structure of the world."[8]

In the early thirties, when a radical change was taking place in Wittgenstein's thinking, we find the older conception of philosophy still at work alongside the new. For example, in lectures[9] he noted three stages in philosophical progress: first, seeing the commonsense answer to a problem, then getting into the problem so deeply that the commonsense answer seems unbearable, and finally, getting from that situation to the commonsense answer again. Suppose we are presented with the claim that since we cannot know we are not dreaming, no one can know there is a table on which he is writing. The commonsense reply is simply that we do have knowledge of the existence of such things. G. E. Moore, in the course of defending common sense, asserted that we do know many things; only we don't know *how* we know. This sounds like a matter-of-fact account of our knowledge. If the reply is in fact this, then the final phase of philosophical activity consists in justifying a commonsense truth. Against this stands the following explicit statement in *The Blue Book*: "There is no commonsense answer to a philosophical problem. One can defend common sense against the attacks of philosophers only by solving their puzzles, i.e., by curing them of the temptation to attack common sense."[10] And this cure is to be effected "by looking into the workings of our language."[11] His thesis is that "by commanding a clear view of the use of our words"[12] we can make the problem "completely disappear."[13] Philosophical problems, he says, "are, of course, not empirical problems,"[14] and it is a persistent mistake to think that they are. The mistake is made natural by the form in which the problems are phased. "The characteristic of a metaphysical question is that we express an unclarity about the grammar of words in the *form* of a scientific question."[15] For this reason the first rule of procedure in investigating a metaphysical proposition is "to destroy the outward similarity between it and an experiential proposition."[16] This is to be done by showing that "it hides a grammatical rule."[17] The latter comment may stand in need of clarification, but it does indicate that Wittgenstein considers attention to language rather than to nonverbal fact as the proper occupation of the philosopher. "Your questions relate to words," he says, "so I have to talk about words."[18]

These and other of his pronouncements show that he takes it that philosophical problems are misconceived if one expects to find a *solution,* true or false. The misconception is analogous to that of a man who on being told he cannot marry his widow's sister sees it as a legal or moral injunction which he must find ways to circumvent. Once he sees it for what it is, the initial problem disappears. It is worthwhile noting that all he needs to attend to is the words by which what looked like a legal or social prohibition was expressed, whereupon he sees there is no *problem* to solve. Dissolving a problem by seeing that it has neither a true nor a false answer, and solving a problem by finding what the true answer is, cannot both be philosophical goals. Since the one is effected by investigating language and the other by investigating fact, it is strange that there should be any confusion about which procedure it is relevant to embark on. But one only has to remember that very often the words of a metaphysician "can also be used to state a fact of experience,"[19] as Wittgenstein points out, to realize how great is the potentiality for being misled by the indicative form of expression. A scientific hypothesis and a metaphysical view, say, about what there is or about the nature of what there is, can look exactly alike. Ostensibly neither is about words. According to Wittgenstein, looking at the metaphysician's language is relevant because it is being used, not to express a factual proposition, but to express a discontent with language in current use. Thus, a metaphysician who denies, for example, the reality of time, is objecting to a linguistic convention, although the way in which the question and the answer are formulated effectively conceals this. Perhaps the best appraisal by Wittgenstein of traditional philosophical study appears in *The Yellow Book*[20] as follows: "The fallacy we want to avoid is this: when we reject some form of symbolism we're inclined to look at it as though we'd rejected a proposition as false. . . . This confusion pervades all of philosophy. It's the same confusion that considers a philosophical problem as though such a problem concerned a fact of the world instead of a matter of expression." If it did concern a fact of the world, it would, in principle, have a solution.

"Problem" and "solution" in their everyday use are antithetical terms. But of the word "problem" as used in philosophy, he writes: "One might say it is misapplied when used for our philosophical troubles."[21] For here it does not have the antithesis, "solution," i.e., discovery of what is true.

This thesis represents more than a revolution in the thinking of the earlier Wittgenstein who in the *Tractatus* wrote: "The belief in the causal nexus is a superstition" (5.1361) and "Theories which make a proposition of logic appear informative are always false" (6.111). It is a revolution in philosophy. The question I want to consider now is whether this new conception of the nature of philosophical theories is carried out when Wittgenstein deals with a specific and important problem: the existence of universals. The explicit aim is to make the problem completely disappear. Does he succeed in "destroying the outward similarity between a metaphysical proposition and an experiential one"? We shall find what looks like an ambivalence of treatment, certainly a treatment which has led some philosophers to suppose that he is merely countering the Platonic position with a denial of the existence of universals. Does his examination of general words and of the claims of metaphysicians about the purported referents of these words conform to the aim of curing the temptation to put forward a view or counterview? Both yes and no answers to this question are plausible.

Briefly expressed, the view to be considered is that in addition to the particular things encountered in everyday experience to which general words apply, there are also abstract entities of which they are the names. As Plato put it in the *Republic,* "Wherever a number of individuals have a common name, we may assume them also to have a corresponding idea or form."[22] And Quine has written, "It is convenient to regard such general names ('wise') as names on the same footing as 'Socrates' and 'Paris': names each of a single specific entity, though a less tangible entity than the man Socrates or the town Boston."[23] About these entities Plato said that "unlike the objects of sense, they have no separate organ, but . . . the mind, by a power of her own, contemplates the universals in all things."[24] Things of sense "may be brought under a single idea, which is called the essence of each. . . . [These] are seen but not known, and the ideas are known but not seen."[25] Were an inventory taken of the contents of the world, these would have to be entered in the ledger along with material objects and events, even though, unlike them, they have no date or place. Russell, like Plato, claimed to be acquainted with universals, and observed that hardly anyone but students of philosophy have recognized their existence. What is puzzling is that some students of philosophy, who are equally competent, claim not to find them and deny their existence. According to Hobbes, "The word *universal* is never the name of anything existent in nature, nor of any idea or phantasm formed in the mind, but always the name of some word or name."[26] The problem is that what looks like a factual dispute about what there is remains unresolved.

Since Wittgenstein treated the problem of universals again and again in his lectures and writings, I should like to consider what looks like support, and perhaps the best support, for the truth of the position that general words name abstract entities. This is provided by numbers. In answer to the question of the Eleatic Stranger, "And numbers are to be reckoned among things which are?", Theaetetus replied, "Yes surely, number if anything has real existence."[27] There necessarily are prime numbers between 5 and 13, and so necessarily there are numbers. The numerals that name them, "7" and "11," do not name concrete, particular entities and so must name something abstract. Furthermore, since there is an infinity of numbers and at any given time only a finite number of numerals, it is natural to think of there being a supply of numbers that outstrips the numerals. When we mention a number greater than the largest number we have thought of up to now, we would not say we created a new number, but rather that we thought of a new number and gave it a name. And no matter how many are mentioned, an infinity remain unthought and unnamed.

Wittgenstein holds that we are misled when we think about numbers in this way. But it needs to be specified in what way we are misled, since one way is traditional and the other revolutionary. To hold a *false* theory is to be misled, and to suppose ourselves to be holding a theory when in fact our words only appear to express a theory is also to be misled. Traditionally, nominalists like Hobbes and conceptualists like Locke tried to show that the Platonic theory is false. But if one holds that the words "There are abstract entities among the world's contents" express nothing either true or false, then both proponents and opponents of the Platonic position are misled. It is one thing to resolve a dispute by showing that one of the disputants asserts what is true; it is another thing to remove the dispute by removing the temptation to make either assertion. It can be argued that Wittgenstein's statements about the problem presented by this dispute exhibit an ambivalence about what he is doing: solving a problem or dissolving it. First, I shall cite what appears to be a traditional opposition on his part to a true-or-false doctrine. What he says may have a different point than to expose a mistaken view; but on the surface this is what it appears to be.

It is useful to compare Wittgenstein's words with Locke's words, which were directed against the claim that there is a property common to the things denoted by a general word, and which, if lacking to them, would make them cease to be what they are. "I demand," says Locke, "what are the alterations which may or may not be in a horse or lead, without making either of them to be of another species? . . . We will never be able to know when anything precisely ceases to be of the species of a horse or lead."[28] A change by imperceptible gradations, of a horse into a donkey, makes it impossible to determine the precise point where what is common to all horses is lost. This is taken to show that there is no common feature which constitutes the difference between a horse and a donkey. If there were, its presence or absence would be disclosed to inspection of a horse in the process of transformation. Wittgenstein's words seem to make the same appeal to inspection:

> Consider for example the proceedings that we call "games": I mean board-games, card-games, ball-games, Olympic games, and so on. What is common to them all? — Don't say: "There *must* be something common, or they would not be called 'games'" — but *look and see* whether there is anything common to all. — For if you look at them you will not see something that is common to *all*, but similarities, relationships, and a whole series of them at that. To repeat: don't think, but look! — Look for example at board-games, with their multifarious relationships. Now pass to card-games; here you may find many correspondences with the first group, but many common features drop out, and others appear. . . . And the result of this examination is: we see a complicated network of similarities overlapping and criss-crossing. . . . I can think of no better expression to characterize these similarities than "family resemblances."[29]

The opposite of this outcome of examining games might be claimed with regard to numbers: that 2, for example, *is* the common property of couples. But a claim similar to Wittgenstein's might, in reply, be made in consequence of inspecting cardinal, rational, imaginary, and transfinite numbers. What do all of these have in common? Does $\sqrt{-1}$ have anything in common with the cardinal number 2? Here a Platonist might reply that they would not both be called numbers were it not for possession of a common feature. Which reply is correct is apparently to be decided by inspection, the Platonist maintaining that whatever is apprehended when one grasps the meaning of the word "number" will provide a yes or no answer. The Platonist appears confident that turning our attention to cases of understanding a general world will disclose an abstract object. G. H. Hardy, for example, describes the mathematician's relation to mathematical truths as that of an observer: "I believe," he says, "that mathematical reality lies outside us, and that our function is to discover or *observe* it."[30] Wittgenstein rejects the theory on the basis of what looks to be an empirical, introspective investigation reminiscent of Antisthenes. He asks us to see whether in understanding general words we find their meanings given with them by psychological contiguity — "Here the word, there the meaning."[31] For himself he reports: "When I think in language, there aren't 'meanings' going through my mind in addition to the verbal expressions."[32]

I have assembled here a number of Wittgenstein's remarks the tenor of which certainly suggests that it is a mistake to think there is a common feature to be found in things denoted by a general term, and that understanding a general term is an inner process directed to a kind of object, namely, the word's meaning. A number of philosophers have construed these remarks in this way, that is, as intended to show the Platonic position to be false, for example, George Pitcher in a chapter entitled "The Attack on Essentialism."[33] I think it is fair to say that Wittgenstein's comments lend themselves to this interpretation, and for this reason I have spoken of the ambivalence of his approach to the claim that general words name abstract entities. But it may be that no ambivalence exists and to suppose it does means that the *point* of Wittgenstein's putative examination of what it is *in things* that is denoted by a general word and also what is *before the mind* when one grasps the word's meaning is misunderstood. Is it directed to eliminating the question about the existence of universals rather than to combating a false answer to it? There is some reason to suppose that it is. In any case, independent of a new interpretation of these remarks, there is support for holding that he is attempting to dissolve, or dispel, rather than solve a problem.

Wittgenstein's departure from the traditional view that in addition to the things general words apply to there are abstract entities named by them, and that these are what general words mean, is signalized by his directive: replace "meaning of a word" by "use of a word," and "understanding a word" (i.e., apprehending its meaning) by "being able to use the word." The point of this directive is to loosen the hold of a linguistic obsession, which, as he commented in lectures, "is not recognized or even recognizable as an obsession."[34] The obsession is exhibited in the language the philosopher uses. The philosopher says there *must* be some common feature of things in virtue of which they are called by the same name, that thought *must* have an object just as surely as do the senses. He insists, that is, that understanding general words *must* consist in the presence of meanings to the mind, and that the difference between words with meanings and those without meaning *must* be the presence or absence of an accompaniment. In lectures Wittgenstein said: "Every philosophical problem contains one particular word or its equivalent, the word 'must' or 'cannot.' When you ask yourself what happens in your mind when you hear or use a sentence in which the word 'plant' occurs, you immediately tend to say there must be an image before your mind, either an image of a particular plant or, if not this, then a Galtonian photograph. But on examination you find there is no image. When you discover this you tend to say you must have something like it: 'If it is not an image it must be something more subtle.' . . . This 'must' is a sign of a philosophical problem."[35]

Philosophy, he says, "arises out of prejudices — prejudices in favor of one form of description,"[36] and we have to be set free from "the fascination which forms of expression exert upon us."[37] In the case of the problem at hand, this means being set free from the picture suggested by the noun phrase "meaning of a word." In the presence of a noun we feel we ought to be able to point to something it denotes. "We have the idea that the meaning of a word is an object,"[38] and that having a mental image and grasping a meaning differ only in that "a different content is proffered — is present — to consciousness."[39] Or again, that a word and its meaning are but different kinds of objects: "You think of the meaning as a thing of the same kind as the word, though also different from the word. Here the word, there the meaning."[40] The temptation to try to find a substance corresponding to a substantive is, he says, "one of the great sources of philosophical bewilderment."[41] Many words do stand for things that can be pointed to, but many do not, and "meaning" is one of the latter. What money buys cannot always be pointed to, e.g., permission to sit in a theatre, a title, one's life.[42] And yet we tend to compare words and their meanings with money and the things bought rather than with money and its uses.[43]

But now why is the latter comparison the correct one? In saying that "meaning" does not stand for an object, even an ethereal one, is Wittgenstein merely taking a philosophical position opposed to Platonism? The therapy he suggests for dealing with the Platonist's assertion is not a more careful inspection, but a linguistic examination, an examination of the words occurring in the expression of the position, yet not in the context of a philosophical assertion, but "in their original home,"[44] i.e., in a natural setting. The Platonist says that understanding a word is a mental process of apprehending an object, which is its meaning; and its meaning, in contrast to the things it applies to, is the feature common to all the things in virtue of which they are called by the same name. Instead of trying to answer the question "What is the meaning of a word?", Wittgenstein suggests examining what is meant by "explanation of the meaning of a word."[45] We shall thereby learn something about "the grammar" of the word "meaning," since explanation of a word's meaning turns out to be an account of its *use*. It is natural to take the noun phrase "meaning of a word" to have a naming use, like proper names or names of specific colors or general nouns like "cat." The uses of these expressions vary, as explanations of their meanings show: some can be explained by means of a definition, or by illustrating their use in sentences, or by pointing to what they apply to, and all three types of explanation are open to some of them. The differences in their meanings show up when we observe the differences in their explanations. Seeing the difference in explanation of the word "cat," say, and "meaning of a word," Wittgenstein says, "will cure [us] of the temptation to look about . . . for some object which [we] might call 'the meaning.' "[46] To keep this difference from being obscured he suggests replacing the phrase "meaning of a word" by "use of a word," since the latter phrase, unlike the former, does not suggest an "object coexisting with the sign."[47] It should be noted that in the early pages of *The Blue Book* Wittgenstein called it a mistake to look for a coexistent object. This can be taken as an indication of ambivalence about what he was doing.

It might be asked what virtue there is in highlighting a difference between the word "meaning" and other substantives. Wittgenstein would say that this is to highlight a *grammatical* difference. His use of the word "grammatical" admittedly departs from ordinary usage, inasmuch as textbook grammar does not preclude the use of nouns that appear to stand for objects but are not so used. It is part of the grammar of the word "time" and "meaning" that it is sensible to speak of the measurement of the one but not of the other. To urge replacing "meaning of a word" by "use of a word" is to highlight a fact about the use of the substantive "meaning," namely, that it has no ostensive definition. We do not explain the meaning of the word "meaning" by directing attention to an object. Platonists nevertheless hold that the meaning of a numeral a is an ideal object. Wittgenstein remarks that saying this "is evidently supposed to assert something about the meaning, and so about the use of 'a'. And it means of course that this use is in a certain respect similar to that of a sign that has an object, and that it does not stand for any object."[48] The suggestion of the antithesis "real"/"ideal" is that these terms differ as do "red" and "blue" and are at the same time similar in their use to characterize objects. Wittgenstein remarks that "when we perceive that a substantive is not used as what in general we should call the name of an object, and when therefore we can't help saying to ourselves that it is the name of an aethereal object . . . we already know the idea of 'aethereal objects' as a subterfuge."[49]

Wittgenstein's invitation to try thinking of the meaning of a word without thinking of the word itself, despite appearing to ask for a Gedanken-experiment, can be interpreted as a means of showing us something verbal, namely, that it is not one of the criteria for the application of the word "meaning" that it refer to an accompaniment of a word. I think it might be argued that a similar interpretation can be placed on other things he has said which I first interpreted as ambivalence over whether his task was to show the Platonic position to be *false*. For example, when he asks us to note the difference between experiencing a sequence of images and grasping the meaning of a sentence, the point of this may be verbal, namely, that it is sensible to say we have a parade of images on hearing the sequence of words "cerise, sepia, crimson," but not that we have a parade of the meanings of the words in a sentence we understand. For if the meaning of a word is its use, it is not sensible to speak of a parade of uses. To put it in a way that Wittgenstein might himself have done, the use of a substantive is not a substance, refined or gross. The verbal point of this statement is to tell us something about the meaning of a noun phrase "meaning of a word" and of nouns in general. Similarly, to call attention to the fact that in some cases we can cite no mental process accompanying words we understand is one way of saying that the presence of a mental process is not one of the criteria for the application of the phrase "understands a word." The therapy against the temptation to cover up this fact is to replace "understands a word" by "is able to use a word." Again, to note that we use general words in cases where we can single out no common feature in virtue of which the words apply to a number of things is a way of saying that the presence of a common property is not a necessary condition for the application of a noun or adjective. To insist on a definition giving "the essence" of a thing, as did Socrates, is in many cases to seek a boundary where the language does not provide one. "What still counts as a game and what no longer does? Can you give the boundary? No. You can *draw* one; for none has so far been drawn."[50]

The Platonist knows these facts about the use of language as well as Wittgenstein. So what is the Platonist doing when he says that the intangible, invisible essences are apprehended by the eye of the mind? Let us revert to the best support for the claim that a true theory about what there is is being announced. Numbers, each named by a numeral, provide the most persuasive examples. The dispute between the Platonist and the nominalist is over the statement "Numbers are objects." Since introspection will not decide its truth-value, and neither disputant is moved by any considerations to give up his claim, the statement is evidently not empirical. It would appear that each of the opponents wants his words to be taken to express a necessary truth. Let us look at what is required for a sentence to say what is necessarily true. (This will give us an insight into why Wittgenstein called necessary truths "rules of grammar.") For a sentence to express a necessity there must in fact be some established convention about the use of words occurring in it. E.g., the fact that "Vixens are female foxes" expresses a necessary truth is equivalent to the fact that it is a convention of English that "female fox" applies to everything "vixen" applies to. Being a female fox is the accepted criterion for applying the word "vixen." Here we have an example in which the boundary criteria are precisely drawn, and the dictionary states what they are. In the case of many sentences expressing necessary truths—e.g., "A number whose digits sum up to 9 or a multiple of 9 is divisible by 9"—they do so in virtue of rules for the use of words derived from rules for the use of other words. The sentence "Numbers are objects" is as simple as the first example, in that whether it expresses an *a priori* truth should be decidable without recourse to anything beyond the dictionary. But the dictionary reports no convention to the effect that "object" does or does not apply to what "number" applies to. Are both Platonists and nominalists making a mistake then about what the linguistic facts are? Wittgenstein's reply is, by implication, no, for he holds that each is expressing his discontent with the fact that no convention exists. So each sets his own boundary, one which "will never entirely coincide with the actual usage, as this usage has no sharp boundary."[51] A boundary does not exist; it is drawn. But since the words "Numbers are objects" mentions no words and cannot therefore be about linguistic conventions, it appears to express a true-or-false theory about numbers rather than to recommend fixing usage. By means of the nonverbal idiom the Platonist conceals from others, and also himself, that he "wishes for a notation which . . . uses more closely similar forms of expression than our ordinary language."[52] His form of speech creates the illusion, pervasive throughout philosophy, that the problem "concerns a fact of the world instead of a matter of expression."

What Wittgenstein does is to destroy the similarity between this metaphysical proposition and an experiential proposition by exposing the purported grammatical rule which is hidden by the sentence the Platonist utters. Associated with the fact that a sentence expresses an *a priori* proposition is an empirical truth about conventional usage, which operates like a rule. But if a sentence is uttered which purports to express something necessary although no convention exists to support the claim that it in fact does, then we may take it that a philosopher is not making a mistake — since he knows usage — but is saying that there ought to be such a convention. He is dissatisfied with our present notation. And when he says that numbers are objects, or more generally, that meanings are objects, we can see what linguistic boundary he wishes to draw, what notation would satisfy him. It is one in which numerals, and in general, the word "meaning," function as names — as their surface grammar suggests. Their substantive form holds him captive, in the way in which an unrecognized obsession does. Here the Platonic obsession is a grammatical one. Impressed by the common grammatical form of the word "meaning" and other substantives, he redraws its boundaries so as to stress the similarity. It is made to fall under a stretched use of "proper name."

A.A.

NOTES

1. *Philosophical Investigations,* p. 47.
2. *The Blue Book,* p. 62.
3. Ibid., p. 18.
4. *Wittgenstein's Lectures, Cambridge 1932–1935* (edited by Alice Ambrose), p. 99.
5. *Philosophical Investigations,* op. cit., p. 49.
6. Ibid., p. 43.
7. Ibid., p. 53e.
8. *An Inquiry into Meaning and Truth* (New York: W. W. Norton Co., 1940), p. 429.
9. *Wittgenstein's Lectures, Cambridge 1932–1935,* op. cit., p. 109.
10. *The Blue Book,* op. cit., pp. 58–59.
11. *Philosophical Investigations,* op. cit., p. 47.
12. Ibid., p. 49.
13. Ibid., p. 51.
14. Ibid., p. 47.
15. *The Blue Book,* op. cit., p. 35.
16. Ibid., p. 55.
17. Ibid.
18. *Philosophical Investigations,* op. cit., p. 49.
19. *The Blue Book,* op. cit., pp. 56–57.

20. Notes taken by Margaret Masterman and Alice Ambrose of lectures and informal discussion in the intervals between dictation of *The Blue Book,* called *The Yellow Book. Wittgenstein's Lectures, Cambridge 1932–1935,* p. 69.

21. *The Blue Book,* op. cit., p. 46.

22. Bk. X, Sec. 596 (Jowet Translation).

23. *Mathematical Logic* (Cambridge, Mass.: Harvard University Press, rev. ed., 1951), p. 119.

24. *Theaetetus,* Sec. 185.

25. *Republic,* Bk. VI, Sec. 507.

26. *The English Works of Thomas Hobbes,* vol. 1, p. 20, edited by Sir William Molesworth, London, 1839.

27. *Sophist,* Sec. 238.

28. *Essay Concerning Human Understanding,* Bk. III, Ch. III, Sec. 13.

29. *Philosophical Investigations,* op. cit., pp. 31–32.

30. *A Mathematician's Apology* (Cambridge: The University Press, 1940), pp. 63–64.

31. *Philosophical Investigations,* op. cit., p. 49.

32. Ibid., p. 107.

33. *The Philosophy of Wittgenstein* (Englewood Cliffs, N.J.: Prentice-Hall, Inc., 1964).

34. *Wittgenstein's Lectures, Cambridge 1932–1935,* op. cit., p. 99.

35. Ibid., see p. 78.

36. Ibid., p. 115.

37. *The Blue Book,* op. cit., p. 27.

38. Comment reported by John Wisdom from a Cambridge Moral Sciences meeting, p. 87, *Paradox and Discovery.*

39. *Philosophical Investigations,* op. cit., p. 175.

40. Ibid., p. 49.

41. *The Blue Book,* op. cit., p. 1.

42. *Wittgenstein's Lectures, Cambridge 1932–1935,* op. cit., p. 30.

43. Ibid., p. 46.

44. *Philosophical Investigations,* op. cit., p. 48.

45. *The Blue Book,* op. cit., p. 1.

46. Ibid.

47. Ibid., p. 5. It should be noted that in the early pages of *The Blue Book* Wittgenstein called it a mistake to look for a coexistent object. This can be taken as an indication of ambivalence about what he was doing.

48. *Remarks on the Foundations of Mathematics,* p. 136.

49. *The Blue Book,* op. cit., p. 47.

50. *Philosophical Investigations,* op. cit., p. 33.

51. *The Blue Book,* op. cit., p. 19.

52. Ibid., p. 59.

VII

Two Paradoxical Statements

In his *Tractatus Logico-Philosophicus* Wittgenstein makes the surprising remark that every mathematical proposition must be obviously true. His entire statement (6.2341) is the following: "The essential characteristic of mathematical methodology is that it deals with equations. This implies that every proposition of mathematics must be self-evident" (my translation). One thing that makes his assertion surprising is that he could not have failed to know that some propositions, e.g., the proposition regarding the trisection of an angle by straight edge and compass, were thought to be true and subsequently shown impossible. How could he have made his statement in the face of what he undoubtedly knew? It is perhaps possible to avoid the difficulty by taking Wittgenstein to mean by his words, not that all *a priori* propositions were self-evident, but that all *true a priori* propositions were self-evident, that all that is necessary to know their truth-values is to apprehend them. On this interpretation of Wittgenstein's words we are faced with another equally perplexing difficulty. For, again, he could not have been ignorant of the fact that there have been mathematical statements whose truth was unknown and later demonstrated.

It is not, to be sure, rare or unusual for a philosopher to advance a statement which, to all appearances, plainly goes against known fact. G. E. Moore has explicitly called our attention to this bizarre phenomenon, but it cannot be said that philosophers have been made anxious about it or that it has stirred up a feeling that it should be looked into. As is known, Moore's account of this perplexing phenomenon is that it takes place in a "philosophic moment." Moore gives no explanation of his term, apparently thinking that it needs none. The only possible reason for Moore's omission is that by "philosophic moment" he meant nothing more esoteric than the time when we are doing philosophy. It is *philosophy* that casts a spell over our minds and blinds us to glaring inconsistencies. Norman Malcolm, apparently under Moore's influence, has remarked that "philosophical reasoning has a peculiar power to blind us to the obvious."[1] He has made no attempt to explain the mysterious power possessed by philosophical reasoning; neither has he attempted to explain in what way reasoning which has this property differs from reasoning which does not. It is noteworthy that Malcolm did not give a thought to the peculiar power he attributes to philosophical reasoning. But philosophy is all of a piece, and the alleged power of philosophical reasoning to blind must reside in *all* of philosophy. It is time to become realistic about philosophy, face up to its shortcomings, and try seriously to seek an explanation.

Throughout its entire history as a reasoned discipline philosophy has been unable to establish a single uncontested proposition: intractable disagreements cluster around every one of its claims. It undoubtedly was a perception of this disconcerting fact which, in part at least, elicited a complaint from Moore which he privately expressed to friends. In one letter he wrote: "Philosophy is a terrible subject: the more I go on with it, the more difficult it is to say anything at all about it which is both true and worth saying. You can never feel that you have finished with any philosophical question whatever: got it finally right, so that you can pass on to something else."[2] It is interesting to note that he never gave expression to his unhappiness about philosophy in his published writings, not even in his *Commonplace Book.* The thought cannot fail to pass through one's mind that it was intended for private consumption and should not be made public.

A second paradoxical proposition, also put forward in the *Tractatus,* is the following: "All inference is made a priori" (5.133). To realize that this proposition presents a perplexing paradox we need only be aware that Wittgenstein must have known that many inferences are not *a priori,* e.g., inferences about the weather, the behavior of people, etc., etc. W. V. Quine, who claims that philosophy is a "non-fiction" discipline,[3] states that the quest of the philosophical physicist is to lay bare the "inner nature" of things.[4] The quest in the present essay is to lay bare the inner nature of Wittgenstein's two propositions and in this way improve in some measure our understanding of the workings of philosophy.

It is easy to see that the words "All inference is made a priori" do not express an empirical proposition, an inductively arrived at generalization. Wittgenstein, as well as any other philosopher who adopts his philosophical view, did not examine cases to which the word "inference" correctly applies and conclude that *probably* all cases to which the word correctly applies are *a priori.* Inductive evidence for an empirical proposition involves the theoretical possibility of an upsetting instance, which is to say, a describable countercase. A philosopher who maintains that all inference is *a priori* cannot say what a counter instance would be like, any more than a mathematician can say what it would be like for a number to be the greatest prime.

Once it is seen that the words "All inference is made *a priori*" are not being used to express a proposition about the nature of inference, a proposition to the investigation of which an examination of cases is relevant, it is natural to think they are being used to make a verbal claim about the correct use of inference terminology. Construing the words as expressing a proposition about the proper use of a set of familiar terms, the claim is that "*a priori*" applies to whatever the word "inference" (and equivalent words) correctly applies to: that established usage dictates the application of the one term to whatever the other term ranges over. So-called ordinary language philosophers place a linguistic construction on paradoxical philosophical utterances, such as "Time is unreal" and "We do not really see things." They are represented as going against the use of expressions occurring in ordinary language and as implying that such everyday expressions as "sees a table" and "I was kept waiting all of fifty minutes" are mistaken, or better, that these expressions have no descriptive function in the language. Similarly with regard to the view that all inference is *a priori,* or that in a correct inference the antecedent *entails* the consequent: the underlying explication is taken to be that a large number of ordinary applications of the term "inference" are improper and that its proper applications are confined to those inferences that are made *a priori*. In sum, paradoxical philosophical views are understood as *attacks* on ordinary language.

G. E. Moore, the most important defender of philosophical common sense, made the following remark about the view that we do not really see things: "Some people may no doubt think it very unphilosophical in me to say that we ever can perceive such things as these [doors and fingers]. But it seems to me that we do, in ordinary life, constantly talk of *seeing* such things, and that when we do so, we are neither using language incorrectly, nor making any mistake about the facts—supposing something to occur which never in fact occurs. . . . I am not, therefore, afraid to say that I now perceive that that is a door, and that that is a finger."[5] Norman Malcolm has said: "I expect that some will be puzzled as to how anyone in his right mind can *deny* that we see doors and know that pencils exist."[6]

We cannot seriously entertain the idea that a philosopher who embraces the paradoxical view that we do not see things is not in his right mind or that he is mentally unbalanced, any more than we would think that a person who has strange, unbelievable dreams is deranged. Our own behavior is entirely different from what it would be if we thought him a lunatic. We do not treat him as we would someone we think to be demented: we do not act defensively, humor him, or leave as quickly as possible. The matter would be otherwise if it was *actually* thought that the philosopher meant to say what he seems to be saying. If anyone did think this, then Moore's expression "philosophic moment," the interpretation of which is uncertain, would have an obvious meaning: a moment of lunacy. But there is not the slightest suggestion that anyone harbors uneasiness about the mental condition of the philosopher. Indeed, his utterances are taken seriously and discussed over long periods of time in many different countries and even taught in university courses. An advocate of philosophical paradoxes is not a man out of his senses, nor is he unaware of the facts which to all appearances go against his claims. There can be only one acceptable explanation: this is that the paradoxical views are radically different from the appearance they present. We must suppose the actual nature of a philosophical utterance to be hidden by its apparent nature, just as an arid stretch of land is hidden by an inviting mirage.

The view that all inference is *a priori* is not taken by Wittgenstein to be upset by the existence of what might be called Sherlock Holmes inferences. It has to be construed in a way which makes it impervious to refutation by what is the case. And the fact that Wittgenstein does not accept established inference-terminology as upsetting the second, verbal construction placed on his claim shows that his statement does not actually make the linguistic claim it appears to some philosophers to be making. A possible interpretation of what his view comes to is that it arbitrarily introduces a "holiday"[7] use of "inference," a use which academically contracts the application of "inference" to cover only inferences that are *a priori,* i.e., entailments. This nonconventional use is presented in the indicative form of speech, which is responsible for making it look like a statement which is either about the nature of inference or about inference-terminology. The explanatory power of this interpretation is considerable. It makes understandable the central enigma of philosophy—its ubiquitous, permanently intractable debates. The contracted use is determined by semantic preference, and, like an aesthetic division of opinion, can be disputed endlessly without resolution.

Wittgenstein's other view, namely, that every proposition of mathematics must be self-evident, has a like explanation. There can be no doubt that he made his claim while knowing perfectly well that the truth-values of many mathematical propositions have been and in some cases remain unknown, e.g., the Goldbach theorem that every even number can be represented as the sum of two primes. And some well-known mathematical propositions thought to be true were eventually proved false. It might be noted that if the truth of a logically necessary proposition were evident, then all that would be required to know that an unknown *a priori* proposition is not true is to see that its truth does not lie on its surface. Mathematicians would certainly be spared a great deal of uncertainty and labor. Putting this aside, it poses no difficulty to see that Wittgenstein's view that mathematical propositions are self-evident, like his view that all inference is made *a priori,* is not arrived at by an inductive procedure. It is easy to see why the utterance cannot be construed as an inductive generalization. To realize this, it is only necessary to keep in mind the fact that he rejects *any* cases which might be taken as going against it.

Again, as in the case of the preceding proposition, there is a strong tendency to place a linguistic construction on it, a construction which implies something about the correctness or incorrectness of the use of terms occurring in everyday language. Wittgenstein has said, "Your questions relate to words; so I have to talk about words."[8] And the general working idea behind a great deal of contemporary philosophy is that by its inner nature a philosophical statement is linguistic. It is interesting as an aside that C. D. Broad lays this development, which he thinks highly undesirable, at Moore's door.

The verbal construction placed on the ontologically formulated utterance — ontologically formulated since it mentions no term and, moreover, creates what is for many the unshakable idea that it is about nonlinguistic realities — is that it is about the use in the language of the terms "mathematical proposition" and "self-evident": it is to the effect that the second term correctly applies to whatever the first term applies to.

If we resist invoking occult forces, which bestow on philosophical reasoning the power to blind one to known facts of verbal usage or which can make us accept inconsistencies between what we believe to be true and what we know to be false, or, what is the same thing, which enable us to believe propositions we know to be false, then only one possibility presents itself: there is no inconsistency, and philosophical reasoning does not blind us to facts of linguistic usage. F. H. Bradley has remarked that "Metaphysics is the finding of bad reasons for what we believe upon instinct."[9] If Bradley is correct about this, then the reasoning leading to a view is not the reason for its being held; its function is different from that of a mathematical demonstration. Bradley's words serve to remind us that reasoning which one philosopher finds persuasive leaves another philosopher cold: its power to "blind" seems to be selective.

Now, if there is no inconsistency between the use in the language of terms referring to nonentailment inferences and the proposition that the term "made *a priori*" correctly applies to cases to which the word "inference" properly applies, then the proposition cannot be understood as making a factual claim. Instead, it must be construed as surreptitiously introducing an academically contracted use of "inference," a use which prohibits its application to nonentailment inferences. In the special language game of the philosopher, nonentailment inferences are not to be called "inferences." Wittgenstein has said that the philosophy of mathematics is an idleness in mathematics, and his remark can easily be seen to hold for inference practice: philosophical inference talk is an idleness in the making of inferences. An illusion-creating, gerrymandered term like "inference," not meant for actual adoption, can contribute nothing to the *work* which we assign to inference terminology.

It might be suggested that in holding this view about the hidden nature of philosophy I imply that philosophy has magical properties of concealment which prevent philosophers from seeing their discipline aright even after immersing themselves in it for hundreds of years. Putting aside such an implication, one realistic explanation of the nature of their subject is that they do not see what they *do not wish* to see. But there is more to it than this. The serious explanation has to bring in the unconscious part of the mind, which was first scientifically investigated by Freud. According to Freud and his followers, past and recent, conscious processes have their roots in the unconscious, which modifies and determines them in various ways. Thus an utterance which at the conscious level of the mind conveys or appears to convey a certain idea will at the deeper level of the mind express an unconscious fantasy or wish.

To return to our example, the words "all inference is made *a priori*" present the conscious idea that a discovery about the nature of inference or about inference talk has been made. For the unconscious, we may permit ourselves to conjecture, these words refer to a Spinozistic fantasy: the mind can know everything by deduction alone. Intellectual narcissism may be the governing force of the inner dream the words stand for in our unconscious. The words express a subjective overestimation of our mental powers that is necessary to ward off the feelings of insecurity and inadequacy from which everyone suffers. It is understandable that we would protect a conscious idea, correct, incorrect, or philosophical, which plays the role of giving us unconscious consolation.

M.L.

NOTES

1. *Knowledge and Certainty,* p. 180.
2. Quoted in Sotheby's brochure (London) listing Moore's writings which were to be put on sale.
3. *Word and Object* (Cambridge, Mass. and New York: The Technology Press of M.I.T., and Wiley, 1960), p. 275.
4. "Philosophical Progress in Language Theory," *Metaphilosophy* 1(1970), p. 2.
5. "Some Judgments of Perception," *Philosophical Studies,* pp. 226–227.
6. *Knowledge and Certainty,* op. cit., p. 175.
7. Wittgenstein's word.
8. *Philosophical Investigations,* p. 49.
9. *Appearance and Reality,* p. xiv.

VIII

The Yellow Book Notes in Relation to *The Blue Book*

The contents of the Yellow Book[1] connect very closely with problems taken up in *The Blue Book,* which to my mind contains the most revolutionary ideas in the works of Wittgenstein. Philosophers have been so concerned with trying to picture him as a conventional philosopher, with a place in an established philosophical tradition, that his contributions to the understanding of philosophical problems have been ignored or muted. That he himself was aware of the change of outlook on philosophy which took place in the early years after his return to Cambridge is evident in the following statement in *The Blue Book*: "One might say that the subject we are dealing with is one of the heirs of the subject which used to be called 'philosophy'."[2] At that time, Wittgenstein evidently considered it to be the only important work left to be done in philosophy. Nevertheless, he fully realized the objection traditional philosophers would make: "Why should what you do here be called 'philosophy'? Why should it be regarded as the only legitimate heir of the different activities which had this name in former times?"[3] His awareness of the difference between his new conception of philosophy and the historical conception is clear in this Yellow Book excerpt: "Suppose someone said, 'My craving is to get a general comprehensive picture of the universe. Can you satisfy this craving?' I would say 'No.' But if the person says, 'Are you then entirely useless to me?', I would say, 'Possibly not. Let us see whether doing such and such or thinking such and such a way will, not satisfy your craving, but make you cease to have it. This may happen. But it may equally happen that your craving is not taken away; in this case I can do nothing for you.'" This statement is consonant with the position expressed subsequently in the *Philosophical Investigations*: ". . . the clarity we are aiming at is indeed *complete* clarity. But this simply means that the

From *Crítica,* Vol. IX, No. 26, 1977, with minor changes. Reprinted by permission of the publisher.

philosophical problem should *completely* disappear."[4] As he said in lectures, not the solution of philosophical problems, but their *dissolution,* is the goal. He recognized that this aim is destructive of what most people consider valuable in philosophy. Thus, in the *Investigations,* he wrote: "Where does our investigation get its importance from, since it seems only to destroy everything interesting, that is, all that is great and important? (As it were all the buildings, leaving behind only bits of stone and rubble.)"[5] His answer was: "What we are destroying is nothing but houses of cards and we are clearing the ground of language on which they stand."[6]

As is known, in this period Wittgenstein found the source of philosophical problems in language. "Philosophy, as we use the word," he said, "is a fight against the fascination which forms of expression exert upon us."[7] And also, "Philosophical problems are solved . . . by looking into the workings of our language."[8] The reference to language is the key to what John Wisdom called "the Wittgenstein revolution"[9]: the drastic change in the conception of philosophical activity and of its future direction. The extensive literature of philosophy pictures the philosopher as a persistent seeker after truth. And at the same time it is a record of the continuous disagreements over whether truth has been found.[10] Various historical figures — Kant for one, Descartes for another — have taken explicit note of this disconcerting fact. Descartes deprecated the lack of stable results in metaphysics as compared with the steady accumulation of secure results in mathematics. But it seems not to have occurred to philosophers that something in the nature of philosophical views, rather than a shortcoming on their own part, precludes a truth-value decision on them. Wittgenstein turned his mind to discovering what gave philosophical views the air of being factual claims, and disagreement about them the appearance of disputation over fact. His conclusion was that their source was a verbal muddle, that the philosopher is misled by his own language into supposing he is solving a problem. Instead of aiming at a decision about where the truth lies, future investigation should focus on determining how the philosopher's use of words manages to create the idea that a true-or-false answer exists. The implication of a number of his remarks, both in *The Blue Book* and in the Yellow Book, is that the fact-stating form of speech produces the illusion that a theory about matters of fact is being advanced. Quite usually, philosophical pronouncements have an air of paradox about them, and the arguments given for them are puzzling because they seem cogent even to those to whom the conclusion appears obviously false. Their seeming cogency is a sign that "we are up against trouble caused by our way of expression."[11]

General comments such as these are what Wittgenstein called "hints" or "pointers." During the informal discussions recorded in the Yellow Book a question was raised about what he meant by "hints," to which he replied that they were "remarks that may set you on the right track in solving a problem. But I could leave out all of the hints, and just treat of special problems. However, people often cannot imagine what I am talking about when they hear me dealing with some special difficulty, and they only understand what I am driving at when they begin to understand my general remarks, my hints." One of these hints, found in the Yellow Book, I shall take as a general guide in dealing with a special problem (a problem to which almost half of the informal discussion was given over). The hint is the following: "The fallacy we want to avoid is this: when we reject some form of symbolism, we're inclined to look at it as though we'd rejected a proposition as false. . . . This confusion pervades all of philosophy. It's the same confusion that considers a philosophical problem as though such a problem concerned a fact of the world instead of a matter of expression." It need hardly be remarked that, traditionally, philosophical problems appear to concern just what he says they do not: a fact of the world, and not a matter of expression.

In order to give substance to the general hint it is useful to compare briefly an example of the traditional treatment of a philosophical problem with Wittgenstein's treatment of it. Descartes' investigation of mind and body gives us a good illustration of Wittgenstein's thesis[12] that philosophical questions have been approached as one would a scientific problem because they sound as though they are questions about fact of which we do not know enough rather than questions about language. Consider Descartes' question, "What, then, am I?". He gave as his answer, "a thinking thing" (*Meditation* II), and proceeded to delineate its features: "When I consider the mind, that is, when I consider myself in so far only as I am a thinking thing, I can distinguish in myself no parts, . . . for it is the same mind all entire that is exercised in willing, perceiving, . . . etc." (VI). "It is plain that I am not the assemblage of members called the human body" (II). "There is a vast difference between mind and body, in respect that body, of its nature, is always divisible, and that mind is entirely indivisible" (VI). "Although I conceive that I am a thinking and non-extended thing, and that a stone, on the contrary, is extended and unconscious, there being thus the greatest diversity between the two concepts, yet these two ideas have this in common that they both represent substances" (III). In these passages we have a typical philosophical investigation of the nature of one's self, an argument for not identifying it with one's body, and a conclusion that there are two kinds of entities, the one thinking and the other extended. The entire discussion is conducted in what might be called the fact-stating idiom. The impression is that we have been given an account of the features we ourselves, and our bodies, in fact possess.

Without pursuing questions about the self, I shall merely contrast how Wittgenstein approached them in the Yellow Book. By collating what he said at various places the differences can readily be seen. His question sounds Cartesian: "Is the person A the same thing as A's body?", he asks. But his answer makes it clear that he thinks words, not the phenomena to which they refer, to be the only relevant subject matter for investigation:

That the name of a person refers to a human body is clear enough if only you consider how you would introduce A to someone. On the other hand we know that a person changes his body during his life-time, by growing up, etc. Furthermore, the following case is conceivable, that someone comes into my room and says, "I'm your friend Smith, though I don't look it. My body has changed overnight while I slept." . . . What would we do to test the truth of what he said? I think we would ask him a lot of questions about his past; and we should say he was the man he claimed to be if he could tell us all the details of his life which we knew Smith could have told us. Another criterion we might apply would be whether Smith's former body had disappeared and his second body had come into existence in its place. . . . These considerations show that the proper name "A" and the expression "A's body" do not have the same use, at least not if we decide to use the above criteria for the identity of A. But now be careful not to think that these considerations show that besides A's body there is something else, another object, which is A. You must refrain from looking for a substance when you see a substantive—but not from thoroughly examining the use of a word. (YB)

This directive is elaborated in what follows:

Suppose one answers the question, "Who remembers last year's earthquake?", with "I," pointing to a body. There is a queer mistake, hard to explain, in considering that pointing to a body when one answers "I," is an indirect way of pointing to the self. It is bound up with counting objects in visual space, where we understand what we oppose our bodies to. We can count bodies, but how do we count selves? What do I oppose myself to? We're inclined to say that names for selves refer to entities connected with bodies. . . . Compare supposing that each of us has a self like myself with supposing that everybody has a shilling (though I know only that I myself have one). In the latter case the act of supposing might be done with a drawing. Part of the game of supposing that other people have a shilling is being able to make a picture. The sense of the word "shilling" is given by the use language makes of it, and part of what we might do to explain any sentence containing "shilling" would be showing a picture. . . . The supposition of having a self is very different from that of having a shilling, although "Each of you has a self" sounds like "Each of you has a shilling." Seeing how different they are . . . may make you more reluctant to say "although other people can't be imagined without their bodies I could nevertheless be imagined without mine." But suppose we had selves without bodies, what about language? How should we make ourselves understood? . . . Voices might be imagined as coming from various places, but it might easily be the case that the same voice was heard at once in several different places; and then what use would the word "I" have? (YB)

Recall that when Smith said "I'm Smith, though my body has changed," "the proper name referred in one way or another to a human body; for Smith in his new body had to remember his old body" (YB). At the same time, the example of Smith's two bodies shows that " 'I' and 'this body' can't be interchanged, even though 'I' only has meaning with reference to a body. . . . But if you discover that the word 'I' doesn't mean 'my body,' i.e., that it's used differently, this doesn't mean that you've discovered a new entity, the ego, besides the body. All you've discovered is that 'I' isn't used the same way as 'my body'" (YB).

This is enough to illustrate how Wittgenstein examines the Cartesian question, as though it does not concern a fact of the world but rather a matter of expression. But it leaves one with a feeling of dissatisfaction because it does not make clear what the Cartesian philosopher is doing with language when he says the concept *mind* represents a substance; and the puzzles about the self do not disappear. The stated goal, dissolving a problem, has yet to be reached. Wittgenstein's views on the nature of positions philosophers put forward and on philosophers' use of language are directed to this goal. By filling out and supplementing things Wittgenstein said in *The Blue Book* and Yellow Book, we can use a philosophical position often associated with dualistic views, namely solipsism, to illustrate how these metaphilosophical views function to make a puzzling position disappear. Three important general guides govern Wittgenstein's treatment of philosophical problems, and will be illustrated here by the problem of our knowledge of other minds. These are: (1) that philosophical problems are not empirical problems; (2) that the philosopher, dissatisfied with current language, presents a language innovation under the guise of stating a matter of fact; (3) that the revised terminology is idle in the language of use.

First, consider the thesis that a philosophical problem is not empirical, as applied to the following form of solipsism: I cannot know what goes on in the mind of another, or whether anything goes on, or whether indeed there is another mind. The following questions of the solipsist seems to challenge a commonsense, factual belief: "How can I know that another person has a pain, or whether what he has when he says he has pain is like what I have when I have pain?" His answer is that I cannot, that one can only know what one experiences oneself. Only if I could have *his* pain could I know what he is experiencing. But there is no possibility of two people having the same pain. It is this last assertion, offered in support of the claim that one cannot know what others' experiences are, or even that there are experiences other than one's own, that Wittgenstein returned to again and again. His avowed task was to destroy the picture created by such words as these: "I cannot experience anything except my own experience. I can see my red, but I can never see yours. I can feel my emotion, but not yours. Even if your anger infects me, so that I feel it in sympathy with you, it is yet, in so far as I feel it, *my* anger, not yours."[13] The picture conjured up by these words is of private ownership, and of private access to what is owned, each mind being related to its contents in this exclusive and privileged way. To all appearances the words are intended to give a picture of the psychological facts.

Whether they in fact do give such a picture is made doubtful by a question analogous to one raised by Wittgenstein in another connection:[14] Does the philosopher mean that all his past experience has shown that he has never had the same feeling as another, and that he is therefore justified in the general claim that sharing anyone's feeling is not psychologically possible? Wittgenstein remarks that "when we say 'I can't feel his pain,' the idea of an insurmountable barrier suggests itself to us."[15] The picture of an obstacle that prevents my entering into your experience and sharing your thoughts and feelings is like that of a locked door which bars the way into your study. But the solipsist's support of his position makes it plain that unlike a locked door, there is no conceivable way of circumventing this obstacle. Thus, Stace argues: "Even if you can telepathically transfer a mental state, say an image, from your mind to mine, yet when I become aware of it, it is then *my* image, and not yours. I can never be you, nor you me."[16] We might add that even if, per impossible, I were someone else, I could not be said to have his image, for my having someone else's image requires a person other than myself whose image I am having. Obviously, if I *were* someone else there would not be two people sharing an image. So long as I am I and he is he, there is no having his pain, and hence no knowing what he is feeling.

Now what is the nature of the impossibility which prevents me from having someone else's pain? The physical structure of human bodies excludes the possibility of my having pain in someone else's tooth. What never in fact happens is nevertheless conceivable; it is merely a fact of nature, which could be otherwise, that it is not possible for my pain to be located in another's body. But that my pain should belong to another person as well as to myself, the solipsist implies, is a *logical* impossibility. As A. J. Ayer put the matter, "It is logically impossible for a sense-experience to belong to the sense-history of more than a single self."[17] It is to be noted that the impossibility of my having someone else's experiences is supported by the *a priori* reason that I cannot be he. Wittgenstein remarked that when the words "can," "cannot," and "must" are met with in philosophy, the sentences in which they occur are being used to express propositions which are secure against falsification. That it often appears that a fact is being asserted is sometimes because the same sentence can be used to state a fact of experience.[18] (One can, for example, imagine circumstances in which the sentences "I can't know what is in his mind," "Motion is impossible," "Only I exist" would function in this way.) In *Zettel* Wittgenstein said that "the essential thing about metaphysics" is that "it obliterates the distinction between factual and conceptual investigations."[19] He therefore set about to "destroy the outward similarity between a metaphysical proposition and an experiential one,"[20] and this requires dispelling the outward likeness between a necessary proposition and an empirical one.

A philosopher who gives "I am I and he is he" as a reason for his view that no two people can have the same pain is not deriving an empirical conclusion, which means that the sentence "I can't have his pain" is not used to express an empirical proposition. A logical impossibility, not a physical impossibility, is being asserted. In this use, according to Wittgenstein, the sentence "hides a grammatical rule."[21] This characterization of necessary propositions is central to his explanation of the philosopher's activity, namely, that in arguing for a "view" a philosopher evidences a dissatisfaction with ordinary language. Despite the nonverbal, empirical air surrounding sentences which use the logical "can't" (such as "I can't have his pain"), these sentences, according to him, "do not refer to a matter of experience at all, but only to a form of expression we have adopted and which we could perfectly easily chuck aside. They are statements about a convention which we have made" (YB). The characterization of necessary propositions as "rules of grammar" has caused Wittgenstein to be called a conventionalist, and there is much justification for this label. But we can make his point about the import of a philosophical utterance, now understood as intended to express a necessity, without subscribing to the view that a sentence making no mention of words, e.g., "Cats are animals," is about words. This can be done by considering *sentences* which express necessary propositions, rather than the propositions they express. This approach, which prevents the confusion of necessary propositions with verbal propositions, is due to Morris Lazerowitz.[22] It achieves Wittgenstein's aim of explaining how a philosophical sentence which appears to state "a fact of the world" while being, in the philosopher's use, the vehicle of a necessary truth, is connected with a linguistic convention. The way in which the necessity of a proposition is bound up with a verbal matter is the following: the statement that a sentence S expresses a necessary proposition is equivalent to a statement about the usage of words occurring to S.

To see this, consider two sentences in current language which parallel the sentence "It is impossible for two people to have the same pain," one expressing a necessary proposition and one a fact of experience: "It is impossible for a prime number greater than 2 to be even" and "It is impossible for a horse to overtake a cheetah." The statement that a horse cannot overtake a cheetah could in principle be false. And in general, in the case of every sentence of the form "x cannot . . ." which expresses an empirical proposition, we know what it would be like for the situation asserted by "x does . . ." to obtain. "Cheetah that is outrun by a horse" describes something whose existence is denied by the sentence in which it occurs. A similar account of sentences expressing necessary propositions will, however, not do. Where the "cannot" refers to a logical impossibility, the sentence does not deny the existence of something it *describes*. Unlike a physicist, a mathematician who tells us what cannot be does not *describe* what cannot be; for he does not describe what in principle *could* be. In general, in the case of mathematics this is to say that in sentences of the form "x cannot exist," *x* does not have a descriptive function. To return now to the example, "An even prime greater than 2 does not exist," we can see how the fact that it expresses an *a priori* necessity is bound up with a verbal matter: the fact (a) that this sentence expresses a necessary proposition is equivalent to the fact (b) that "even prime greater than 2" describes no number. In knowing fact (a) about the sentence in which "even number greater than 2" occurs, we know that in the language of mathematics this phrase has no use—although the verbal fact about the phrase is not what the sentence expresses. Wittgenstein did not develop the detail required for explaining how the necessity of a proposition is bound up with a verbal matter, but I think the explanation here is consonant with his thesis about philosophical views.

Consider now the philosophical sentence, "It is impossible for two people to have the same pain." Taken as expressing a necessary proposition, it prevents the phrase "having the same pain" from describing the experience of two people. Seeing that this is the point of the philosopher's utterance brings to light his discontent with our present language and the revision his nonverbal mode of speech conceals. It is plain that as English is used it is proper to say "You are having the same headache I have," "We both had the same feeling when we heard the news," etc. Ordinary English does not proscribe its use, and in ordinary circumstances the solipsist would without hesitation describe his pain as the same as another's. He does not bring his ordinary talk into line with his philosophical talk. If he insists in a "philosophic moment," to use Moore's term, that another's pain cannot be his, that he spoke inaccurately before and should have instead said "His pain is exactly like mine," then Wittgenstein's conclusion seems to be the right one: "He is saying that he doesn't wish to apply the phrase 'he has got my pain' or 'we both have the same pain.' . . ."[23] By advancing his statement as though it expressed a necessary truth he is giving vent to his dissatisfaction with current usage and is changing it in a way that suits him better—all this masked by the fact-stating form of speech in which things rather than words are referred to. Behind the delusive façade of rejecting a proposition as false, he is altering an ordinary mode of speech. "Having the same pain as yours" is rejected in favor of "having a similar pain to yours."

The philosopher gives no notice that he is legislating "You and I have the same pain" out of the language, and is unaware that his activity is purely linguistic. He is duped by the indicative, fact-stating form of the words "Everyone's experiences are his alone" into the illusion that they express a psychological truth, and fails to see that he is merely introducing revised terminology. Wittgenstein made the same point in the following well-known but insufficiently discussed passage: "[The philosopher] is not aware that he is objecting to a convention. He sees a way of dividing the country different from the one used on the ordinary map. He feels tempted say, to use the name 'Devonshire' not for the county with its conventional boundary, but for a region differently bounded. He could express this by saying, 'Isn't it absurd to make *this* a county, to draw the boundaries *here*?' But what he says is: 'The *real* Devonshire is this.' We could answer: 'What you want is only a new notation, and by a new notation no facts of geography are changed.'"[24] This passage graphically makes the point that the philosopher is in some way dissatisfied with current language. Moreover, where the metaphysician supposes himself to be exploring a terrain for new facts, Wittgenstein represents him as merely manipulating terminology. Once this is seen, the philosopher's erroneous idea of his investigations tends to disappear, and should completely disappear when the linguistic sources are uncovered.

In exploring the sources of the revision, Wittgenstein begins in the Yellow Book by pointing out what he calls the difference in grammar of the word "have" in "Miss Ambrose does not have the fountain pen; I have it" and "Miss Ambrose has toothache. I have toothache." In the case of the latter pair, an asymmetry strikes us, namely, that there is no hypothesis about the statement "I have toothache." If there were, it would be proper English to say "I think it's I who has toothache" (YB). We are tempted to express the difference by saying that I can know that I have toothache but not that she has (YB). But he asks us to note that if we express ourselves in this way we are emphasizing a difference between "I have" and "she has" in a manner which bears only a surface analogy to the difference between "I have a gold tooth" and "She has a gold tooth." We seem to bring out the difference by saying that I can know both that I have a gold tooth and that she has but not that we are both in pain. What we have to see is that we are saying something different when we use a similar form of words: that to say I know that I have a gold tooth but cannot know that she has is to assert a matter of empirical fact, supported by my being unable to look into her mouth; whereas to say I can know I have pain but not that she has is to highlight a difference in "the grammar" of "I have" and "she has." Wittgenstein says of our ordinary notation that "it draws a boundary round a rather heterogeneous set of experiences—mine, yours, hers," and, in this notation, the difference between the uses of the words "I," "you," and "she" is minimized. Each designates the proprietor of a toothache. A notation can stress, and it can minimize, and the solipsist is tempted to change the emphasis—by assigning to the pronoun "I" a unique position in the language. That this is what he is doing is hidden behind the appearance of an assertion about pain and knowing (YB)—in particular, about the possibility of *my* knowing.

Consider now the consequences of the solipsist claim that "only I feel my pain," taken as expressing a necessary proposition. If what it expresses were necessary, then phrases such as "our having the same pain" would be excluded from being used to describe any state of affairs, and "our having different pains" would be made to cover all conceivable cases of our being in pain. This is to say that "our having different pains" would lose its antithesis. In *The Blue Book* Wittgenstein remarks on the "typically metaphysical" use of a word or phrase, "namely without an antithesis; whereas in their correct and everyday use vagueness [for example,] is opposed to clearness, flux to stability, inaccuracy to accuracy."[25] The objection to this revision of usage is that depriving one of a pair of antithetical terms of its use in sentences that convey information destroys the function of both, as when a tiller is detached from the rudder. Wittgenstein stated this general principle in the Yellow Book by saying that "a word to which no other word can be contrasted is of no use." In the present context, preventing the phrase "our having the same pain" from applying to any experience makes "our having different pains" idle. For the latter will no longer distinguish between possible cases of two people being in pain. Since our having the same pain is not a possibility, "our having *different* pains" will cover all conceivable pains of ours, and will have no more descriptive force than does "our having pain"; and "All people in pain have different pains" will convey no more factual information than "All people in pain are in pain." Now in ordinary English "Two people have the same pain" has a use. A nurse, for example, might explain giving two patients the same sedative by saying they have the same pain. Unless the solipsist makes restitution by means of a form of words which does the work of "They have the same pain," the words "Only I feel my pain" will not do the kind of work he thinks they do, namely, "express a kind of scientific truth,"[26] an important fact about the psychological make-up of people (YB). Instead of being a factual proposition, "Only I feel my pain" reduces to the contentless tautology, "All pains felt by me are pains felt by me." It is clear that if the solipsist does make linguistic reparation so that the new language can express the fact that we have the same feeling, then nothing is gained.

It will be useful now to consider the solipsist position which "I alone feel my pain" was intended to support, namely: "I can know only my own experience, not what anyone else's is; about someone else I can only conjecture. I may believe someone is in pain, but not being he, I can never know this." Here again the words have the air of making a factual assertion, but the solipsist must be understood to use them to express a necessary proposition. For he excludes the only possible evidence for someone else being in pain, namely, bodily behavior, including speaking and writing as well as moaning. It is logically inconceivable that any evidence should be adequate for knowledge. This means that the phrase "knowing that Smith is in pain" is deprived of its use. The consequence with regard to the contrast words "believe," "conjecture," "suppose," "imagine," and the like, now emerges clearly. They no longer have their former function of demarcating a boundary beyond which lies possible knowledge. "Believe but do not know" stands for no contrast. The solipsist uses the phrase in stating his position, but it is mere appearance that either "believe" or "know" is used with its antithesis intact. The suggestion of the solipsist's language is that there is a goal which we cannot reach. But in fact his language provides no goal; indeed, it logically precludes it (YB). And so "believe," etc., lose their contrast use, and therefore their use. There is no point in saying that we believe Smith is in pain if nothing better than belief is even theoretically open to us.

The solipsist might counter that "believe" still serves to distinguish between an attitude to others' experiences and the knowledge I have of my own. But consider his use of "know" in "I know I am in pain." In what J. L. Austin called the standard case, where the experience is clearcut and the word "pain" unquestionably applies, it runs counter to usage to say "I believe I am in pain." It is just because of this fact that I cannot say "I know." What more does "I know I am in pain" say than "I am in pain"? As Wittgenstein observed, "know" is used where I can also use "doubt," not where "doubt" is logically excluded.[27] It may well have been a source of dissatisfaction to the solipsist that ordinary language does not mark off explicitly "I have pain" from "He has pain" by allotting knowledge to the one and belief to the other. But the words by which he expresses his position about the experiences of others employs the distinction between "know" and "believe" while at the same time legislating "know" out of use — by destroying the distinction. This is an indication that the nature of his claim about the limits of knowledge and the role of supporting arguments has been misconceived.

The solipsist will insist that the distinction is preserved: that the word "know" is left a restricted use to preface statements about my own experience, and "believe" and related words are given an enormously expanded use. But if within the stretched use the solipsist gives the word "believe," he tries to distinguish, for example, believing Nixon would be impeached from believing litmus paper will turn red in acid, say by distinguishing degrees of probability, then ordinary language may as well be left alone. There would be no point whatever in introducing "believes with a high degree of probability" to do the work of "knows." Furthermore, the new notation would contain the seeds of the solipsist's discontent with the old: he could ask whether our belief that others have pain has a high degree of probability or not. One of Wittgenstein's provocative remarks in the Yellow Book was that what the philosopher says is all wrong, what the bedmaker says is all right.

A.A.

NOTES

1. Notes taken in the academic year 1933–1934, when Wittgenstein chose for dictation of *The Blue Book* five students: H. S. M. Coxeter, R. L. Goodstein, Margaret

Masterman, Francis Skinner, and me, a group which was later augmented. The Yellow Book consists of notes taken by Margaret Masterman and me on informal discussions in the interval between dictation of notes taken by us and by Francis Skinner on lectures Wittgenstein gave at times during the year when he stopped dictating. References to the Yellow Book, some of which is unpublished, will be abbreviated by YB.

2. *The Blue Book,* p. 28. This subject is the one for which Morris Lazerowitz coined the term "metaphilosophy."

3. *The Blue Book,* op. cit., p. 62.

4. *Philosophical Investigations,* p. 51.

5. Ibid., p. 48.

6. Ibid.

7. *The Blue Book,* op. cit., p. 27.

8. *Philosophical Investigations,* op. cit., p. 47.

9. In a personal letter.

10. Unaccountably, Wittgenstein appeared to take no notice of this fact.

11. *The Blue Book,* op. cit., p. 48.

12. *Wittgenstein's Lectures, Cambridge 1932–1935* (edited by Alice Ambrose), p. 99.

13. W. T. Stace, *The Theory of Knowledge and Existence,* p. 67.

14. *The Blue Book,* op. cit., p. 16.

15. Ibid., pp. 55–56.

16. *The Theory of Knowledge and Existence,* op. cit., p. 67.

17. *Language, Truth and Logic,* 2nd. ed., p. 125.

18. *The Blue Book,* op. cit., pp. 56–57.

19. *Zettel,* p. 82.

20. *The Blue Book,* op. cit., p. 55.

21. Ibid.

22. See especially *The Structure of Metaphysics,* pp. 265–271, and *Studies in Metaphilosophy,* pp. 46–56.

23. *The Blue Book,* op. cit., p. 54.

24. Ibid., p. 57.

25. Ibid., p. 46.

26. Ibid., p. 55.

27. *Philosophical Investigations,* op. cit., p. 221.

IX

Wittgenstein and Linguistic Solipsism

Philosophers frequently find themselves captive to a paradox. They find themselves unable to avoid arguments apparently directed against common sense. This makes them defend positions which, as John Wisdom says, "no one would, or no . . . one but a madman would, or no . . . one but a madman or a philosopher would."[1] G. E. Moore's way of dealing with attacks on common sense was first to take them at face value as attacks on obvious truths, and then, by examining the language philosophers use to express a position and their arguments for it, to show the absurdity of the resulting logical consequences. Analyses of the implications of positions were put in the service of defending common sense. For example, Moore's reply to the skeptic's claim that we cannot know that material things exist was, in his well-known words, to "translate the claim into the concrete." The skeptic's position he translated as follows: "Suppose that now . . . instead of saying 'I have got some clothes on,' I were to say 'I think I've got some clothes on but it's just possible that I haven't.'" His concluding comment was: "For me now, in full possession of my senses, it would be quite ridiculous to express myself in this way, because the circumstances are such as to make it obvious that I don't merely think that I have, but know that I have."[2]

Wittgenstein's assertion that philosophical problems are solved by "looking into the workings of our language"[3] might lead one to suppose that here we have a consensus between two important philosophers on how to approach a problem. But Wittgenstein's attention to the language of philosophers had an entirely different aim than the defense of common sense. He explicitly denied that there is a commonsense answer to a philosophical problem.[4] In his view a philosophical problem is a symptom of a verbal muddle engendered by an obsession with the form of speech in which it is phrased, which when straightened out will effect, not a solution to the problem, but its disappearance. He describes his treatment of a problem as being

139

"like the treatment of an illness,"[5] its aim being to cure one of the penchant to ask questions and seek true answers. "One can defend common sense against attacks by philosophers," Wittgenstein says, "only by curing them of the temptation to attack common sense."[6] Philosophical arguments for a paradoxical position *appear* to present reasons for accepting what is obviously false. But to be content with the appearance is to misconceive the point of the arguments and the nature of the conclusion. What needs to be done is to determine, not whether the argument is valid, and the conclusion true, but to see that the philosopher's use of words produces the illusion that a true-or-false conclusion is to be had. It is an illusion fostered by the fact-stating form of speech in which the inference is expressed. The purpose of philosophical reasoning which appears to attack, say, the reality of material objects or the claim to have knowledge of them, is not to convince anyone of a paradoxical fact but to express dissatisfaction with a notation—the notation which is ordinary language. "We sometimes wish for a notation," Wittgenstein says, "which expresses a difference more strongly . . . than ordinary language does, or one which . . . uses more closely similar forms of expression than our ordinary language."[7] Wittgenstein's picture of the philosopher is very different from the philosopher's picture of himself as a scientist establishing what the real state of affairs is. He sees the philosopher as urging the alteration of a convention to which he objects, without recognizing the linguistic obsession that motivates him. According to Wittgenstein: "He sees a way of dividing the country different from the one used on the ordinary map. He feels tempted, say, to use the name 'Devonshire' not for the county with its conventional boundary, but for a region differently bounded. He could express this by saying 'Isn't it absurd to make *this* a county, to draw the boundaries *here*?' But what he says is: 'The *real* Devonshire is this.' We could answer: 'What you want is only a new notation. . . .'"[8] The metaphysician and the scientist use a common form of speech in the expression of their problems—neither makes reference to anything verbal; and both appear to assert facts. But when the philosopher takes such problems to be scientific ones Wittgenstein says he "treats them perfectly hopelessly—as if they were questions of fact of which we do not yet know enough instead of questions about language."[9] His view is summed up in the Yellow Book as follows: "The fallacy we want to avoid is this: When we reject some form of symbolism, we're inclined to look at it as though we'd rejected a proposition as false. . . . This confusion pervades all of philosophy. It's the same confusion that considers a philosophical problem as though such a problem concerned a fact of the world rather than a matter of expression."[10]

In giving this account of Wittgenstein's view of philosophical problems it should be made clear at once that this is not the only view to be found in his work. Many things he says sound indistinguishable from what a traditional philosopher says. A case could be made for supposing he attempted to refute views as false. Such attempts are nothing new in philosophy. What

I should like to do here is to bring out the new and revolutionary part of his work, which has largely been ignored by the philosophical establishment. I have cited several instances of iconoclastic general remarks on the nature of philosophical problems, and I now wish to apply them to a specific view attributed to Gorgias, namely, that communication is impossible. In this context Wittgenstein's thesis would be that under the guise of giving reasons for a factual statement regarding the possibility of communication, Gorgias is articulating his discontent with our language. Inasmuch as Gorgias' claim is still unrefuted, it is clear that we need some other appraisal of it than that it is false and the argument for it inconclusive. Wittgenstein's perception of how a philosopher changes language when he argues for a paradox will help us see that Gorgias' thesis does not concern a matter of fact and that his arguments merely create the appearance of going against a common belief. I shall also need to deal with a subsidiary problem which is a consequence of Gorgias' negative answer to the question, "Is communication with others possible?", namely, "Can there be a language with which one communicates with oneself—albeit *only* with oneself?" In other words, "Can there be a private language?" Given that the answer to both questions is negative, language cannot exist. Both of these are bound up with the further question "Can I know what goes on in another's mind?" and with its negative answer by the solipsist.

Now, if reasons can be marshalled against the claim that there exists intrapersonal communication, i.e., against there being a common, public language, then it is natural to retreat to the claim that one can at least understand one's own words. A solipsistic language, one which has a use only for private soliloquy, is the natural consequence of accepting the impossibility of knowing what others mean. Let us now consider the reasons for saying that the meanings anyone else assigns to his vocabulary cannot be known.

Presumably the possibility of communication between two persons rests on each being able to know what the other means by his words. The common-sense account of how we know this is that in the case of many words one needs merely to point out things to which the words apply. The word "cat" is explained by pointing to a cat, the word "red" by exhibiting a red thing. Barring occult means such as telepathy, the only way of conveying what is meant by general words is to show how they are used. The philosopher's objection to this account is readily seen, namely, that I could never know that showing you my use of a word prompts you to attach the same meaning to it as I do. And unless I know what meaning you attach to my words I cannot know that I have conveyed my meaning to you.

Suppose we take the Platonic view that the meanings of words, as compared with the mental acts of apprehending them, are objects capable of being entertained by different people, just as according to common sense, tables can be seen by a number of perceivers. Consider the abstract entity, or universal, as such objects are called, which is named by the general word "red." Suppose that we both in fact have the same universal before our minds when we understand the word. It can be argued that no one could know that someone else uses the word to name that universal. For me to know that you mean by the word "red" what I mean by it I should have to know that you apply it to color instances like those to which I apply it, that is, to similar sense data. At most, I can have only indirect evidence that you do so. The fact that you apply it, for example, to a scarf that I call red is no guarantee that there is a red datum in your visual experience. You might consistently apply the word "red" to objects I would call green if I had your visual experience, and I should be none the wiser. To be sure that you use the word to denote the property I use it to stand for I would need more than the evidence provided by your behavior. All behavioral evidence is in the same case. It can be argued that I can never know that you mean by "pain" what I mean by it. When you say you are in pain I can only infer from your behavior that you attach the same meaning to your words as I do. To know that you mean what I mean I would need to enter into your mind and experience your seeing of the color data and your feeling of pain. This I could do only by being you. But if I *were* you, it would not be a case of my knowing what someone *else,* someone *other* than myself, means when using the color word or pain word that *I* use. If I were identical with you, there would be no *me* to wonder about *your* thoughts. Two minds cannot be one and still be two. Thus, it may be maintained quite generally that no one can know that he and his hearer mean the same by each other's words. We are left with the picture of the whole of society living in a tower of Babel, all behaving, by some miracle, as though each knew what the other meant. As Morris Lazerowitz put it to me, Leibniz's divine pre-established harmony would have to be invoked to avoid a cosmic improbability.

If one sees no escape from the skeptic's conclusion, then each person is reduced to what seems to be a modest claim about himself, viz., "I at least know what *I* mean by my words." What *I* mean by "red" is what I experience when I look at *my* image, and there is nothing inferential about my knowledge. When I say to myself "This is red," I do not look at any outer behavior and conjecture how I am using the word "red." I have myself given the name to this kind of visual impression, and I need not test the correctness of my application by referring to a physical sample or someone else's agreement with me in applying the word "red" to a thing like the sample. Of this communication to oneself Wittgenstein says, "Some people philosophizing might be inclined to say that it is the only real case of communication of personal experience because only I know what I really mean by 'red.'"[11] Although this position represents a retreat from the idea that we use language to communicate with each other, its appeal is that it makes clear where certainty is possible, namely, about what we mean by the words we use in communicating with ourselves. No one else can understand my explanation to myself of the meaning of "red" since no one else can know what I am referring to by "this" in "I mean by 'red' what I experience when I look at *this* image." What the word "this" refers to is strictly private to me; I have exclusive access to it.

But even the claim that I know what I mean is not free from difficulties. Objections spring up from various quarters, some of the traditional kind a philosophic skeptic would raise and some of a quite different kind which Wittgenstein raises. Consider what giving words meaning in a private language would be like. This appears to be a simple thing to do. I assign a meaning to the word "red," for example, merely by fixing attention on a visual image I am having and saying "I now mean *this* by 'red.'" That is, I give "red" an inner ostensive definition. I show myself what the word is to refer to by an inward looking. The purpose of concentrating on my experience is to impress upon myself an association between name and visual datum, this with an eye to future uses of the word in the same way, that is, for images like *this* one. As in defining any other word, one undertakes to fix its use. Once having defined "red," when I say "*This* is red" or "I am seeing red" I communicate a personal experience to myself if I am using the word "red" consistently with the rule my private definition lays down.

Now the skeptic might very well object that when on a given occasion I say to myself "This is red" I have to rely on my memory of the visual datum to which I assigned the word "red" to know that what I am saying is true. My memory might be mistaken, and there is no means of checking it. When I check my memory of my childhood home, say, I may compare it with a photograph. But what is expressed by a sentence of a private language can have no such outer check. It might seem to me that I was applying the word "red" to similar data, whereas I was not doing so. How would I discover whether in fact I was? The visual image by reference to which I defined "red" is gone, and possibly I do not rightly remember what kind of color impression entered into the definition, or even whether it was a *color* impression instead of a taste sensation. Even if some special feature of the image I have when I say to myself "This is red," such as vivacity, has been laid down as the criterion for the correctness of a memory impression, I could not be sure it was present. I could not be sure the present image is vivacious *enough*. I could never get beyond its seeming to me that my use of language is in conformity with the original verbal stipulation. The skeptic's objection puts into permanent question the claim that I do know what I mean by my words. If I cannot know this, a private language is not possible. The linguistic solipsist, as Lazerowitz put it, is a Robinson Crusoe who can no more speak to himself than to his man Friday.

This brings us to an objection Wittgenstein raised in *Philosophical Investigations* against the possibility of a private language which turns attention to the language by which its proponent describes his assignment of meanings to his own words. About a private definition, Norman Malcolm, in reviewing the *Investigations,* writes as follows: "It [is] a success only if it [leads] me to use the word correctly in the future. In the present case 'correctly' would mean '*consistently* with my own definition.' . . . Now how is it to be decided whether I have used the word consistently? What will be the difference between my having used it consistently and its *seeming* to me that I have? Or has this distinction vanished?" The answer to this question is connected with the following important facts about a private language: it cannot be taught to me, and it is not a language whose words I can be said to *learn.* Compare now how we are taught and how we come to learn the uses of words in ordinary language, in particular, the phrases "accurate memory impression" and "application of a word to the same things." Teaching and learning are accomplished by the agency of things and persons, both of which are outside my impressions. The *test* by which we confirm that we have applied a word to things like that used in its ostensive definition is not a mere memory check, though of course we do sometimes check one memory against another. Wittgenstein's example of the latter is checking the recollection of a train's departure time with the memory image of the timetable. But unless the image of the timetable could itself be checked for correctness, that image could not confirm the correctness of the recollection. A private language precludes my testing the correctness of a private word's application or the correctness of a memory impression by reference to things designated by words of a public language. On the private language thesis there is no possibility of being taught the correct use of "same" in "same things denoted by 'red.'" I am the sole arbiter of whether *this* datum is the same as an earlier one. What I call the same *is* the same, and what seems to me correct *is* correct. That I remember the connection between word and datum rightly will have no test. Wittgenstein says that this "only means that here we can't talk about 'right.'"[13] In ordinary language the phrases "seems to be correct, but is not" and "seems to be correct and is correct" mark actual distinctions. In a private language the distinction between "correct" and "seems correct" disappears. So to advocate the possibility of a private language by saying that a person need only remember his definition of a word in order to know its present application is correct, i.e., to know that he applies it consistently to the same kind of thing as was referred to in his ostensive definition, merely pantomimes ordinary language. Since he uses his words in such a way that they can make no distinction between what seems to be and what is, between the same impression and a different impression, they cannot be used to defend his position.

Let us now turn to a semantical principle whose application has even more serious repercussions for the two philosophical theses under discussion: that a private language is possible and that a public language is impossible. The importance of this principle has not been sufficiently realized, perhaps because Wittgenstein did not give it explicit formulation. The principle is that if a word is deprived of its antithesis, the word itself loses its use.

To illustrate, when Hobbes said all desires are selfish, he meant to preclude the word "unselfish" from being used to describe any conceivable desire. But if this word is deprived of its application then "selfish" loses its use in the language to characterize desires. It is important to note that antithetical terms are of two different kinds. Some, like "swift" and "slow," "far" and "near," can be applied correctly to the same thing at different times. Even though one of the two does not in fact apply to anything, so long as there could conceivably be things to which it applies, it retains its function to characterize some among possible things and distinguish them from others. Other pairs of words, e.g., "odd" and "even," are of such a kind that what the one applies to cannot conceivably be described by the other. A number which is odd cannot conceivably be even, and vice versa. The fact that it is logically impossible for the number 3 to be even, that is, that the antithetical property cannot apply to it, does not, however, imply that "even" has no use. For "even" has a use to select some out of a set of numbers.[14]

Wittgenstein said the philosopher uses words "in a typically metaphysical way, namely without an antithesis."[15] Let us see how this characterizes the linguistic solipsist. It will be argued that in consequence of his position the solipsist has no language left by means of which to express it. Consider now the following statements comprising his view: "Only I can know what my words mean," "I mean *this* by 'red,'" "On future occasions of my use of 'red' I need only remember its definition to know I am supplying it to the same sort of thing." Compare the use of the pronoun "I" in these statements with its use in ordinary language, and ask how the linguistic solipsist is to learn the meaning of this word. In ordinary language the pronoun "I" is a contrast term to second and third person pronouns, and is taught as such. There can be no such teaching of pronouns in a logically private language. In fact, the words "you" and "they" and "we" cannot be defined, and must drop out. But in this case, on our semantical principle, "I" loses its function as a contrast term to other pronouns, and also drops out. So to speak, when the "I-thou" distinction vanishes, the "I" vanishes with it. In consequence, the linguistic solipsist does not have the language available for saying "I, and no one else, know what my words mean." Even proper names drop out, for I cannot say "*I* am Alice Ambrose." Wittgenstein put the matter graphically in the following way: what the solipsist wants is not a notation in which the ego has a monopoly, but one in which the ego vanishes,[16] i.e., a notation in which the first person pronoun has no place. In the *Tractatus* he stated that "whereof one cannot speak, thereof one must be silent."[17] As it turns out, the linguistic solipsist is reduced to silence.

It will be recalled that the possibility of a private language was presented as a position of retreat before the attack on the possibility of a public language. It is now seen as being no position, so that what we are left with is the thesis that neither a private nor a public language can exist. Let us return to the view that there can be no such thing as communication with others by means of language. Inasmuch as the search for a conclusive argument against this doctrine has been so fruitless in the past, let us try Wittgenstein's approach, that is, see whether an investigation of the language of the philosopher will lead to the problem's disappearance. Wittgenstein described himself as "bringing words back from their metaphysical to their everyday usage."[18] "When philosophers use a word," he said, "[e.g., the words] 'knowledge,' 'being,' . . . 'I,' 'name' . . . one must always ask oneself: is the word ever actually used in this way in the language game which is its original home?"[19] His question suggests that it is not. We have already seen that the word "I," despite appearances, does not have its usual use in the language of the linguistic solipsist, since it has lost its antithesis. The semantic principle of antithetical terms can again be employed in connection with the view that no two people can understand each other. It will be held that though the philosopher employs words occurring in everyday language, he only seems to be using them with their antitheses intact.

The impression he gives of using language normally is strengthened by a fact Wittgenstein notes, namely, "that the words of his assertion can also be used to state a fact of experience."[20] We can easily imagine situations where it would be true to say the words of one person are not understood by the other, nor could they be—for example, when the two speak alien languages. But in such cases we can describe how they get to know what each other's words mean. The philosophical statement that no one can know what another means is different. Here it is being asserted that such knowledge is logically impossible. The argument for the position is to the effect that a logically impossible condition, viz., one person being identical with another person, would have to be met if two people were to understand each other. The linguistic correlate is that the phrase "knows what another means" has no more descriptive use in the philosopher's language than "round square" has in ours. "Knows" and "does not know" are no longer contrasting terms which can be used in the same sort of circumstances at different times and in different circumstances at the same time. This is to say they are not like the terms "swift" and "slow," which we can use to describe one thing as now swift but previously slow, and two different things simultaneously. But neither are they like the other and different kind of antithetical terms "odd" and "even." It will be recalled that although it is logically impossible for each of the two to apply to the same number, and that even so, this does not imply that because "even" has no use—to characterize, e.g., the number 3— it, and therefore the term "odd" likewise, has no use. It might appear that the philosopher's use of "know" in "knows what another person's words mean" is like "even" in "3 is even," and that the fact that it has no application to the meanings of others need not deprive it of all use.

This appearance is delusive, as the following shows. What secures a use for both "odd" and "even" in our arithmetic is the fact that each has application to members of the same natural number series. Suppose now there were an arithmetic which, from the vantage point of our own arithmetic, we should describe as having only odd numbers. Then, in the language of *that* arithmetic, it could not be said that all numbers are odd. For in it "even" would have no application whatsoever. An analogous situation obtains for the claim that no one can know what another person's words mean. Unlike "odd" and "even" in our arithmetic, "knows" in the philosopher's language does not have an application to the meanings of others' words in any instance whatever. On no conceivable occasion of the use of words by others can one know what is meant. And thus the phrase "does not know" also loses its use. That the philosopher's words appear to mark a distinction, as they do in everyday speech, is seen to be delusive. "Does not know," to use a figure from Wittgenstein, is like a tiller without a rudder.

Now there is a rejoinder open to the solipsist which deserves attention. On his position "does not know" and "know" both retain a use inasmuch as they serve to mark the distinction he makes explicit in saying "I cannot know what another person means by his words but I know what I mean." But note the use of "know" in "I know what I mean," and compare it with its everyday use, which the solipsist does not give up. I quote from the *Investigations*: "One says 'I know' where one can also say 'I believe' or 'I suspect'; where one can find out. . . . 'I know . . .' may mean 'I do not doubt . . .' but does not mean that the words 'I doubt . . .' are *senseless,* that doubt is logically excluded."[21] The solipsist uses "know" in this connection without its antithesis "doubt"; the phrase "doubt about what I mean by 'red'" he excludes from use. When Nixon said "I know what I said and I know what I meant" he assuredly thought that "I know what I meant" was unassailable. Although others might challenge his claim to knowing what he said, any questioning of that claim could be settled by the tapes; but supposedly no one could challenge his own knowledge of what he meant. Leaving aside challenges of his memory, one can see that "knowing what I mean" is no defense if "not knowing" applies to no possible instance of what I mean by my words.

The adjectives "public" and "private" provide a further illustration of the principle of antithetical terms. Ordinarily these adjectives can be used to characterize the same language at different times. Words once common to many users could come to have meaning to only one person, the one who deciphers them; and language which is private to one person may be made public property, e.g., the words of Pepys's diary or da Vinci's script. It is easily seen that despite the fact that the adjectives "public" and "private" seem to have similar characterizing functions in philosophical usage, they do not. A factually private language could be decoded and become public, a logically private language cannot. This means that "private" has no antithesis, inasmuch as "public" has no theoretical application to any notation. Thus, "private" is precluded from characterizing any language. In calling attention to these facts about the philosopher's talk, I am not saying that his words assert what is false, but that his use of them is such that the sentence "No one can know what anyone else means, although I know what I mean" fails to make the distinction it appears to.

Finally, it is important that some comment be made on Wittgenstein's view that a philosophical position represents dissatisfaction with the language in use. Since the skeptic's arguments are not explicitly directed towards any verbal matter—to all appearances they are concerned with knowledge, not the word "knowledge"—the bearing of Wittgenstein's view is unclear. However, what the skeptic appears to attempt, namely, to establish the logical impossibility of anyone knowing the meanings of words used by others, does have a verbal, though implausible, concomitant. This is that the expression "knows what others mean," like other expressions denoting logical impossibilities, has no descriptive use. If in fact the skeptic committed himself to this verbal consequence, then he would be guilty of a mere mistake about usage. Since in ordinary circumstances he employs the distinction between knowing and not knowing what others mean precisely as we all do, some other account of the intent of his arguments must be given. He presents his theory with assurance, yet his assurance cannot rest on a fact about communication or a fact about usage. Wittgenstein asserts that it is because the philosopher is not stating an opinion that he can be so sure of what he says.[22] According to him, the philosopher, under the guise of stating an opinion, is instead introducing an innovation in usage, although he is unaware that he is objecting to a convention. "We sometimes wish for a notation," Wittgenstein says, "which stresses a difference more strongly . . . than ordinary language does."[23] In the Yellow Book he notes that ordinary language draws a boundary around a rather heterogeneous set of experiences—mine, yours, and his—and in this notation the difference between the use of "I," "you," and "he" is minimized. The pairs "I am in pain," "He is in pain" and "I mean x by the word w," "He means x by the word w" look like the pairs "I have a gold tooth," "He has a gold tooth" and "I write w," "He writes w." Seeing that there is no hypothesis about my meaning x by w or my being in pain, so that it is not proper English to say "I believe x is what I mean by w," "I believe I am in pain" induces the skeptic to express the difference by saying "I can know what I mean but not what he means." This has the effect of restricting the use of "know" so that it applies only to what one means oneself, and widening the application of "do not know" to cover what others mean. Revising the scope of the word "know" in this way serves to stress the difference in usage between "I" and other pronouns. But instead of saying "Let the use of 'know' be confined to what I mean by a word w," the solipsist says "Only I really know what I mean by w." He hides the revision behind an indicative statement about knowledge. Morris Lazerowitz has offered an explanation of why the solipsist does this, namely, that the indicative form creates the illusion of announcing a discovery and is used primarily for this reason. For one cannot suppose that the revision the solipsist covertly introduces is intended for acceptance in practice. His own linguistic behavior attests to this *not* being his intent; he continues to speak with the vulgar. This in no way gainsays the fascination of the game he plays with words, nor the challenge and fascination to be had by seeing through his game.

A.A.

NOTES

1. *Philosophy and Psychoanalysis* (Oxford: Basil Blackwell, 1953), p. 173.
2. *Philosophical Papers,* pp. 227–228.
3. *Philosophical Investigations,* p. 47.
4. *The Blue Book,* pp. 58–59.
5. *Philosophical Investigations,* op. cit., p. 91.
6. *The Blue Book,* op. cit., pp. 58–59.
7. Ibid.
8. Ibid., p. 59.
9. *Wittgenstein's Lectures, Cambridge 1932–1935,* p. 99.
10. Ibid., p. 69.
11. "Notes for Lectures on 'Private Experience' and 'Sense Data,'" *Philosophical Review* LXXVII (July 1968), pp. 276–277.
12. *Knowledge and Certainty,* pp. 98–99.
13. *Philosophical Investigations,* p. 92.
14. I owe this distinction to discussions with Morris Lazerowitz.
15. *The Blue Book,* op. cit., p. 46.
16. "The Yellow Book." References here are to the unpublished part of the notes.
17. *Tractatus Logico-Philosophicus* (6.54).
18. *Philosophical Investigations,* op. cit., p. 48.
19. Ibid.
20. *The Blue Book,* op. cit., p. 57.
21. *Philosophical Investigations,* op. cit., Section 354, p. 221.
22. *The Blue Book,* op. cit., p. 60.
23 Ibid., p. 59.

X

Reason and the Senses

Philosophy suffers from a baffling malady which philosophers apparently have no wish to acknowledge or address. They behave as though it does not exist, and calling their attention to it does not elicit the expected reaction of concern. But it does in fact exist, and until the ailment is understood and correctly diagnosed, the nature of technical, academic philosophy is veiled from our understanding. For all we know, it may turn out not to be the high-level investigation of reality it is taken to be. One has only to think of alchemy, the predecessor of chemistry, to realize that this has become a possibility. The idea to be reckoned with is that philosophy — the philosophy of Plato, Descartes, Hume, Kant, Russell, etc. — is semantic alchemy: it uses terminology to produce a delusive appearance that reality is under investigation and that theories about things are being advanced. To give a preliminary example of the illusion-creating use of language, a person who declares that assimilation is genocide[1] is not using language in the normal way to state a fact, but is instead doing things with terminology which create the impression that he is doing so. It is easy to see that a disagreement over whether assimilation is genocide could go on endlessly, with a final resolution always like the horizon, beyond reach.

The intellectual ailment philosophy suffers from is fruitless disagreement, which without exception attaches to every one of its theories. From the beginning, philosophers have been locked in debate over their theories, which often vary only in the language used to express them, perhaps to avoid monotony and to give the impression of progress. Philosophers add *new* theories to their collection of claims, but they never succeed in *establishing* any of them. The Cambridge University philosopher G. E. Moore wrote to one of his learned friends: "Philosophy is a terrible subject: the more I go on with it, the more difficult it is to say anything at all about it which is both true and worth saying. You can never feel that you have finished with any philosophical question whatever: got it finally right, so that

150

you can pass on to something else."[2] On the whole, however, philosophers do not complain about their subject; instead, they behave like a complacent Tantalus, and even defend their plight when it is called to their attention.

Consider for a moment the so-called theory of universals (also called essences, abstract ideas, forms). This theory has had a long and troubled history. Bertrand Russell has remarked: "General words such as 'man' or 'cat' or 'triangle' are said to denote universals, concerning which from the time of Plato to the present day, philosophers have never ceased to debate."[3] Parenthetically, it may be pointed out that Russell himself changed sides a number of times in the debate, sometimes maintaining that universals exist while at other times insisting, with equal cogency, that they do not exist. In one of his Platonic phases he wrote the following panegyric about the realm of abstract, supersensible objects: "The world of [universals] is unchangeable, rigid, exact, delightful to the mathematician, the logician, the builder of metaphysical systems, and all who love perfection more than life"[4]—as against the world of everyday things, which is "fleeting, vague, without sharp boundaries."[5] There is an apocryphal tale about an exchange between Plato and the cynic Diogenes who challenged Plato by claiming that he could see tables but not the universal *tableness*. To this Plato retorted that Diogenes' remark showed that, although he had eyes, he had no intelligence. The retort might be called a slanderous witticism, for, of course, Plato knew perfectly well that Diogenes was an able thinker. In our own day the dispute has been carried on around the so-called Principle of Verification in sense-experience, embraced by some and rejected by others.

Russell has remarked that "hardly anybody except students of philosophy ever realizes that there are such entities as universals."[6] There are several different ways of arguing for their existence, the simplest of which identifies the meaning of a general word, such as "horse" or "tree," as a universal. To express the claim in Russell's way, "nearly all the words to be found in the dictionary stand for universals."[7] As is well known, the debate about universals, and not only about whether they exist but also about their nature, has had a remarkably vigorous history and has attracted the most acute thinkers. Like other interminable divisions of opinion, there is no prospect whatever of a resolution. Arguments on all sides are repeated and the stalemate continues, without decrease in vigor or enthusiasm.

The longevity of philosophical disputes has been dismissed or shrugged off as being of no consequence by some thinkers who do give it momentary attention. In defense of their discipline they point out that the sciences, including mathematics, have their unsolved problems and clashes of opinion, without anyone making a fuss about it. But it is quite plain that the firm foundations on which science rests leave no room for a Cassandra. A philosophical debate is quite unlike a scientific difference of opinion. In the scientific case, a disagreement occurs when not all of the relevant facts are known, and it vanishes when the missing facts become available. If we think realistically about the debate over whether abstract objects exist, we can see that it is carried on in the presence of all the facts necessary to settle the question—if the question is indeed about the facts of the case. How, then, are we to understand a problem the answer to which everyone knows, but with respect to which opposing positions are nevertheless taken? Until we can give a satisfactory answer to this question, philosophy is enshrouded in mist and remains an enigma to our understanding.

One contemporary philosopher, Ludwig Wittgenstein, has made a number of observations which, if followed through, lead to a possible explanation of the perplexing failure to resolve philosophical disagreements. Although he is perhaps the most frequently discussed philosopher of this century, his insightful remarks have failed to attract any attention or to provoke the least interest. One reason for this neglect may be that philosophers have been deterred by the oracular tone of his writings. The oracle of Delphi, according to Heraclitus, neither utters nor hides her meaning, but shows it by a sign; and Wittgenstein's special remarks may also show something about philosophy by a sign. It would seem plain, however, that even though he may have created an obstacle by the manner in which he presented his remarks, there is no accounting for the complete lack of interest in them. And it *may* be that they are in some way perceived as containing an iconoclastic, unwelcome idea of the *nature* of philosophy, an idea that is destructive of its seeming to be an elite, high-order investigation of what there is.

Let us now take up a major division which goes back to the very beginnings of philosophy—the conflict between rationalists and empiricists. A. J. Ayer has characterized philosophical rationalism in the following way: "The fundamental tenet of rationalism is that thought is an independent source of knowledge, and is moreover a more trustworthy source of knowledge than experience; indeed some rationalists have gone so far as to say that thought is the only source of knowledge."[8] More than two thousand years earlier, Parmenides had urged us to heed not the blind eye nor the resounding ear but to use only "the test of reason" in our investigation of what there is. Contesting the Parmenidean thesis, Empedocles urges the use of the senses: "But come, examine by every means each thing how it is clear, neither putting greater faith in anything seen than in that which is heard, nor keep from trusting any of the other means in which there lies the possibility of knowledge. Know each thing in the way in which it is clear."[9] These words express no more than a counter-claim to Parmenideanism and only contribute to the accumulation of claims on one side of the strange bifurcation that has intractably divided philosophy. As is well known, Ayer counts himself a philosophical empiricist and believes that there is an argument which conclusively shows rationalism to be fallacious. He attempts to remove the support that rationalism requires by denying that there could be any necessary truths which are truths about the world. That is, he holds that if a truth is logically necessary, it is not about the world; and if it is about the world, it is not logically necessary. Wittgenstein put it in the following way: It is not required that we look at the weather to know that it is either raining or not raining, and the fact that it is raining does not *make* it true that it is either raining or not raining. The latter is true no matter what the weather is like, and so says nothing about the weather.

Ayer does not, to my knowledge, give a special reason for the claim that a logically necessary truth is not a truth about the world. This claim is a consequence of a nominalistic view which he and others have adopted. According to this view, necessary propositions are really verbal. It is readily seen that a proposition about words is not about things. Ayer has asserted that analytic, or logically necessary, truths convey no information about nonverbal matters. Rather, they "enlighten us by illustrating the way in which we use certain symbols. Thus if I say, 'Nothing can be coloured in different ways at the same time with respect to the same part of itself,' I am not saying anything about the properties of any actual thing; but I am not talking nonsense. I am expressing an analytic proposition, which records our determination to call a colour expanse which differs in quality from a neighbouring colour expanse a different part of a given thing. In other words, I am simply calling attention to the implications of a certain linguistic usage."[10]

The conventionalist view of logical necessity, according to which *a priori* propositions are really verbal, is itself a philosophical view and, as one might expect, it is the subject of intractable disputation. It might be pointed out that Ayer has not tried to meet the charge that on his view of logical necessity, a necessary proposition is not necessary. Putting this aside, however, it is hardly sound procedure to rest an important theory on insecure, controversial grounds. It may be useful to present a general reason, gleaned from C. I. Lewis,[11] for the thesis that all nonempirical truths, including synthetic *a priori* propositions, are incapable of conveying information about things. It is a reason which appears to make no use of philosophical ideas. A logically necessary truth is true no matter what changes take place in the world. The world could be entirely different from its present state, or even fail to exist, without altering the truth-value of the proposition. Expressing this in terms of the currently popular idea of "possible worlds": it is true for all possible worlds, or better, it is true no matter which possible world is the actual world. And it would remain true if there were no world whatever. It therefore says nothing about what there actually is, any more than a so-called truth-table tautology does.

When one thinks on it, it must impress even the blithest of philosophers as incredible that the opposition between rationalism and empiricism could be so durable. One side or the other may temporarily go into a decline, but, like the titan Antaeus, it eventually springs back with renewed strength and vigor. Another feature which must perplex philosophers, whatever their particular persuasion, is that in the conduct of their everyday lives they disregard their philosophical positions as if irrelevant, and talk and behave in the ordinary, familiar ways. In this respect empiricists and rationalists do not differ in the slightest. The Parmenidean heeds his eyes and ears in traffic just as we do. He does not close his eyes and ears and make his way across the street by using "the test of reason." When Diogenes walked before the assembled philosophers who had come to Zeno's lecture in Athens on the impossibility of motion, there could be no doubt of Zeno's sincerity. He was not an intellectual trickster. But neither can there be any doubt that he was aware of the fact that *he* had walked to the lecture room.

On the empiricist side of the division, intellectual anomalies make their appearance which throw empiricism, i.e., what it actually is, into a mystifying light. It is important at the outset to realize that philosophical empiricism is not itself an empirical form of investigation. Very often, the talk is like that of someone conducting empirical research, comparable even to such an elementary observation as that friction between bodies generates heat. Ayer, who himself gave the title *British Empirical Philosophers* to one of the books he coedited, apparently fell dupe to the idea that philosophers employ scientific procedure. Like Empedocles, the philosophical empiricist holds the senses to be instruments for obtaining information about things, but he does not *use* any of the senses to support his view. No more than a moment's reflection is required to make plain that empiricism urges the use of what no one would in fact dream of giving up, not even a Parmenidean. One of its special findings may suffice to show the *kind* of 'scientific' work empiricism does: for example, the existence of a thing, say, the sheet of paper before me, is an *hypothesis,* and can never be more than an hypothesis. The reason given for this claim is that, regardless of the number of actual sense-tests, there is always the *logical* possibility of a confuting instance coming up, which prevents the hypothesis from ever becoming certain. This reason applies equally to the bodies of other people, as well as to my own body. The strangeness of a professor saying to his class that it is his intention to show that their existence, as well as the existence of their classroom and his own body, are uncertain and can never be more than hypothetical, must be apparent to everyone, including the professor who argues for the view.

Outwardly, rationalism and empiricism look to be poles apart, but they have something important in common. This is the *method* by which they obtain their results: neither uses observation or experimentation in its investigations. Empiricism equally with rationalism employs thought alone on whatever material is being considered. It has to be admitted that philosophers sometimes use language which suggests the idea that they are doing an empirical piece of work—a careful scrutiny of a phenomenon, or an experiment, or a search. Wittgenstein, who stated that philosophical propositions are not empirical, suggested that we "look and see"[12] whether objects belonging to a set of resembling things, such as games, have something in common. Regardless of what he was in fact implying by his words, a powerful impression is created that looking will decide for us the truth-value of a frequently held Platonic theory. One thing needs to be pointed out: that from the earliest days of philosophy, controversy has surrounded the question as to whether being similar implies having a property in common.

It has already been noted that an *a priori* true proposition is not about the world, which is to say that its truth-value is not determined by what the world is like. No empirical examination of things or groups of things will be relevant to the claim made by the proposition. Bertrand Russell declared that $2 + 2 = 4$ even far out in space, one suggestion of his words being that if we went far enough out into space we might find $2 + 2$ failing to equal 4. This may be nothing more than a piece of Russellian humor, for the *place* where there are $2 + 2$ things has nothing whatever to do with the fact that they are equal to 4 things. If Wittgenstein is to be consistent with his idea that philosophical propositions are not empirical (the only accepted alternative being that they are *a priori*), then looking can play no role in their determination. In particular, no amount of looking will help decide whether similarity involves having a common property. How are we to understand Wittgenstein's apparent failure to remember his own claim that philosophical propositions are not empirical, and how are we to understand his piece of advice, which looks to be empirical?

Those who are familiar with technical philosophy will know that the perplexing anomalies pointed out here barely scratch the surface. Poe's *Purloined Letter* shows how easily what is in plain view can go unseen, and especially if there is inner resistance against seeing. The effective technique that one tends to fall back on is the psychological mechanism of suppression,[13] a kind of self-blinding process. However, resistance to knowledge has always given way to knowledge, even if only slowly and irregularly. Freud's words in *The Future of an Illusion* are worth citing: the voice of reason is soft but persistent and eventually makes itself heard.

Ayer has written that "One of the main objects of this treatise [*Language, Truth and Logic*] has been to show that there is nothing in the nature of philosophy to warrant the existence of conflicting philosophical parties or 'schools.'"[14] His reason is as follows: "The function of the philosopher is not to devise speculative theories which require to be validated in experience, but to elicit the consequences of our linguistic usages. That is to say, the questions with which philosophy is concerned are purely logical questions. . . ."[15] It is not easy to see the reason for saying that the questions of philosophy are purely logical. Indeed, if they were, then the disputes would be resolved, as they eventually are in mathematics and logic. For example, the question as to whether our perception of things is direct or indirect, or the question whether abstract entities exist, are not questions that anyone would expect to find dealt with in logic. Leaving this point aside, there can be no doubt that philosophy in all of its parts is in a ferment of disputation.

The problem of explaining its disagreements would certainly be simplified if the work of philosophy were nothing more than "to elicit the consequences of our linguistic usages." But regardless of whether the disputes are warranted, they do in fact exist, and there seems to be no way of making them disappear. Ayer continues with the following words: ". . . although people do in fact dispute about logical questions, such disputes are always unwarranted. For they involve either the denial of a proposition which is necessarily true, or the assertion of a proposition which is necessarily false. In all such cases, therefore, we may be sure that one party to the dispute has been guilty of a miscalculation which a sufficiently close scrutiny of the reasoning will enable us to detect. So that if the dispute is not immediately resolved, it is because the logical error of which one party is guilty is too subtle to be easily detected, and not because the question at issue is irresolvable on the available evidence."[16]

Anyone who makes the claim that the existence of a philosophical disagreement implies that at least one of the disagreeing parties has made a mistake is taking a surprisingly rosy view of philosophical disagreements. For the *fact* is that philosophical disputes do not get resolved and that philosophical "miscalculations" do not get corrected. Only an overstrong wish could make one forget that the Zeno arguments against motion are still in dispute. Consider the following nonphilosophical problem. A renegade general who was captured by his own troops was sentenced to death by a firing squad. At the time of the execution the commanding officer reconsidered the situation and decided to give the general the option of either being shot or shooting himself. He elected to shoot himself. Did he commit suicide? People invariably divide on the question as to whether the general committed suicide. Those who say "Yes" give as their reason that he killed himself while having the option not to. Those who say "No" contend that the general did not have a choice between life and death. Restated in terms of entailment-claims, the question is whether choosing to shoot oneself instead of being shot entails committing suicide. Restated linguistically, the question is whether "committed suicide" correctly applies to whatever "chose to shoot himself rather than be shot" applies to. Each of the parties to the dispute knows the *reason* for the position of the other, and would unyieldingly resist the suggestion that he had made a miscalculation.

The constant temptation in philosophy is to take sides and to contend that arguments for rejected views are mistaken. A feature to be noticed regarding these arguments is that it is possible to change one's mind a number of times about their validity without anything not already known about them emerging. It is by no means rare for a philosophical argument to impress a philosopher as being conclusive, later to lose its force for him and be given up, regain its force, and so on. It would seem that the validity of a philosophical argument, unlike the validity of a piece of evidence in science, is determined by *preference*. This can, perhaps, be most easily seen by extending the case of the renegade general. Suppose it turns out that the general and his relatives are Catholics, who cannot be buried in consecrated ground if they have committed suicide. The practical consequences of the decision that he was guilty of suicide are plain, and they tell us what considerations bear on the decision. This would be out of the question if there were an entailment relation between the general's electing to shoot himself under those circumstances and his committing — or his not committing — suicide. In the present problem it is not actual linguistic *usage* which dictates or prohibits the application of "commits suicide" to what the phrase "elects to shoot himself" is correctly applicable. Rather, it is a decision to *fix* a use of the word "suicide" where language provides no rule. It should be pointed out that actual usage need not be a hindrance to introducing a new use which goes against a piece of established use: preference again plays the deciding role.

The important similarity between the question about the renegade general and philosophical questions cannot fail to make an impression unless inhibited by a strong investment in philosophy. The main difference seems to be one of dignity. The problems under investigation by philosophers concern "ultimate reality," to use Bradley's phrase, whereas the question regarding the renegade general seems to be merely one of terminology. Freud somewhere describes our ego and the role it plays in our mind with the words, "His Majesty, the Ego." It is understandable that when something conflicts with our self-esteem we tend to erect defensive barriers, and the greater the threat to our pride the more difficult it will be to break down the defenses. The mind has a number of strategies it can use, one of which is like the punishment meted out to a member of a Pennsylvania Dutch community who has broken a taboo. He is subjected to what might be called the "obliteration treatment": no one speaks to him, sees him, or hears him. It is not a wild speculation that this is the prevailing, perhaps largely unconscious, attitude toward any explanation of the nature of philosophy which deflates it in the eyes of philosophers, punctures their semantic balloon. Anyone who can overcome the tendency to take flight from the unpleasant will soon see that the problem of the renegade general provides us with a new way of looking at philosophical problems, and that it improves our understanding of the central enigma of philosophy.

Wittgenstein has asked: "Where does our investigation get its importance from, since it seems only to destroy everything interesting, that is, all that is great and important? (As it were, all the buildings, leaving behind only bits of stone and rubble.)"[17] His answer is that "What we are destroying is nothing but houses of cards and we are clearing up the ground of language on which they stand."[18] In lectures Wittgenstein has sometimes said that philosophical problems are not the kind of problems which have solutions: they have *dissolutions*. The alarming possibility, the skeleton which must be kept locked away at all costs, is that philosophy is only the imitation of a discipline and that "clearing up the ground of language" on which it stands will do nothing more than make it vanish.

Philosophical rationalism, which appears to reject our senses as avenues of knowledge, turns out not to be about our senses at all. Like everyone else, the rationalist heeds his eyes, uses his tongue and ears the way people normally do. When thrown into doubt about a thing, he knows how to check with his senses. Nor does he change his talk in the conduct of his ordinary life. He lectures to the learned but he talks and acts with the vulgar. The rationalist's philosophical statements about the senses make no factual claims about them. And realizing this naturally leads one to the idea that the statements are about sense-terminology. The verbal claim that many philosophers believe these statements to be making is that words like "hears," "tastes," and "sees" have no correct or proper use in the language. But this interpretation cannot be the right one either. For calling attention to the fact that "hears" has a correct use in the language and that sentences like "He heard the clock ticking on the wall" make literal, descriptive sense, could only call attention to what the philosopher already knows. Such facts would not make him give up his philosophical position, however. He would not deny that "hears" has a use in *ordinary language,* and his accompanying behavior would carry with it the suggestion that by his view he did not intend to deny a known fact of usage. He does not in fact reject established usage, yet he maintains his view as if he is not embracing an inconsistency.

The rationalist view makes neither a claim about our five senses nor one about the actual use of sense-terminology. This, taken together with the debates surrounding it, suggests, and even lends plausibility to, the idea that a terminological innovation is being introduced. In the spirit of a game being played with language, sense-terminology is deleted from the language but the deletions are made in the nonverbal mode of speech, i.e., the form of speech in which words are not mentioned. Presented in what might be called the ontological form of speech, the utterance creates the illusion that things, rather than words, are being referred to. Depending upon whether a philosopher finds the illusion attractive, he will argue either for or against the introduction of a notation which departs, academically, from the language in actual use. The argument can continue without end because preference, not fact, is at issue.

A similar explanation holds good for empiricism, i.e., the cluster of views which appear to imply that our senses are required for obtaining information about the world. Taken as making a factual claim, these words win no attention and can only have the effect of making us wonder why anyone would go to the trouble of uttering them. For who in fact would ever dream of denying the important job our senses have in everyday life. Only in philosophy would it be taken seriously, which means that philosophy stands in need of explanation. Again, if we give up the idea that empiricism presents factual claims about our five senses, it seems natural to think it makes a verbal claim about sense-terminology, namely, that such terminology has a proper use in the language. Considered by itself, apart from rationalism, the view it opposes, it is hardly worth the saying. In philosophy it seems *important* to maintain that, e.g., the word "sees" has a descriptive use, whereas in everyday life the assertion that the word has literal sense would either offend us, as if to imply unusual ignorance on our part, or make us wonder about a person who fancied himself to be informing us about a common term. It should be obvious that no one thinks of resorting to the standard way of settling disputes about actual usage: an authoritative dictionary. This surprising amnesia indicates that actual usage is not in question. Moreover, viewed in the context of the philosophical rationalist-empiricist debate, it can only be thought of as a psychological counter to rationalism. Read in this way, the appeal to actual use is to be understood as representing the decision to retain perception nomenclature, this as a move in a semantic game. Part of the importance the game has for the contestants is the appearance of rival scientific theories being at issue, an appearance generated by the ontological form of speech used. The philosophical theories would fade away like the Cheshire cat's grin if the verbal mode of speech were to replace ontologically formulated utterances.

The empiricist sometimes represents himself as a super-careful scientist. This picture of the philosopher is produced by the philosophical view that we can believe in the existence of something with more or less probability but that certainty is *in principle* beyond our reach. The implication would seem to be that we are never justified in asserting that we *know* that a thing exists, e.g., the sheet of paper before me. Some years ago, Bertrand Russell recounted an exchange between himself and Hans Reichenbach as they watched a lunar eclipse from Reichenbach's yard in Los Angeles. As the moon drew nearer the sun Russell said, "Now will you say that it is certain the eclipse will occur?" Reichenbach's answer in each instance was, "No, but it is more probable than before." When the moon was in eclipse Russell said, "Now you surely *will* say it is certain that there is an eclipse." Reichenbach's response was, "Not certain, but very, very probable." A mathematician who sat next to me during Russell's lecture whispered, "I don't care what Reichenbach calls it; I call it certain." The point brought out by the mathematician is that the word "certain" does have a current application to perceived things. When for some reason we are made doubtful about a thing, e.g., whether what is in the fruit basket is an orange, we make certain by feeling, looking, tasting, etc. What philosophers like Reichenbach and Ayer have done is to exorcise from the language the term "physically possible" and leave only the term "logically possible," so that after any number of sense-tests, no matter how great, it remains logically possible that the next sense-test will go against the previous ones. The word "probable" has been stretched beyond its present use and the word "possible" has been identified with the term "logically possible"—all this for the sake of creating the illusion that the philosopher is even more careful than is the scientist.

M.L.

NOTES

1. It is of some interest to note that the *New York Times* (June 6, 1971) carried an article stating that "the world's gypsy population is facing the threat of 'genocide by assimilation.'"

2. Quoted in Sotheby's brochure, *The Papers of G. E. Moore O.M.* (London, 1979), listing Moore's writings which were to be put on sale.

3. *Philosophy* (New York: W. W. Norton & Co., Inc., 1927), p. 53.

4. *The Problems of Philosophy* (Oxford: The Oxford University Press, 1943, seventeenth impression), p. 156.

5. Ibid.

6. Ibid., p. 146.

7. Ibid.

8. *Language, Truth and Logic,* p. 73.

9. *Selections from Early Greek Philosophy* (New York: T. S. Crofts and Co., 1934). Edited by Milton Nahm, p. 129.

10. *Language, Truth and Logic,* op. cit., p. 79.

11. Not necessarily held by him.

12. *Philosophical Investigations,* p. 31.

13. Suppression is to be distinguished from repression. To suppress is merely to cast out of one's thinking, not to relegate to the unconscious.

14. *Language, Truth and Logic,* op. cit., p. 133.

15. Ibid.

16. Ibid.

17. *Philosophical Investigations,* op. cit., p. 48.

18. Ibid.

XI

Being and Existence

It would seem plain enough to anyone who takes the trouble to observe the behavior of philosophers that philosophy is saturated with Parmenideanism, in one or another of its forms. This offers the only explanation of how the philosopher is able to imagine that he is advancing claims about what there is, and that he is revealing new things about the world around him. O. K. Bouwsma has remarked on a mystifying difference between the non-philosophical explorer of the world and his philosophical counterpart. The former *goes to* the things he reports on; but the philosopher—e.g., Spinoza, who plotted the scheme of things in the seclusion of his study—obtains his special knowledge of what exists in detachment from the world, as if the world was unnecessary to his investigation. Instead of examining the things he reports on, the philosopher gazes into concepts, i.e., the literal meaning of general words, or he scrutinizes the use of expressions in a language, or he does something that we normally consider equally unrelated to the task of obtaining knowledge about the existence or nature of things. All this, together with playing down the stubborn fact that philosophy cannot boast a single uncontroversial proposition, compels the conclusion that the aim of philosophy is not the pursuit of knowledge but a sham imitation of such a pursuit. Many important philosophers have expressed discontent with the condition of philosophy; one of G.E. Moore's letters has condemned philosophy in the words of someone who feels betrayed by what he has held in the highest esteem. His words bear repeating: "Philosophy is a terrible subject: the longer I go on with it, the more difficult it seems to say anything at all about it which is both true and worth saying. You can never feel that you have finished with any philosophical question whatever: got it finally right, so that you can pass on to something else."[1] It is a strange thing that Moore never allowed such thoughts to intrude into his published writings. In my many discussions with him not the smallest hint manifested itself. The impression is that a private scandal was not to be made public.

It is hard not to think that a subject which is practiced in the less well lighted part of the mind and requires blinding oneself to an unwelcome, irremovable fact will be accompanied by a weakened sense of reality. Consider Bertrand Russell's discussion of the philosophical theory of realms of existence:

> It is argued, e.g., by Meinong, that we can speak about "the golden mountain," "the round square," and so on; we can make true propositions of which these are the subjects; hence they must have some kind of logical being . . . . In such theories, it seems to me, there is a failure of that feeling for reality which ought to be preserved even in the most abstract studies . . . . To say that unicorns have an existence in heraldry, or in literature, or in the imagination, is a most pitiful and paltry evasion. What exists in heraldry is not an animal, made of flesh and blood, moving and breathing of its own initiative . . . . There is only one world, the "real" world . . . it is of the very essence of fiction that only the thoughts, feelings, etc., in Shakespeare and his readers are real, and that there is not, in addition to them an objective Hamlet . . . . The sense of reality is vital in logic, and whoever juggles with it by pretending that Hamlet has another kind of reality is doing a disservice to thought. A robust sense of reality is very necessary in framing a correct analysis of propositions about unicorns, golden mountains, round squares, and other such pseudo-objects.[2]

Moore's brother, Sturge Moore, described Yeats's talk as "dream soaked," which suggests that Yeats lacked a "robust sense of reality"—a lack that may well be an asset in a poet or an artist. We would have similar thoughts about a person who is convinced that there actually are leprechauns or that Hamlet, the golden mountain, and the gods on Olympus really exist. The matter is altogether different with "the round square." To imitate Spinoza, "not even God can bring a round square, or greatest prime number, into existence," to which might be added that neither could He conceive or imagine a round square or greatest prime. Unlike leprechauns and the golden mountain, which could, in principle, exist, what the terms "round square" and "greatest prime number" refer to cannot be apprehended: it makes no literal sense to say "The round square exists," either in reality or in the imagination. Such a sentence as "A mathematical prodigy has imagined a round square or written down the greatest prime number" is devoid of intelligibility. A robust or weakened sense of reality can play no role in connection with what is logically impossible: a weakened sense of reality cannot make us accept a logically impossible concept, nor could a robust sense of reality make us reject it, the reason being that the phrase expressing it does not describe anything.

Against the notion that there are many universes of discourse Russell declared that "there is only one world, the 'real' world." For Russell, "What exists in heraldry is not an animal, made of flesh and blood, moving and breathing of its own initiative. What exists is a picture, or a description in words." The implication of these words is clear. They are not directed against the empirical claim that in addition to horses and goats there are unicorns and winged serpents; rather, they are directed to the nonempirical, philosophical proposition that unicorns exist in heraldry as "flesh and blood" creatures, that Hamlet is a fictitious character which is yet a real person, and that the gods peopling Olympus are living beings who nevertheless are mythical.

It needs no arguing to see that the concepts *heraldic flesh and blood unicorn, fictitious real person, mythological living god* are logically impossible concepts like *greatest prime number* and *round square.* And to the acceptance or rejection of a logically impossible concept a sense of reality, strong or weak, is not relevant. But to say, as Russell says, that "a robust sense of reality is very necessary in framing a correct analysis of propositions about unicorns, golden mountains, round squares, and other pseudo-objects" is to surround the theory with an empirical air. We may well say that philosophers are practiced at making their theories appear to be about things, pseudo or otherwise.

The kind of work with nomenclature underlying the theory of domains of existence is by now familiar. It consists of a nonwork-a-day rearrangement of terminology which, when presented in the form of speech in which terms are used rather than mentioned, creates the intriguing appearance of an elite science, one that dispenses with both observation and experiment. It will be remembered that Thomas Aquinas called philosophy "the Divine Science," which is to say that philosophy is the kind of science that can be conducted within the mind.

The first thing that comes through regarding the semantic substructure on which the philosophical theory rests is the academic regrouping of logically impossible concepts with noncontradictory, uninstantiated concepts. This is given recognition, whether conscious or not, by listing *the round square* with *the golden mountain, unicorns,* etc. To put the matter more accurately, terms which, because they stand for logically impossible concepts, have no descriptive use in the language, are artificially classified with terms that do have descriptive use, as well as with terms that function as names, e.g., "Hamlet" or "Zeus." The second terminological innovation, essential to Parmenidean theory, is the introduction of a stretched, if linguistically idle, use of the term "has a denotation," which dictates its application to all expressions which are counted as having descriptive import. Together with the stretched use of the word "denotation," the phrase "there exist" (or "there are") is given a use which permits its occurrence in indicative sentences whose descriptive parts have logically impossible meanings.

J. Laird represents another attempt to modify the Parmenidean thesis that it is impossible to think of what does not exist, or that "thought and being are the same." He raises the question whether 'being' and 'existence' are identical, and goes on to write:

An apparently clear distinction between the two was familiar in British philosophy some little time after the turn of the century. The idea was that 'being' was a genus of which 'existence' and 'subsistence' were distinct species. Anything a man could name or appear to think about was said to "have being," but of the entities which were said to "have being" only some existed. The things or (shall I say?) thingumbobs that were said to subsist were said, at any rate in certain quarters, to comprise a remarkably motley collection of universals, fantasies, dream-castles, hallucinations, contradictions—in short a collection in which some very respectable thingumbobs rubbed shoulders with a whole lot of promising candidates for a Miltonic limbo.

The basis of the theory appears to have been that every thought, however absurd, must refer to something; which something, consequently, must "have being" in some intelligible sense. It was impossible to hold that all such objects-of-thought existed—for the thingumbobs included round squares which couldn't exist, and thingumbobs like Mr. Pecksniff which didn't exist. All, however, were said to "have being."[3]

The idea to which the terms "exists," "subsists," and "has being" give rise is that in addition to such things as apples and giraffes, which are capable of various kinds of behavior and interactions, there are shadowy objects which do not exist but which subsist or have being. To put it metaphysically in Leibniz's way, they are objects which "stretch forth to existence."[4] But this idea is not in fact appropriate to the philosophical thesis, for what does not exist is intangible to the senses even though it has being. What does not exist cannot, regardless of anything else, be tasted, felt, smelled, seen, or heard. The phrase "tastes a lime which does not exist" denotes a logical impossibility and thus has no descriptive use in the language.

The reasoning leading to the theory that only some among conceivable objects exist but that all have being is that since every thought must have an object and since some thoughts are of chimerical objects, such as phoenixes and cyclops, which do not exist, these objects must nevertheless have being. A giraffe has being and also exists; a winged horse only has being. Both are objects of thought, and every thought must "refer to something." This comes to the Parmenidean thesis that "thought and being are the same."[5] The view that thought must have an object makes an entailment-claim: *being a thought* entails *having an object of which it is the thought*, such that "is a thought but does not refer to anything" describes no theoretical possibility. Elsewhere, it has been shown that an *a priori* claim is a verbal claim about usage presented in the nonverbal form of speech.[6] Thus, the verbal reality of the putative entailment is that "refers to something," or "has an object," applies to whatever "is a thought" applies to.

In the ordinary way of speaking, a person who told us that he was thinking of something that does not exist but that nonetheless has being would only bewilder us; the phrase "does not exist but has being" would be taken to imply "does not exist but exists." This shows that the philosophical use of "has being" does not correspond to any of its ordinary uses, just as the philosophical use of "subsists" does not correspond to any of its ordinary uses. It is unrealistic to suppose that, over a long period of time, philosophers have labored under the mistaken notion that a term has a use in the language which it does not in fact have. It is equally unrealistic to imagine that those who reject the view have failed to notice the mistake and for this reason have not pointed it out to their adversaries.

What has happened? A possible explanation, if perhaps an emotionally unwelcome one, is that no mistake is involved in the view that every conceivable thing has being although not every conceivable thing exists. Instead, an old term is being presented in a new role, a role not intended for practical adoption but introduced for the sake of the semantic illusion it brings into existence. This is the illusion that a person who thinks of what does not exist thinks, not of nothing, but of *something,* as demanded by the formula that thought must have an object. Parenthetically, the formula which is presented as an *a priori* truth has only verbal content and makes no claim about the nature of thought. It is not hard to see that "has an object" uses "object" in a stretched sense to cover what it is not normally used to cover.

To return to the matter under discussion, if in answer to the question "What are you thinking about?" I say "I am thinking about Aladdin's lamp and wish that it existed and was mine," it would be incorrect to maintain that because Aladdin's lamp does not exist I was thinking of nothing. And if I were to add, "What I am thinking of 'has being,'" I would be saying no more than that I was thinking of Aladdin's lamp. This makes clear that the philosophical role of "has being" is to create an illusion, i.e., the illusion that Aladdin's lamp *in some way* exists. To put it metaphorically, "has being" does not stand for a halfway house to existence, but the phrase creates the impression that it does. A philosopher who declares that a thought must "refer" to something suggests by his words that there is something to which he wishes to direct our attention. But what he is actually doing is introducing an academically stretched use of "refer."

M.L.

NOTES

1. See essay X, "Reason and the Senses," p. 150.
2. *Introduction to Mathematical Philosophy* (London: George Allen & Unwin, Ltd.; New York: The Macmillan Co., 1919), pp. 169–170.
3. *Mind* LX (July 1942), pp. 249–250.

4. "On the Radical Origin of Things," *New Essays Concerning Human Understanding* (Chicago, London: Open Court Publishing Co., 1916), trans. by Alfred G. Langley, appendix, p. 693.

5. *Selections from Early Greek Philosophy,* p. 115.

6. See, for example, chapter 3, "Necessity and Language," in my *Language of Philosophy* (Dordrecht, Holland; Boston, Mass.: D. Reidel Publishing Co., 1977).

XII

Mathematical Generalizations and Counter-Examples

"A truth, necessary and universal, relative to any object of our knowledge, must verify itself in every instance where that object is before our contemplation."[1] These words of William Whewell's, quoted with approbation by John Stuart Mill, provide a natural picture of mathematical generalizations, as truths about their subject matter, and as holding, once demonstrated, for each particular instance. The description could equally well serve for natural laws inductively arrived at. As is well known, Mill asserted the identity of the two sorts of generalization. He characterized the proposition $2(a + b) = 2a + 2b$ as "a truth coextensive with creation." He went on to say that "these algebraic truths are true of all things whatever."[2]

This description of "truths necessary and universal" is made questionable by the peculiar relation of mathematical generalizations to counter-examples. If under standard physical conditions a case occurred in which water did not freeze at 32°F, the present natural law to the effect that water freezes at this temperature would be upset. A counter-instance, which is perfectly imaginable, would show the generalization to be false, although the truth of the generalization would remain conceivable. In general, an empirical statement of the form $(x)fx \supset gx$ has two possible truth-values, and the same is true of the statement of the form $fa. \sim ga$ which is formally inconsistent with it. The case is otherwise with mathematical generalizations. First of all, examples of the form $fa. \sim ga$ are sometimes taken to be exceptions and sometimes not. When Euler discovered that for $n = 5$, $2^{2^n} + 1$ is factorable, the generalization that for all n, $2^{2^n} + 1$ is prime was immediately discarded from number theory. On the other hand, given a circle in a

plane, what is represented by the following diagram, was

not taken to upset the proposition that it is cut by every straight line in the plane. Instead, it was said to be cut by line AB through imaginary points. For some time, whether or not $x^2 = -1$ presented an exception to *every equation of nth degree has n roots* was under debate. Did it have no roots or two nonreal roots? No comparable situation exists with regard to empirical generalizations, and even in the case in which everyone would say of an example that it was a counter-example and thus falsified the mathematical generalization, there are puzzling differences which challenge the natural, parallel description of such generalizations. Wittgenstein stated that "the mathematical general does not stand in the same relation to the mathematical particular as elsewhere the general to the particular."[3] What is it about the nature of a mathematical generalization that makes it difficult to describe its relation to particular cases which are formal exceptions? What accounts for apparent exceptions being subject to mathematicians' decisions in some instances and not in others? These are questions which need to be considered.

Light can be thrown on the puzzling extension of a generalization to cover what appears to be a counter-example by looking first at recognized exceptions which might be taken to present no puzzle, inasmuch as they seem to show the same thing exceptions show about empirical generalizations, namely, their falsity. But they in fact do not show the same thing, and seeing this helps us see how apparent exceptions can be brought under a general description. Consider Mersenne's conjecture that the only prime p for which numbers of the form $2^p - 1$ are prime are 2, 3, 5, 13, 17, 19, 31, 67, 127, and 257. F. N. Cole showed that for $p = 67$, $2^p - 1$ is factorable, and some decades earlier $2^p - 1$ was shown to be prime for $p = 61$. Cole's presentation of his result at a mathematical meeting was greeted with applause, and Mersenne's conjecture "vanished into the limbo of mathematical mythology."[4] There was no question but that it had been shown to be false. But describing the role of the exception in this way, as falsifying the proposition that for all and only those primes p cited, $2^p - 1$ is prime, obscures the essential difference of the generalization, its exceptions, and their relation from corresponding inductive analogues. What the exceptions show is the self-contradictoriness of the generalization. And the proposition that there is a prime p that yields a factorable number of the form $2^p - 1$, and also the special proposition that $2^{67} - 1$ is factorable, are logically necessary. In describing "the collision between the general and special proposition," Wittgenstein said, "The special case refutes the general proposition from within, not in an external manner . . . it does not refute it as the existence of a one-eyed man refutes 'All men have two eyes.'"[5] A mathematical generalization of the form "All f's are g's" asserts an entailment. If it holds, it could not, in principle, fail to hold; if it does not hold, there is no theoretical condition given which it would hold.

These features, as distinct from those of empirical generalizations and their exceptions, actual or theoretical, are of course obvious, and only as one begins to reflect upon them do there appear to be any difficulties. Quite apart from the fact that something having all the earmarks of an exception is sometimes not taken to be such, in cases where a counter-example would certainly be taken to show the self-inconsistency of an asserted entailment various puzzling questions arise, having to do with the subject matter of necessary generalizations. The following remark and query by Wittgenstein are a hint which I shall pursue: "What makes a merely internal generality questionable is the fact that it can be refuted by the occurrence of a single case (hence by something extensional). But what is the collision here between the general and the special proposition?"[6]

If, with Mill, one looks on necessary propositions as having for their subject matter a totality of elements of a given kind, there seems to be no difficulty about what this "collision" is. If "All *f*'s are *g*'s" predicates *g* of every individual having *f*, then a counter-instance is related to the generalization as "not every" to "every." This is how inductive generalizations and their exceptions are related. But a careful look at entailment propositions makes extremely questionable the natural inclination to take them to be assertions about a totality of elements, whether the elements are, as Mill held concerning geometry, "such lines, angles, and figures as really exist"[7] (since "that science cannot be supposed to be conversant about non-entities"[8]), or, as Russell sometimes held, universals, in contrast to the particular which may fall under them. What needs to be determined is whether necessary propositions can be correctly described as having a subject matter at all. On the face of it, the denial that they do have a subject matter seems bizarre, and anyone who undertakes to hold it must take into account considerations which support interpreting mathematical generalizations as statements about a set of elements. These considerations are various and should be set out in their most favorable light.

The first consideration bears directly on the topic of this study. If a counter-example is taken to refute a generalization, how does it effect a falsification if the generalization is not about a totality of elements within the range of the function $fx \supset gx$? How does the exception, of the form $fa. \sim ga,$ connect with the generalization? And how does the existential proposition of the form $(\exists x)fx. \sim gx$ contradict it? Seemingly, the existential proposition must be construed as asserting the existence of at least one entity. Another consideration, which suggests an analogous treatment of mathematical and inductive generalizations in respect of their subject class, is the procedure by which mathematicians often come to believe that a generalization holds. There can be little doubt that an examination of special cases of a generalization—a procedure which parallels the collection of inductive evidence—has led mathematicians to try to discover a proof. Fermat, for example, must have tried out a number of values of *n* and *p* before attempting to prove that for any integer *n* not divisible by the prime *p*, $n^{p-1} - 1$ is divisible by *p*. What is more natural than to describe this theorem as a truth about the totality of integers not divisible by *p*, a truth suggested by special cases, and once demonstrated, applicable to others? Mathematics is often looked upon as a kind of natural history of various domains of elements.[9] The language of numbers encourages this idea. The numerals behave like proper names serving to tick off members of the infinite stretch of numbers. Constructive existence proofs rest on the principle that from fa, $(\exists x)fx$ follows: if a named object has a property f, the existence of something having f is guaranteed.

The idea that the mathematician's field of investigation is a set of *objects* apparently has the merit of not creating the problem of explaining how an exception to a mathematical generalization connects up with the generalization. An exception shows that some member of the subject class fails to have a property which the generalization asserts all members to have. But one consideration makes it questionable whether there is any merit in talking about mathematical and empirical propositions in a like way. This is the unaccountable division of opinion as to the supposed subject matter of mathematical propositions. As is well known, the objects constituting their subject matter have been variously held to be real objects, ideal objects, mental constructs, or symbols standing for no objects whatever. There are no new facts in addition to known facts that could decide which account is correct, which is to say that everything required for coming to a decision is already known to everyone. And this raises the question whether what Wittgenstein called an extensional interpretation of mathematical statements — i.e., one which assumes the existence of a domain of objects over which their variables range — can be either correct or incorrect. The bearing of this question on describing the refutation of a mathematical generalization of the form $(x)fx \supset gx$ as being effected by an object having the properties of f and *not-g* is obvious.

To describe the refutation of an empirical generalization in this way is unobjectionable. An empirical proposition has two equally conceivable possibilities open to it, and the effect of a counter-instance is to exclude one of its possible truth-values without rendering it logically impossible. The case is quite otherwise with a mathematical proposition. As Wittgenstein pointed out, in mathematics "all" and "necessary" go together. A true mathematical generalization can be restated as an entailment and cannot, in principle, be false, whereas a true inductive generalization, no matter how certain and no matter how great the number of confirmations, is not restatable as an entailment. Concerning the relation of a counter-instance to a mathematical generalization, I wish to bring out a paradox which at first sight seems to be unavoidable. It can be put in this way: Establishing the special proposition of the form $fa . \sim ga$ to be true, i.e., necessarily true, does not show that the putative proposition to which it is taken to be an exception is false, but instead shows that *there is no proposition to which it is an exception*. This paradox can easily be constructed from C. H. Langford's view that self-contradictory expressions have "no unitary meaning," and hence express "no single proposition."

I shall try to find an escape from this paradox via an account of necessity.

Unless we take cognizance of the feature of necessary propositions which will be pointed out, there is no escape from the paradox, which arises from the following considerations. The mathematical generalization to which we find an exception (often surprisingly) is shown to be logically impossible. The question is: Could we have conceived it? Can one conceive what is logically impossible? Can one conceive that 6 is less than 5, or that in a bouquet of ten flowers, twelve were tulips? By no effort of mind is what is *logically* inconceivable capable of conception. The situation is obviously different from that in which a proposition is unthinkable because the sentence expressing it is too involved and complicated for us to grasp its meaning. In accordance with Langford's view, the sentence "All numbers of the form $n^2 - n + 41$ are prime" expresses, not an *unthinkable* proposition, but no proposition at all. To claim that prior to discovering a factorable number of this form (when $n = 41$) we entertained a proposition which, as it turned out, is logically impossible, is to claim that what is inconceivable was nevertheless conceived. That there is a factorable number of this form is an *a priori* truth, and to suppose that the universal generalization is conceivably true comes to supposing that the negation of the existential proposition is conceivable, which it is not. What establishing its truth shows is that there is no generalization. The paradox is that there is then no proposition on which the counter-instance bears. And this is to say the exception is not an exception.

It is not part of my intention to enter into the philosophical debate over whether self-contradictory expressions are meaningless. I have tried to make explicit the paradox of entertaining the truth of a logically impossible proposition and the further paradox of there being *no* proposition to which a counter-example is an exception; both have been set forth as a step to finding a way of avoiding the two paradoxes and to finding a nonparadoxical way of construing the relation between a mathematical generalization and its exception. About both paradoxes I wish to say that it is philosophical talk about *propositions*[12] which gives rise to them. Talk about mathematical propositions and exceptions to them imitates talk about empirical propositions whose counter-examples rule out one of their possible truth-values. By going over to talk about the use of terminology with which necessary propositions (in contrast to nonverbal empirical propositions) are connected, we shall find that we cannot formulate the paradox arising when we try to specify the relation of the mathematical proposition to its exception. Resorting to this procedure will also enable us to account for the extension of generalizations to cover cases which in verbal appearance are inconsistent with them.

It is required first to say something about the connection between *a priori* propositions and the use of words occurring in their expression. In order to avoid conventionalism, which is itself a philosophical view, I shall begin by considering *sentences* that express entailments. Take the sentence "All lions are feline," which can be translated into a sentence asserting an entailment between *being a lion* and *being feline*. That the sentence expresses a necessary proposition is of course an empirical fact, and depends on a fact about the use of words in it. It is a linguistic convention of English that "feline" applies to whatever "lion" correctly applies to. One can know "All lions are feline" expresses a necessarily true proposition by knowing this fact of usage. Such is not the case with sentences expressing empirical generalizations, e.g., "Lions are carnivorous." To get to know that this sentence expresses a truth it is necessary to examine things, not verbal usage: the fact that "carnivorous" applies to whatever "lion" applies to is not determined by usage, but by a fact of nature. Sentences which express entailments are in an ambiguous position. They make no assertion about the words occurring in them, and so cannot be said to express verbal facts, yet they give us only verbal information.[13] Knowing a fact about the conventional use of certain words or phrases in sentences expressing entailments is in simple cases like the above *all* that one needs to know in order to know that the proposition denoted is true. Were this not the case, examining word-usage to determine whether the proposition expressed by "All lions are feline" is true would be irrelevant. For convenience I shall refer to this feature of necessary propositions as their verbal aspect. It is a feature which serves to explain the fact that necessary propositions have a role with respect to the use of language which empirical, nonverbal propositions do not have.

Wittgenstein has remarked that "a proposition which is supposed to be impossible to imagine as other than true has a different *function* from one for which this does not hold."[14] He characterized a mathematical proposition as having "the dignity of a rule,"[15] a rule, or standard for the use of words, which "shews us what it makes SENSE to say."[16] The fact that a proposition is necessarily true, which connects with an empirical fact about the words in the sentence expressing it, serves to preclude certain sentences from conveying anything. On recognizing the necessity of *All lions are feline,* one sees that the words "I saw a lion which was not feline" have no use to convey information. The descriptive part of this sentence, "lion which is not feline," has no use to describe anything; it denotes nothing conceivable. Arithmetical propositions such as $25 \times 17 = 425$ serve as a standard by which, for example, the correctness of a count of squares in a rectangle 25 squares long by 17 wide is measured. Because of the acceptance of a linguistic convention, $25 \times 17 = 425$ is incorrigible; differing results of counting will not show it to be false. The remarkable agreement of mathematicians concerning the necessity of a proposition rests on their undeniable accord in the use of language. That "425" can be substituted for "25×17" and that $25 \times 17 = 425$ is necessary are counterparts. Although the necessary proposition makes no mention of number-words, its employment is to legislate that the sentences "The rectangle I drew had 25×17 squares" and "The rectangle I drew had 325 squares" cannot be used to express the same fact.

Seeing the connection between a necessarily true proposition and the use of the words in the sentence expressing it provides an escape from paradoxes constructed from talk about an entailment proposition being upset by a counter-example. Clearly, it is proper English to say that a counter-example refutes a mathematical generalization. Thus, it is incumbent on one to show the meeting place of the two without at the same time falling into paradoxes which result from describing the exception in the usual way, i.e., as revealing the proposition whose truth one entertained to be a logical impossibility. Suppose we say that we wish to test the hypothesis that all numbers of the form $n^2 - n + 41$ are prime by examining cases. This is a convenient way of saying something more awkward but less likely to cause philosophical puzzlement, namely, that we wish to determine whether the *sentence* "All numbers of the form $n^2 - n + 41$ are prime" expresses a necessary truth. To ask whether this sentence expresses a necessary proposition is to ask whether the phrase "being prime" is correctly applicable to every number to which "being of the form $n^2 - n + 41$" applies. Suppose it is shown that there is a value of *n* for which $n^2 - n + 41$ is not prime, i.e., the value 41. This is to show that the existential proposition and the special proposition which implies it are both necessary. The sentences expressing these latter propositions will have a similar interpretation to that of sentences expressing entailments: in knowing the propositions they express to be *a priori,* what we know will be facts of usage (although these facts are not mentioned by the sentences). This interpretation can be carried out as follows. Consider the translation into quantifier notation of the sentence "There is a number *n* for which $n^2 - n + 41$ is not prime": "$(\exists n)n^2 - n + 41$ is not prime." The fact that this sentence expresses a necessity is equivalent to the fact that some sentence resulting from substitution on "*n*" in "$n^2 - n + 41$ is not prime" expresses a necessity. That is, within the language of numerals at least one numeral "*n*" is so used that "$n^2 - n + 41$ is not prime" expresses a necessary truth. If "*n*" is "41," then the fact that "$n^2 - n + 41$ is not prime" expresses a necessary truth prevents the expression "$n^2 - n + 41$ and prime" from being used to describe the number resulting from substitution of "41" for "*n*." To say that "There is a number *n* such that $n^2 - n + 41$ is not prime" has a verbal feature is to say that in knowing that the sentence "*a* is of the form $n^2 - n + 41$ and not prime" expresses a necessary proposition for some specification of *a,* we know a fact about the use of the numeral "*a*" and certain predicate expressions.

We can now state quite generally what is meant by the "collision" between a generalization and an exception. That a mathematical sentence of the form "$(x)fx \supset gx$" purports to express a truth is equivalent to its purporting that "*f* but not *g*" has no use. The verbal correlate of an exception which in fact upsets a generalization is to the effect that "*f* but not *g*" has a use; so the actual convention simply contradicts the purported convention. To entertain the claim that a certain sentence expresses a necessary truth is to entertain an empirical, verbal proposition which is refuted by the fact that the negative of the sentence makes a true claim about a convention. The paradox of there being no proposition on which the exception bears is avoided, because it arises from the propositional idiom, that is, from looking at the modal property of a mathematical proposition rather than at its verbal aspect. If the question whether or not a mathematical generalization of the form $(x)fx \supset gx$ is necessary is replaced by the question whether or not the sentence of the form "$(x)fx \supset gx$" expresses an *a priori* truth, the paradox can no longer be formulated. Whether a sentence expresses an entailment between f and g is an empirical question about a linguistic convention: about the application of "g," given that "f" applies. The verbal correlate of finding a counter-example $fa. \sim ga$ to a purportedly true generalization is showing an empirical proposition about the purported convention to be false, i.e., establishing that "g" in fact does not apply to whatever "f" applies to. Showing an empirical proposition to be false obviously does not come to showing that there was no proposition to begin with. Puzzles about believing on "inductive" grounds that a mathematical generalization $(x)fx \supset gx$ is true can also be avoided by construing the belief as one to the effect that each sentence of the form "$fa \supset ga$" expresses a necessary proposition, that is, to the effect that conventional rules dictate in each case the application of "g," given that "f" applies.

What I have not tried to explain here is how the philosopher's use of language gives rise to the paradoxes: that a proved exception to a generalization shows that what was conceived could not have been conceived and that there is no proposition on which an exception bears. What use of "impossible proposition" or "self-contradictory proposition," both of which have an actual use in the language, is responsible for the paradoxes which can so easily be constructed? The answer to this question requires a wider investigation than is undertaken here, where the aim has been to show that another way of formulating the relation between a generalization and its exception avoids the paradoxes. The direction of such an investigation is indicated in the last section of Morris Lazerowitz's essay entitled "Philosophy and Necessity". For the present I would like to meet a possible objection to the means I have used for avoiding the paradoxes: the reformulation of the assertion that a generalization has an exception. For it might be thought that the account given here of necessarily true generalizations and of necessarily true existentials is merely the conventionalist position which equates a necessarily true proposition with a proposition about usage. But it is not being held that the proposition that all f's are g's is verbal; rather, the statement that the sentence "All f's are g's" expresses a necessary truth implies the existence of a convention which prevents the application of "f and not g." Nor is the existential proposition of the form $(\exists x)fx. \sim gx$ verbal; rather, the statement that the sentence "There is an f which is not g" expresses a necessary proposition implies that "f and not g" has an application.

Before leaving the treatment of counter-examples which upset generalizations it is necessary to consider the contention that a *non*linguistic fact, namely, that 41 is a value of n for which $n^2 - n + 41$ is not prime (established by an examination of numbers) informs us that the phrase "of the form $n^2 - n + 41$ and not prime" correctly applies when $n = 41$. It has been argued that the sentence "For $n = 41$, $n^2 - n + 41$ is not prime" expresses something necessary by virtue of an established verbal fact. But it might be countered that inspection of abstract entities shows "not being prime" to stand for an internal property of $41^2 - 41 + 41$, just as "being a fox" stands for an accidental property of certain animals. What lies back of this reply is that numbers are objects and that "value of n for which $n^2 - n + 41$ is not prime" sets off one class of objects from another. Here we have arrived at a metaphysical position. According to the Platonist, the necessary proposition that there exists a factorable number which is a value of $n^2 - n + 41$ entails the existence of at least one number and hence the existence of at least one abstract object. Further, the existence of objects of the latter sort would be necessary since the consequence of a necessary proposition is also necessary. The presupposition of the last step in this chain of consequences is purportedly an entailment proposition: that numbers are abstract objects. Nominalists would dispute the existence of any sort of object named by a numeral. Now, whether or not the exact connection between an entailment proposition and a verbal fact has been correctly described here, there can be no doubt that there is a connection. Otherwise, appeal to the dictionary would be irrelevant to deciding (as it is in simple cases) whether a proposition is necessary. It is clear that the dictionary is of no help in deciding between conflicting accounts of the domain of number theory. It neither justifies nor gainsays that "object" and "number" have a connected application. Hence, at a minimum, it can be said that there is no ground for holding a mathematical generalization to be an assertion about a totality of objects, or that it is confirmed or refuted by examination of objects.

By attending to the verbal aspect of *a priori* propositions we can now explain how it is possible for generalizations to cover cases which have the verbal appearance of being exceptions. If mathematical generalizations are about a totality of elements all of whose properties are internal to them, it is inexplicable that whether a generalization is upset by an apparent counterinstance should rest on a *decision*. The following pairs of propositions are examples of cases where a consensus (not examination of the properties of mathematical objects) determined which proposition remained operative within a given branch of mathematics, or whether both are somehow accommodated.

Any two lines of a plane intersect; Parallel lines do not meet

Given a circle in a plane, it is intersected by every straight line; Lines whose minimum distance from the perimeter of a circle is a do not intersect it

Every equation of nth degree has exactly n roots; $x^2 - 1$ has no roots

All linear equations have solutions; For $a > b$, $n + a = b$ has no solution

a^n is defined only for positive integers > 0; $a^0 = 1$, $a^{1/2} = \sqrt{a}$, $a^{-1} = \frac{1}{a}$

Prime numbers are divisible only by themselves and 1; 1 is not prime.

In the case of each of these pairs, something like a decision was made, for good reason, which in effect incorporated the exception under the generalization and mitigated the seeming contradiction. The question is: How are we to describe the extension of a generalization to cover a formal exception? How are formally inconsistent propositions to be reconciled? And the further question is: Why is this possible in some cases and not in others? Consider the first pair of propositions. Within Euclidean geometry "parallel lines" is defined to mean lines which do not meet. Thus the established convention guarantees the necessary truth of *parallel lines do not meet.* Is this inconsistent with its being true that any two lines of a plane intersect? Similarly with the second pair of propositions. Can it be the case both that every straight line of a plane intersects a circle in that plane and that some lines in the plane do not? As for the third pair, its mathematical history is well known. The equation $x^2 = -1$ was at first said to have no solution, and later Gauss's proof was accepted as establishing that every such equation has a solution. Before the "introduction" of negative numbers a similar situation existed with regard to equations of the form $n + a = b$. The equation $n = 5 - 8$ was apparently an exception to the generalization that all linear equations have a solution. The proposition to the effect that an equation has no solution is a modal proposition: it asserts the logical impossibility of there being one. When $n = 5 - 8$ was given a value it was like arranging that something which is logically impossible be a truth.

The apparent inconsistency between the members of the last two pairs of the above list is resolved by an implicit re-definition, in the one case of exponentiation, in the other of "prime number." A re-definition of "a^n" extends it to cases where n is not integral or not greater than 0, and a re-definition of "prime number" restricts its application to numbers greater than 1. Each has its point, in the first case to extend laws of exponents already proved, in the second to preserve the law that any integer can be resolved into a product of primes and in only one way. Were 1 to count as a prime, 12 could be represented as the product $1 \cdot 2 \cdot 2 \cdot 3$, $1 \cdot 1 \cdot 2 \cdot 2 \cdot 3$, etc. These cases have in common with the incorporation of exceptions under generalizations that the accommodation effected between the propositions of a pair is *notational.* In some instances, the notational change is like a change of boundaries on a map: "no facts of geography are changed."[17] In the case of the generalization that any two lines of a plane intersect, parallel lines are accommodated by describing them as meeting at infinity. Thereby nothing different is said than is said by "Parallel lines do not meet." And by means of a new convention, viz., that "lines meeting at infinity" applies to whatever "parallel lines" applies to, the two propositions *Any two lines of a plane intersect* and *Parallel lines do not meet* are reconciled. Reasons can even be given to justify the new convention. As a line through a point outside a fixed line is rotated from 90° to 180°, it intersects the fixed line farther and farther out, so that "at the limit" it can be said to "intersect it at infinity." The limit is thus incorporated in the series. Thereby the description of parallel lines is made continuous with that of all other lines. A similar notational change occurs when a line that would naturally be described as *not* intersecting a circle in a plane is described as intersecting it in imaginary points. The generalization that a circle in a plane is intersected by every line is thus preserved. It is clear that what has been preserved by a kind of grammatical ruse is the convention that "circle in a plane not cut by some line in it" shall have no use.

It might be thought that the mathematician would have no such latitude where numbers are concerned, that truths about these are fixed by their nature and forced upon us, not decided by us. But eventually it was mathematicians, not the mathematical facts, which decided whether $x^3 + x^2 + x + 1 = 0$ had three roots, one of which is $+\sqrt{-1}$. The invention of the symbolism "a + bi" is heralded by some mathematicians as "the introduction of complex numbers," as though the mathematician could create existents as well as notation. (Dedekind said, "negative and fractional rational numbers are formed by a new creation.") On the other hand, even after the symbolism was invented Descartes denied that there were three roots of the cubic equation cited; as late as 1770 Euler wrote: "All such expressions as $\sqrt{-1}$, $\sqrt{-2}$, etc., are impossible or imaginary numbers, since they represent roots of negative quantities, and of such numbers we may truly assert that they are neither nothing, nor greater than nothing, nor less than nothing, which necessarily constitutes them imaginary or impossible."[18] Nevertheless Euler made use of these expressions. Calculations involving them enabled theorems to be proved which did not involve them, for example, Cardan's proof that 10 could be split into two parts the product of which is 40 (5 + $\sqrt{-15}$ and 5 − $\sqrt{-15}$). With the acceptance of Guass's proof that *every* equation has a solution, *n* roots for an equation of *n*th degree, these symbols and the rules for calculating with them came to have an established place. The equation $x^2 = -1$ was no longer an exception. This case is analogous to the acceptance, after some debate over negative numbers, of such an equation as $n + 8 = 5$ as having a solution. The decision in both cases, to preserve the generalization, meant making a new part of mathematics continuous with the old.

When a decision is made between two apparently conflicting statements, such as are cited in the list set out here, there are of course considerations determining it. The considerations show the pairs of examples to be quite different from each other. In some cases, what is achieved by the decision is uniformity of description, and this is evidently the point of the change. What Wittgenstein said in another connection applies here: "Everything said in the one [notation] can, of course, be said in the other. But the two draw different boundaries . . . and a notation can stress, or it can minimize [a difference]."[19] The redescription of parallel lines as meeting at infinity, and of lines not intersecting a given circle of the plane as intersecting it in imaginary points illustrate this type of decision. The characterization of 1 as not prime, in order to permit a uniform description of all integers as the product of primes in only one way, is a similar, though also differing, example. But where a *proof* is given which extends the domain of mathematics, i.e., makes an addition to it, it is not the case that what is said in one notation can be said in the other; considerations determining the incorporation of the exceptional case cannot be restricted to considerations of uniformity. What has to be examined is the role that proof plays in the incorporation. The fact that there is a proof of the fundamental theorem of algebra might incline one to think that it simply shows it to be *false* that $x^2 = -1$ has no roots, and that the nature of equations of nth degree necessitates this. But this account will not do, inasmuch as the statement "$x^2 = -1$ has no solution" was made because "$x^2 = -1$," prior to Gauss's proof, was taken to be *meaningless*. The rule for finding the roots of a quadratic equation yielded a result to which no meaning had as yet been assigned. Compare the questions: "Has $x^2 + x + 1 = 0$ a real solution?", "Has $x^2 = -1$ a real solution?", and "Has $x^2 = -1$ a solution?" The rules determining the answers to the first two questions do not answer the last one.[20] It was Gauss's proof which *provided* an answer to that question. Before it was produced, "Has $x^2 = -1$ a solution?" was like the question "Can White win in 20 moves?" when the rules of the game are not yet entirely fixed.[21] The fact that the proposition *Every equation of nth degree has n roots* was the result of a series of deductive steps had as its verbal correlate that the sentence denoting it expressed something necessarily true, i.e., that "having n roots" applies to whatever "equation of nth degree" applies to. Acceptance of the proof carried with it acceptance of the new convention.

The role of proof is, as Wittgenstein put it, to persuade one to adopt a rule.[22] With Gauss's proof a genuinely new extension of mathematics came into being, one in which a meaning was conferred on such symbols as "$\sqrt{-1}$", and a new meaning on "root" and "solution." That is to say, "$\sqrt{-1}$" was given a use, and "root" a new use. "It is impossible," Wittgenstein wrote, "to make a discovery of rules of a new sort which hold for a known form. If they are new rules, then it is not the *old* form. . . . For the group of rules first *determines* the sense of our signs, and any change (e.g., supplementation) of the rules means a change in the sense."[23] What is sometimes called extending a concept is less misleadingly called widening the use of a term. For example, we call setting three cups on three saucers in a one-to-one relationship a one-to-one correlation, but what we do when we begin correlating the cardinal numbers with the even numbers is by analogy and by an extension called one-to-one correlation of the cardinals with the evens, though in fact we do not correlate them one-to-one. What we do shows the use the term has. Similarly, Gauss's proof shows what is meant by "root,"[25] and with the acceptance of the proof a wider system in which expressions of the form $a + bi$ occur is invented. Whether or not a proof comes to be accepted depends on how well it makes connections with existing parts of mathematics and on the development it promises in the new part. As one writer said, "When something keeps popping up in [mathematicians'] formulas that seems to make no sense, they will do their best to put sense into it."[26] The road mathematics takes with the newly presented addition is built by that addition, rather than followed out.[27] Prior to Gauss's proof, seeming nonsense resulted from applying the rules for solving equations in the regions of real, rational, or integral numbers; but with its acceptance the seemingly meaningless equation is "brought into relation with such as have a normal solution. . . . The continuity, the connection, with the normal solution is not broken."[28]

A decision made in mathematics thus may be either of two kinds, and sometimes both: one in which a new notation replaces the old without achieving anything more than uniformity of description, i.e., without saying anything different from what the old notation says; and another, in which a new notation is adjoined to the old and given sense, thereby augmenting the body of mathematics. The pair of propositions concerning exponentiation, cited in the list above, are reconciled by decisions which are apparently of both sorts. A new meaning is assigned to the expression "a^n" by giving values to it when n takes 0, fractional, and negative values, and this is done by a proof-like procedure for showing that $a^0 = 1$, $a^{1/2} = \sqrt{a}$, $a^{-1} = \frac{1}{a}$. In general, the expression of a proof is in "the ontological idiom,"[29] and makes no mention of the verbal convention which is its associate. Sometimes, as in N. J. Lenne's justification of $a^0 = 1$ and $a^{1/2} = \sqrt{a}$,[30] the verbal aspect of the necessary propositions which he "proves," and the verbal role of the "proof," are explicit. He begins his proof with the words: "we wish to give $a^{1/2}$ such a meaning that $a^{1/2}.a = a^{1/2+1/2}$."[31] The proof assigns a new meaning to "a^n," and at the same time achieves uniformity of description by extending the laws of exponents, $a^m.a^n = a^{m+n}$ and $a^m \div a^n = a^{m-n}$, to the new values.

So far we have examined the relation of propositions which are formally inconsistent with each other, and have tried to give an account of genuine exceptions to a generalization which avoids paradox and an account of what constitutes the incorporation of an exception under a generalization. Both accounts relied on the fact that purportedly necessary propositions have a verbal correlate: that the empirical, verbal fact that certain expressions do or do not have a use is equivalent to the empirical fact that a certain sentence expresses a necessarily true proposition. A question naturally arises: Why it is that in some cases a mathematician is at liberty to decide whether a sentence expresses something necessary and in other cases is not? One can only answer this question by looking at what the mathematician does when he takes an expression of the form "$(\exists x)fx. \sim gx$" to denote the existence of an exception to a generalization, and what he does when he construes an expression of the form "$(x)fx \supset gx$" to cover a seeming exception. In both cases he gives a justification, sometimes by means of an intricate proof. What needs to be emphasized is that proofs in mathematics are various. Sometimes they are like a calculation according to fixed rules, or like a game whose rules are determinate enough to answer every question; sometimes they justify acceptance of a new rule, and define or redefine a term. Mathematics presents two sides to us, the rigidly necessitated, and the freely decided. "In the one case we make a move in an existent game, in the other we establish a rule of the game."[32] In the first case, we tend to describe a proof as discovered, in the second as invented. When a generalization is upset by an exception the relation between the two is as rigidly determined as that between a calculation and its result. When a generalization incorporates an apparent exception, the process is analogous to justifying a definition or re-definition of a term. The following sums up the opposing descriptions of mathematics: "*So* much is true about saying that mathematics is logic: its movement is within the rules of our language. And this gives it its peculiar solidity, its unassailable position, set apart. . . . What, then—does it just twist and turn about within these rules?—It forms ever new rules: is always building new roads for traffic; by extending the network of the old ones . . . a mathematician is always inventing new forms of description."[33]

A.A.

NOTES

1. J. S. Mill, *A System of Logic* (New York: Harper & Brothers, 1856), p. 163.
2. Ibid., p. 166.
3. Wittgenstein, *Remarks on the Foundations of Mathematics,* p. 146.
4. James R. Newman, *The World of Mathematics* (New York: Simon and Schuster, 1956), vol. 2, p. 503.
5. Wittgenstein, *Philosophische Bemerkungen* (Oxford: Basil Blackwell, 1964), edited by Rush Rhees, p. 214 (my translation).
6. Ibid.
7. *A System of Logic,* op. cit., p. 149.

8. Ibid.

9. *Remarks on the Foundations of Mathematics,* op. cit., p. 117.

10. *Philosophische Bemerkungen,* op. cit., p. 182.

11. See C. I. Lewis and C. H. Langford, *Symbolic Logic,* pp. 476–477.

12. It should be realized that talk about propositions is suspect because the *existence* of propositions is in dispute. It is instructive to compare disagreements over the existence of propositions (and also of universals) with disagreements over the existence of poltergeists.

13. This account of necessary propositions is due to Morris Lazerowitz, who has elaborated it in a number of papers. See especially *Ludwig Wittgenstein: Philosophy and Language,* pp. 234–238, 249–250, and *The Language of Philosophy: Freud and Wittgenstein,* pp. 188–191.

14. *Remarks on the Foundations of Mathematics,* op. cit., p. 114.

15. Ibid., p. 47.

16. Ibid., p. 77.

17. *The Blue Book,* p. 57.

18. Quoted in G. Gamov, *One, Two, Three, . . . Infinity* (New York: The New American Library, 1947), p. 42.

19. "The Yellow Book."

20. See Wittgenstein, *Philosophische Grammatik,* pp. 366–367.

21. Ibid., p. 363.

22. *Wittgenstein's Lectures on the Foundations of Mathematics: Cambridge, 1939* (Ithaca, New York: Cornell University Press, 1976), edited by Cora Diamond, p. 134.

23. *Philosophische Bemerkungen, op. cit., p. 182.*

24. *Wittgenstein's Lectures, Cambridge 1932–1935* (edited by Alice Ambrose), pp. 208–209.

25. Ibid.

26. G. Gamov, op. cit., p. 42.

27. Wittgenstein's Lectures, 1939.

28. *Philosophische Bemerkungen,* op. cit., pp. 214–215.

29. Lazerowitz's description.

30. N. J. Lennes, *College Algebra* (New York and London: Harpers and Brothers, 1929), p. 40.

31. Ibid.

32. *Zettel,* p. 294.

33. *Remarks on the Foundations of Mathematics,* op. cit., p. 47.

XIII

Wittgenstein on Mathematical Proof

In *Remarks on the Foundations of Mathematics,* and elsewhere, Wittgenstein made some general statements about mathematical proof which can only be described as paradoxical. What he says is directed to proofs of propositions for which there is no general method of solution, such as there is for propositions of the form $a \times b = c,$ where a simple calculation is sufficient. His concern is with propositions for which one cannot in advance of proof describe any procedure which will demonstrate them. Examples are: "For all natural numbers $n,$ $2^{2^n} + 1$ is prime," "There is no greatest prime," "Every equation of nth degree has exactly n roots," "Any even number is the sum of two primes." In an earlier study,[1] "Proof and the Theorem Proved," I singled out a group of propositions for which his account of proof seemed correct, and not paradoxical. Examples given were the propositions "$a^0 = 1,$" "$\frac{a}{0}$ represents any number whatever," whose proofs provide justification for introducing or excluding an expression, namely "a^0" and "$\frac{a}{0}$," respectively. But I did not succeed in making his account of deductions of connections between established concepts paradox-free. I should like to return to his account as applied to such demonstrations, with the aim of explaining what justification there is for it, and what his account comes to.

Consider the following statements from Wittgenstein which, taken together, summarize his views about proof:

"If you want to know *what* is proved, look at the proof."[2]

"The result of a mathematical proof gets its meaning from the proof."[3]

[Certain mathematical questions] "give us a sort of hint as to what we are to do, but the proof provides them with content."[4]

From *Mind* XCI (April 1982), pp. 264–272. Reprinted by permission of the publisher.

"Proofs that construct *propositions* make us forget that the *sense* of the result is not to be read off from this by itself, but from the proof."[5]

"The problem of finding a mathematical decision of a theorem might with some justification be called the problem of giving mathematical sense to a formula."[6]

"I should like to say: the proof shews me a new connexion, and hence also gives me a new concept."[7]

"One would like to say: the proof changes the grammar of our language, changes our concepts, makes new connexions. . . . (It does not establish that they are there; they do not exist until it makes them)."[8]

"The question—I want to say—changes its status, when it becomes decidable. For a connexion is made then, which formerly *was not there.*"[9]

These quotations speak for themselves. Their paradoxical consequences are the following:

1. that before proof of the proposition expressed by the sentence "*p,*" "*p*" has a different sense than after proof of *p,* and correspondingly, that the answer to a question concerning the truth-value of *p* does not answer the original question.
2. that a proposition can have but one proof.

To elaborate, if proof gives sense to the concluding sentence "*p*" of the proof sequence of sentences, then prior to arriving at the sentence, either it had no meaning or it had a different meaning. If it had no meaning, then there was no proposition to be proved; and if the concluding sentence "*p*" came to have a different meaning from its original one, the original proposition has not been proved. The proved proposition is not an answer to any question about the truth-value of the initial proposition. In order for a question to be relevant to the *proved* proposition, Wittgenstein agrees that it would already have to have been answered.[10] For "the proof provides it with content."[11] If an interrogative expression does not ask a question about the demonstrated proposition, then what is demonstrated is not an answer to whatever question it did ask. Further, if the sense of the terminal sentence of a proof-sequence of sentences is to be "read off from the proof," then "each proof will demonstrate something which it alone can demonstrate,"[12] so that one and the same proposition can have but one proof.

Now Wittgenstein was not unaware of the difficulties inherent in his claims, and even stated some of them himself. In lectures he asserted that "to say it is the proof which gives sense to the question is absurd because it misuses the word 'question.' "[13] And he asked himself in *Remarks on the Foundations of Mathematics*, ". . . should I say that the same sense can only have *one* proof? Or that when a proof is found the sense alters?"[14] Earlier in the *Remarks* he stated flatly that "Of course it would be nonsense to say that *one* proposition cannot have two proofs — for we do say just that."[15] His comments on these admissions are singularly unhelpful. To the person who says "Then the proof of a proposition cannot ever be found, for, if it has been found, it is no longer the proof of *this* proposition," he replies that "to say this is so far to say nothing at all,"[16] ". . . that these proofs prove the same proposition means, e.g., both demonstrate it as a suitable instrument for the same purpose. . ."[17]

It might be thought that the paradoxes under discussion here arise from Wittgenstein's use of what might be called the mixed mode of speech: the use of "proposition" where "sentence" should be used, or vice versa. To illustrate his ambiguous use of the words "proposition" and "question," his way of describing the role of proof of p in relation to the meaning of the sentence "p" was that "there seem to be propositions which have no sense until we know whether they are true or false,"[18] and also, ". . . a question or proposition does not make sense until a proof, or method of proof, is given."[19] But the difficulty is not removed when put as I have done. "Proof of p gives 'p' a meaning, where p is a proposition and 'p' a sentence." For this also translates into the paradox that the sentence "p" *acquires* meaning when one establishes the truth-value of p: if "p" has a meaning p_1 different from the meaning p_2 which it acquired on proof of p_2, then one has not proved what one set out to prove. The sentence "p" acquires meaning via proof of a proposition which could not have been the goal of the proof. For one proves something different from what one supposed oneself to be proving. Presumably a person who tried to prove p_1 would always demonstrate a different proposition p_2 and would never succeed in doing what he set out to do.

Wittgenstein said both that "one can frame a mathematical proposition in a grammatically correct way without understanding its meaning"[20] and that when a proof is found the sense *alters*. Far from being a correct description of a working mathematician who is trying to solve a problem, these claims appear to be in violation of usage. To say that a proof gives meaning to a statement under consideration and that in the beginning one cannot be said to understand it goes against the common usage of such words as "conjecture" and "suppose." For it is undeniably proper usage to describe Fermat as having conjectured that the sentence "For all n, $2^{2^n} + 1$ is prime" expressed something true; and this implies, in normal discourse, that the sentence had meaning and that it was understood. It must be admitted that very seldom does the word "understand" occur in a mathematician's "proof-talk." Nor are sentences or other symbolism very often described by him as having or lacking meaning. But both terms, "understand" and "having meaning," are connected with terms such as "conjecture" and "suppose" which do occur in the course of what the mathematician does. Thus Wittgenstein's claims are by implication in violation of usage rather than correct descriptions.

Nevertheless, in this paper I wish to hold that there is justification for maintaining both that the meaning a sentence "*p*" has when it is correctly followed by "Q.E.D." is different from the meaning it had before proof was given, and that one proposition can have but one proof. These claims were presented as true accounts of the relation of mathematical proofs to the meaning of sentences denoting the theorems they prove. I shall consider first the reasons which might be adduced for holding that they are true. They rest ultimately on a feature of mathematical propositions which empirical propositions do not have. A sentence denoting an empirical proposition expresses the same proposition no matter which truth-value the proposition has. The truth-value it has is determined by factors external to the proposition. That is, the sentence will express a true proposition if the facts make the proposition true; but the facts might be otherwise, in which case the truth-value of *that* proposition would be falsity. One and the same proposition can have either of two truth-values. By contrast, one and the same *a priori* proposition cannot have a different truth-value than the one it has. It would not be *that* proposition if it had a different truth-value. So a necessarily true *proposition* is never identical with a necessarily false one. This is to say that a sentence expressing a necessarily true proposition must express a different proposition from one that expresses a self-inconsistency.

Consider the sentence "For all n, $2^{2^n} + 1$ is prime." Before it was discovered by calculation that $2^{2^5} + 1$ was factorable, Fermat conjectured that this sentence expressed a truth. Evidently, as the discovery indicates, this came into question. Prior to the calculation both Fermat, who made the conjecture, and Euler, who made the calculation, did not know *which* proposition the sentence expressed, a necessarily true one or a necessarily false one. I think it might with justice be claimed that a person who did not know which proposition a sentence expresses did not understand by the sentence what he understood when he arrived at this knowledge. All he had in the beginning were, in Wittgenstein's words, "signposts for mathematical investigation, stimuli to mathematical constructions."[21] He knew the meanings of the individual words and the fact that their combination was grammatical. This much is required for initiating the proof. But it is surely minimal knowledge. It gives him only "a sort of hint as to what he is to do."[22] What he understood was not only less than but different from what he understood when he came to know which proposition—in this case a necessarily false one—was expressed by it.

Precisely how a sentence acquires an additional meaning with proof may be seen by considering the question asked about the roots of the equation $x^2 + 2x + 1 = 0$, and its answer $(-1, -1)$. Initially, the interrogative "What are the roots?" meant as much and no more than one's explanation of it indicated, namely, "What values of the variable will satisfy the equation, i.e., reduce both of its members to the same term?" By trying out values of the variable, -1 is seen to satisfy it. After the invention of a general formula for solving equations of the form $ax^2 + bx + c = 0$, "roots" meant

$$x_1 = \frac{-b + \sqrt{b^2 - 4ac},}{2a} \quad x_2 = \frac{-b - \sqrt{b^2 - 4ac}.}{2a}$$

With this formula at hand, the sentence "There are two roots of $x^2 + 2x + 1 = 0$" has an augmented meaning: it records the result of a new method which connects coefficients with roots. As Wittgenstein remarked, "I should like to say: the proof shews me a new connexion, and hence also gives me a new concept; the connexion did not exist until it was made."[23] "The question — I want to say — changes its status, when it becomes decidable. For a connexion is made then, which formerly *was not there*."[24] And the answer, in this case $(-1, -1)$, "has more in it than the question. Normally it is not like this."[25]

What Wittgenstein's account serves to point out, and stress, is the difference between showing an empirical proposition to be true, and demonstrating a mathematical proposition. That we understand something different before and after proof singles out a difference which does not obtain when an empirical proposition is verified or falsified. Prior to the discovery of a general method of solving quadratics, one could not have described the solution. In the case of an empirical proposition the method, or methods, of showing it to be true, or false, can be described in advance; and the same proposition will be expressed by the empirical sentence regardless of which truth-value it is shown to have and even if it is not shown to have either.

It is to be noted that only about language do questions about meaning and understanding arise. Sentences, not propositions, have literal meaning (a proposition *is* the meaning of an indicative sentence), and sentences, not propositions, are understood. How then does Wittgenstein's examination of proof of mathematical *propositions* come to involve questions about sentences occurring in the statement of proof? — questions about their meaning and our understanding of them? The answer Wittgenstein gave is that mathematical propositions are "instruments of language."[26] "The proposition proved by means of a proof serves as a rule . . . it shews us what it makes SENSE to say."[27] "Let us remember that in mathematics we are convinced of *grammatical* propositions, so the . . . result of being convinced is that we *accept a rule*"[28] — a rule about the use of words. For example, the proof that it is impossible to trisect an angle by straight edge and compasses convinces us to exclude the expression "trisection of an angle by straight edge and compasses" from describing any operation. It will not make sense to say "I effected the trisection of an angle using only straight edge and compasses." That is, correlated with every proof which is accepted is the acceptance of a rule for the use of language. As Wittgenstein wrote: "I go through the proof and say: . . . I must fix the use of my language in *this* way."[29] By contrast, when one confirms or establishes an empirical hypothesis, such as "Iron has a specific gravity of 7.86," nothing is shown about the use of words. That the words have a use is presupposed by the empirical tests. What is shown by the tests is whether what the words assert corresponds to the facts.[30] With regard to the use of words, the lack of parallelism between sentences which express *a priori* true propositions and sentences which assert empirical facts shows up in the following. The fact that "There is no greatest prime" expresses a true *a priori* proposition is equivalent to the fact that "The phrase 'greatest prime' has no use to describe a number" expresses a true verbal proposition. That is, to know that this sentence expresses an *a priori* truth, all that is required is that we know a fact about the use of the phrase "greatest prime." On the other hand, the fact that "There are no dinosaurs" expresses a true empirical proposition is *not* equivalent to any fact to the effect that "The word 'dinosaurs' has no use" expresses a true verbal proposition.[31] There is no such fact. Indeed, that the word "dinosaurs" has a use is already presupposed by the fact that "There are no dinosaurs" expresses an empirical proposition. What we have to know in order to know that it expresses a *truth* is something in addition to knowing that "dinosaur" has a use, something extra-verbal, namely, that there is in fact no creature falling under the concept *dinosaur.*

We are now in a position to explain the paradox that the meaning a sentence has when it occurs at the end of a proof-sequence is different from the meaning it had when it first came under consideration. On learning that "There is no greatest prime" expresses a true proposition we learn a fact about the use of the phrase "greatest prime," that is, about its meaning. After proof of *There is no greatest prime* we accept the exclusion of "greatest prime" from descriptive use. It is interesting that *reductio ad absurdum* proofs, of which the proof of an infinity of primes is an example, sometimes conclude with "But this is absurd." The absurdity is logical, and as a correlate, the expression "greatest prime" is an absurdity of language. In the context of a mathematical demonstration, "This is absurd" makes an oblique reference to a fact of language, namely, that a certain expression has no use. In the example at hand, what one knows after proof that one did not know before is that "greatest prime" has a self-contradictory meaning. The phrase "greatest prime" could not have been understood from the beginning to have this meaning, else the proof would have been unnecessary. With proof, the use of this phrase becomes fixed. It is to be expected that when it is demonstrated whether or not every even number is the sum of two primes the demonstration will make entirely new conceptual connections, as was done in constructing the formula for solving quadratics. And with new conceptual connections there is a new piece of language. Wittgenstein wrote: "The proof creates a new concept by creating or being a new sign."[32] "Could we say: 'mathematics creates new *expressions,* not new propositions'?"[33]

The proof that $x^2 + 2x + 1 = 0$ has two roots is a typical example of a proof which assigns a meaning to a sentence which in the first place only gives "signposts for mathematical investigation." So it may be useful to pause with this example. On discovery of a general method for solving quadratics, "root" came to mean "values of the form

$$\frac{-b \pm \sqrt{b^2 - 4ac}}{2a},"$$

and hence the sentence "$x + 2x + 1 = 0$ has two roots" acquired a different meaning. As Wittgenstein put it: "The proposition 'this equation has n roots' hasn't *the same* meaning if I've proved it by enumerating the constructed roots as if I've proved it in a different way. If I find a formula for the roots of an equation I've constructed a new calculus."[34] The new calculus is a new piece of language which the proof connects with the concluding "therefore." What appears to be a discovery of truth is the creation of an extension of language in which symbolism is given a use, that is to say, a meaning. In an earlier paper I showed that often so-called proofs, such as the proof of $a^0 = 1$, were better described as giving a reason for introducing a new symbol, in that case "a^0". In this paper I have interpreted Wittgenstein as holding that all proofs which do not make use of an established technique (as do proofs of propositions of the form $a \times b = c$) are justifications for, or involve creations of, new pieces of language. So the difference between proofs which introduce a new symbol and proofs which involve a new combination of symbols is not as great as might at first appear.

If to give a proof is to give a justification for accepting a new use of language, a use consistent with and in addition to the former use, then we apparently have an explanation of the paradox of proving a proposition which is other than the one we set out to prove. But a further consequence of the claim that "the result of a mathematical proof gets its meaning from the proof" is a paradox which has yet to be explained. Wittgenstein's recognition of the consequence is reflected in his questions, "Should I say that the same sense can only have *one* proof?"[35] and "Is it correct to say that every proof demonstrates something to us which it alone can demonstrate?"[36] The answer seems to be yes; and yet he is forced to admit: "Of course it would be nonsense to say that *one* proposition cannot have two proofs — for we do say just that."[37] The paradox lies in the stalemate between the answer and the admission.

The clue to an explanation lies in two claims of Wittgenstein's: first, that "We fix whether there is to be only one proof of a certain proposition, or two proofs, or many proofs,"[38] and second, the fact "that we allow several patterns to be called proofs of the same proposition is due to the application of the symbols in question."[39] For two proofs to prove the same, "It is not enough," he says, "that [they] meet in the same propositional sign."[40] "Two proofs prove the same when what they convince me of is the same—and when is what they convince me of the same?"[41] When they "lead [me] to apply this proposition in such-and-such a way—determine [me] to accept this as sense, that not. . . . The result of our being convinced is that we *accept a rule,*"[42] a rule about the use of an expression. One might suppose that this acceptance is compelled. For it appears that when one goes through a proof and says "I must fix the use of my language in *this* way," one is compelled "to accept this as sense, that not." Wittgenstein denies that when two proofs "meet in the same propositional sign" they determine that the propositional sign rules the same use for the same expression. One proof does not demonstrate that another proof gives the concluding sentence the same applicability.[43] "Why," asks Wittgenstein, "do I always speak of being compelled by a rule; why not of the fact that I can *choose* to follow it?"[44] The suggestion is that what lies ahead of the concluding sentence of two proof-sequences, its application, we can choose. And we usually choose the same thing. It is a fact that people who go through two demonstrations to infer a proposition which is expressed by the same sentence, use that sentence to legislate the *same* use of language. When this is the case they say that the two proofs convince them of the truth of the *same* proposition.

To illustrate, when it is established that $x^2 + 2x + 1 = 0$ has two roots, first by trying out values of the variable and then by use of the formula, instead of describing the two proofs as proofs of two different propositions, it is usual to say that one and the same proposition is proved in two ways. Further, we say that the one proof must give the same result as the other. *Because* people "agree in *getting*"[45] the result -1 (because there is a consensus of action[46]), says Wittgenstein, we lay it down as a rule.[47] And this is different from agreeing that it is true. "To say of the many methods which might be shown you as leading to the same result that they *must* lead to the same result, looks like a prophecy; but really it is a resolution we have made."[48] In a proof one "wins through to a decision."[49] Admittedly, "when two proofs meet it looks as if one had two independent proofs leading to the same result, and not as if one had made them do so."[50]

It might well be maintained that trying out values of the variable to determine the roots of the equation $x^2 + 2x + 1 = 0$, together with observing that the equation is a square, $(x + 1)^2$, shows but one root, whereas calculating the roots by the formula shows two, since we get -1 twice over. In discussing this kind of equation, N. J. Lennes stated that "there is only one root" but that "it is said to have two *coincident roots.*"[51] Here is an example of accepted legislation of a result. The various different proofs of the general theorem *Every equation of nth degree has n roots* are said to prove the same thing in that they are accepted as legislating what we are to say about the number of roots. The application, within mathematics, is to count *n* as the number of roots of an equation of nth degree, though, as Wittgenstein points out, we should not count one and the same chair in this way.[52] Proof, he says, "very often teaches us the most useful form of expression."[53] It is useful to be able to classify $x^2 + 2x + 1 = 0$ and $x^2 + 3x + 2 = 0$ as having the same number of roots. The effect of accepting the various proofs of the general theorem is to rule out the *same* expression, "*the* root of a quadratic equation." And its having the same application regardless of what proves it is one reason for saying that the same proposition is proved by a number of proofs.

I wish to conclude with a brief comment on Wittgenstein's account of proof. Though his language suggests that he supposes himself to be giving a true description of the relation between proofs and the meaning of sentences denoting the theorems they prove, it may be that he is not doing this. He justifies his claim that with a different proof a different proposition results by calling attention to the connection between mathematical propositions and rules for the use of words which set them off so radically from empirical propositions. The addition of a new piece of language effected by a new proof is taken to justify saying that the new proof has not proved the same proposition as did other proofs. It appears to me that under the guise of giving a correct description of the results of different proofs Wittgenstein is citing reasons for altering the use of the phrase "the *same* proposition." In general, the reasons stress the difference between establishing an empirical proposition and proving a mathematical proposition. To say that with a different proof we understand something different, that the same sentence does not express the same proposition, is to *stress* this difference. It may be that what Wittgenstein says of the philosopher, that "all he wants is a new notation,"[54] applies to his own thesis. What he says argues for precluding the use of "the same proposition" and "understands the same" from descriptions of what a proof effects and what we know after proof. He is able to mitigate the resultant paradox by reinstating the use of "same proposition" as a description of proved theorems which, regardless of the proofs, are accepted as legislating the same use of words.

A.A.

NOTES

1. *Essays in Analysis*, pp. 13–25.
2. *Philosophical Grammar*, p. 369.
3. *Wittgenstein's Lectures, Cambridge 1932–1935* (edited by Alice Ambrose), p. 212.

4 Ibid., p. 198.

5. *Remarks on the Foundations of Mathematics,* p. 76.

6. Ibid., p. 153.

7. Ibid., p. 154.

8. Ibid., p. 78.

9. Ibid., p. 138.

10. *Wittgenstein's Lectures, Cambridge 1932–1935,* op. cit., p. 197.

11. Ibid., p. 198.

12. *Remarks on the Foundations of Mathematics,* op. cit., p. 93.

13. *Wittgenstein's Lectures, Cambridge 1932–1935,* op. cit., p. 200.

14. *Remarks on the Foundations of Mathematics,* op. cit., p. 164.

15. Ibid., p. 92.

16. Ibid., p. 164.

17. Ibid., p. 165.

18. *Wittgenstein's Lectures, Cambridge 1932–1935,* op. cit., p. 197.

19. Ibid., p. 199.

20. *Remarks on the Foundations of Mathematics,* op. cit., p. 146.

21. *Philosophical Grammar,* op. cit., p. 371.

22. *Wittgenstein's Lectures, Cambridge 1932–1935,* op. cit., p. 198.

23. *Remarks on the Foundations of Mathematics,* op. cit., p. 154.

24. Ibid., p. 138.

25. *Wittgenstein's Lectures, Cambridge 1932–1935,* op. cit., p. 197.

26. *Remarks on the Foundations of Mathematics,* op. cit., p. 78.

27. Ibid., p. 77.

28. Ibid.

29. Ibid., p. 78.

30. See *Philosophical Grammar,* pp. 370–371.

31. This contrast was first brought out by Morris Lazerowitz. See his *The Structure of Metaphysics,* pp. 267–271.

32. *Remarks on the Foundations of Mathematics,* op. cit., p. 82.

33. Ibid., p. 78.

34. *Philosophical Grammar,* op. cit., p. 373.

35. *Remarks on the Foundations of Mathematics,* op. cit., p. 164.

36. Ibid., p. 93.

37. Ibid., p. 92.

38. *Wittgenstein's Lectures on the Foundations of Mathematics, Cambridge 1939* (edited by Cora Diamond), p. 39.

39. Ibid., pp. 38–39.

40. *Remarks on the Foundations of Mathematics,* op. cit., p. 93.

41. Ibid., p. 92.

42. Ibid., p. 77.

43. Ibid., p. 92.

44. Ibid., p. 193.

45. *Wittgenstein's Lectures on the Foundations of Mathematics, Cambridge 1939,* op. cit., p. 107.

46. Ibid., p. 184.

47. Ibid., p. 107.

48. *Wittgenstein's Lectures, Cambridge 1932–1935,* op. cit., p. 189.

49. *Remarks on the Foundations of Mathematics,* op. cit., p. 77.

50. *Wittgenstein's Lectures, Cambridge 1932–1935,* op. cit., p. 188.

51. N. J. Lennes, *College Algebra,* p. 57.

52. *Wittgenstein's Lectures on the Foundations of Mathematics, Cambridge 1939,* op. cit., pp. 152–153.

53. Ibid., p. 63.

54. *The Blue Book,* p. 57.

XIV

Is Philosophy of Mathematics
"An Idleness in Mathematics"?

The dispute between logicists and intuitionists concerning the applicability of the law of excluded middle to propositions whose expression requires quantifiers ranging over an infinite domain is intimately connected with differing views about the nature of the entities in the domain. Intuitionists challenged the accepted use of the law in mathematics, and thereby raised the general question about what constitutes proof. Along with the question as to the validity of certain sorts of proof, questions have arisen concerning the legitimacy of certain mathematical operations (e.g., set formation in accordance with the axiom of inclusion), and the legitimacy of any use of impredicative definitions. At the core of disagreements over principles lay a number of ill-defined problems about the conception of the finite. These problems arise in part over the conception of an infinite totality (the "consummated infinite"), and in part over the mere fact that individuals in an ordered series having no last member cannot all be examined for possession of a property. It might be supposed that what look to be philosophical questions about the individuals of a domain could be eliminated by the minimal requirement that "the individuals shall constitute a well-defined non-empty class."[1] But it may be that the notion of being well-defined cannot be made clear — for example, when the individuals are real numbers. As is known, the work of Russell in logic, as well as that of Frege, is an attempt to deduce arithmetic from logic. On Bernays's account of Frege, logic is to be viewed as "the general theory of the universe of mathematical objects."[2] These objects are held to exist independently of our constructions, whether they be points, sets of points, numbers, sets of numbers, functions, etc. Godel asserted that we have as good a ground for believing in the existence

From *Bertrand Russell Memorial Volume*. Edited by George W. Roberts (London: George Allen Unwin; New York: Humanities Press, 1979). © 1979 George W. Roberts. Reprinted by permission of the publisher.

of sets, namely, our perception of them, as is given by our perceptions of physical bodies.[3]

These remarks make it appear that work in mathematics is governed by a philosophy of mathematics, in particular, that this is true of Russell's attempt in *Principia Mathematica* to give a foundation to mathematics. The same can be said of the mathematical work of the intuitionists. The cleavage between logicists and intuitionists over the amount of classical mathematics which is logically secure is sometimes thought to reflect a difference of opinion over the character of the entities the propositions of a given branch refer to. This difference would seem to be philosophical. Thus, according to intuitionists, a mathematical entity in the range of a variable is constructed, not discovered; and construction is taken to be a mental operation. An integer, for example, is the result of a mental process. A real number is a sequence of integers for which a method for constructing the nth member of the sequence can be given or a sequence resulting from arbitrary choices. A. Heyting characterizes a mathematical theorem as "a purely empirical fact"[4] — to the effect that a construction has succeeded. An intuitionist mathematician who asserts $2 + 2 = 3 + 1$ is to be understood as saying, "I have effected the two constructions, $2 + 2$ and $3 + 1$, and found that they lead to the same results.[5] Both mathematical entities and the truth-values of mathematical propositions are mind-dependent. It is natural to suppose that the two opposing philosophical positions, conceptualism and Platonic realism, determine whether infinite totalities are to be counted among the values over which a variable ranges, and whether, for example, mathematics should contain the theorem that there are nondenumerably many sets of integers, which Cantor claimed to have proved by using the diagonal argument. If "to exist" means the same as "to be constructed," as it does according to intuitionists, then the existence-theorems within a branch of mathematics will be restricted to what is created by a mind. Creation of numbers has been described as proceeding from "the basal intuition of two-oneness . . . which creates the numbers one and two . . . and all finite ordinal numbers."[6] The application of the law of excluded middle will accordingly be restricted to the domain of entities which the mind can construct. "Constructive" definitions are described quite differently by logicists and intuitionists. According to the former, such definition merely give means for picking out an object from a totality which exists independently and prior to being exhibited.[7] Each such object will either have the property under consideration, or lack it.

In extreme contrast to these two positions, both of which represent philosophical views as bearing on the development of mathematics, stands Wittgenstein's claim that philosophy "leaves mathematics as it is,"[8] that "A 'leading problem of mathematical logic' is for us a problem of mathematics like any other,"[9] ". . . labour in philosophy is as it were an idleness in mathematics."[10] If this claim is correct, then the mathematician need not in the course of his work settle any question of ontology, and a philosophical mathematician who considers it his task to "adjudicate among rival ontologies"[11] will not be doing something requisite for securing the foundations of mathematics. A philosophical problem, in whatever area, is, according to Wittgenstein, misconceived as a problem of deciding what is true; instead, it is to be seen as a puzzle engendered by language, to be dissolved rather than solved. In the present context, one philosophical problem is the ancient one regarding the existence and nature of universals. The *meta*philosophical problem is to understand this problem and consequently the nature of the disagreement between the logicists and intuitionists. According to W. V. Quine, "This opposition is no mere quibble; it makes an essential difference in the amount of classical mathematics to which one is willing to subscribe."[12]

The purpose of this paper is to try to arrive at an understanding of Wittgenstein's opposition to the consensus among mathematicians and logicians on the actual practice of mathematics. In so doing it may be possible to make some assessment of this practice. This is a difficult task if one is to attend to detail. What needs to be decided is whether a philosophical position connects up with the body of mathematics in the sense of having logical consequences for certain of its developments, or whether it is a mistake to suppose it does. I shall argue that some positions at issue are philosophical, and idle, that others which in important respects resemble philosophical positions but appear to be mathematical as well are not idle. In connection with the latter I shall try to specify in what way the development of mathematics is made to depend on them. Before this can be done we shall need to make a distinction between a philosophical view and a statement belonging to mathematics. Because the nature of the opposing claims of intuitionists and logicists is unclear, disputes between the two schools, e.g., over the law of excluded middle, over indirect proof and the extent of acceptable mathematics, over infinite totalities, look to be disputes *within* mathematics which derive from rival theories we all take to be philosophical. Once we get clear on the nature of a philosophical view in general and of the rival claims, and on the relation of philosophical views to the claims, what Wittgenstein meant by a philosophy of mathematics being idle in mathematics may become clear.

Before coming to these central questions it will be useful to review the disagreements between the logicist school associated with Russell and followers of Brouwer, Weyl, and the French "semi-intuitionists." One well-known area of dispute concerned the relation of logic to arithmetic, number theory, analysis, and set theory. Russell's thesis was that logic and mathematics are continuous, in the sense that the concepts of mathematics could be defined in terms of concepts of logic, and that the propositions of mathematics were deductive consequences of the primitives of a formalized logical system. Logic was primary, being the foundation, and laws of logic, such as the law of excluded middle, were taken to be universally applicable. The opposite point of view was that mathematics is primary, that the formal, logical principles it exemplified could not exist prior to its exemplification of them. As N. Bourbaki put it, ". . . logic, so far as we mathematicians are concerned, is no more and no less than the grammar of the language we use, a language which had to exist before the grammar could be constructed."[13] Insofar then as the body of intuitionist mathematics differs from that of classical mathematics, the logical systems which conform to the character of each will differ. As is known, certain proofs occur within classical mathematics which are excluded from intuitionist mathematics, sometimes because the proof is indirect, i.e., has embedded in its structure the principle $p \lor \sim p$. Various systems of intuitionist logic have been set out,[14] and since they codify the logical inferences in intuitionist mathematics, $p \lor \neg p$ (the intuitionist analogue of $p \lor \sim p$) and $(x)A \lor (\exists x)\neg A$ will not appear in them as an axiom or theorem.

Another area of dispute between classical mathematicians and intuitionists concerns the existence of infinitely membered classes — classes whose number is χ_0 or greater. Neither side denies that there is an infinity of natural numbers, but intuitionists will mean by this, not a set of entities which has 2^{χ_0} subsets, but an indefinitely proceeding sequence, one which, as Wittgenstein said, does not have the institution of an end. Terms which can be generated indefinitely in accordance, say, with some rule, will not form a *whole,* that is, a set which can itself be treated as an individual thing. Hence the dispute over the legitimacy of the operation "set of x's," where x ranges, e.g., not only over integers, but over sets of integers, sets of sets of integers, etc.

This dispute has an intimate connection with the dispute over whether every instance of the formula $p \lor \sim p$ *is valid. In the case where x* ranges over an unending sequence of individuals, intuitionists claim that some predicates f are such that the formula $(x)fx \lor (\exists x)\neg fx$ does not hold. For example, for the disjunction, "There either is a greatest pair of primes of the form p and $p+2$, or every pair of this form is such that it is not the greatest," i.e., the number of twin primes is either finite or infinite. In consequence, to use an example from Heyting,[15] the following will not serve to define an integer l: $l =$ the greatest prime such that $l-2$ is also prime, or $l = 1$ if such a prime does not exist. Since this disjunction does not define an integer, it cannot be said that $l = 1$, or that $l \neq 1$. This situation obtains because it is not known whether the sequence of pairs of primes p, $p+2$ is finite or not.

Another instructive example for purposes of contrasting the two schools of thought is the decimal expansion of π. Consider P, "There either are or are not ten consecutive 7's in π," and Q, "There either are or are not ten 7's in the first million places."[16] Finding ten 7's in the first million places will establish the first alternative of both disjunctions, whereas not finding ten 7's in the first million places will establish the second alternative of disjunction Q but not of disjunction P. There is a boundary to the number of steps which must be taken to establish the negative alternative in Q, so that not finding ten 7's has the force of finding there are not ten 7's. In the case of the negative alternative in P, for which we have no *reductio ad absurdum* proof, not finding ten 7's leaves it open, no matter how far we have developed the expansion, whether there is no such sequence or whether we have not persisted long enough to establish the first alternative.

Both logicists and intuitionists would assent to this account of the proof-status of the two alternatives with regard to π, but they differ in what they go on to say. According to logicians like Russell, the fact that neither alternative is *known* to be true does not in the least militate against asserting that one of them nevertheless is true. "There are ten 7's in the infinite development of π" only differs from "There are ten 7's in the first million places" with regard to its proof-status, not with regard to its having a truth-value. If there is one day a proof of one of the alternatives, this proof will show which truth-value it in fact possesses. Similarly for the disjunction "Either there are or are not a finite number of twin primes." Because one of these disjuncts must be true, the disjunction "*1* is the greatest prime such that $1-2$ is also prime, or $1 = 1$ if such a prime does not exist" will define an integer; and the integer is either equal to 1 or it is not equal to 1. Presumably any well-formed declarative expression will serve as a value of p in $p \vee \sim p$.

According to the intuitionist, the existence of propositions of which we can neither assert that they are true nor that they are false precludes our asserting that they are either true or false. The fact that there is no proof either of $1 = 1$ or of $1 \neq 1$ precludes our saying that $1 = 1 \vee 1 \neq 1$. Accordingly, in the logic which Heyting formulates to conform to intuitionist practice in mathematics, $p \vee \neg p$ will not be a theorem. Neither "$1 = 1 \vee 1 \neq 1$" nor "There are or there are not ten 7's in π" is an instance of logical law; that is, $p \vee \neg p$ does not hold universally. This is not to say that $\neg(p \vee \neg p)$ is a theorem of the Heyting system, for some propositions, viz., Q, "There either are or are not ten 7's in the first million places," are instances of $p \vee \neg p$, and are valid. The classical law applies to this proposition because it meets the intuitionist condition for an assertable disjunction $P \vee Q$, namely, that P is assertable or that Q is assertable. Using the usual concepts of the propositional calculus and the concept "p is provable" (symbolized by Bp) and assuming for the latter an axiom system S, Gödel gave an interpretation[17] of Heyting's propositional calculus in which "$p \vee q$" means $Bp \vee Bq$, and from its axioms no formula of the form $Bp \vee Bq$ is provable unless Bp or Bq is provable.[18] This condition precludes $p \vee \neg p$ from being a theorem, and correspondingly, within the intuitionist predicate calculus, $(x)fx \vee (\exists x)\neg fx$ will not be a theorem.

This fact about intuitionist logic reflects an important restriction on proof within mathematics. Given that $(x)fx \vee (\exists x)\neg fx$ is not a theorem, neither is $\neg(x)fx \rightarrow (\exists x)\neg fx$ (and in general $\neg\neg p \rightarrow p$). This means the exclusion of indirect proofs of existence. In accordance with principles of classical logic, a proof of the self-contradictoriness of $(x)fx$ or of $\neg(\exists x)fx$

allows the inference of an existential statement. Indirect proofs are a common means of establishing existence. But it is obvious that the self-contradictoriness of (x)fx might be proved without there being a means for exhibiting something which lacks property f. The same thing obtains for a proof of the contradictoriness of $\neg(\exists x)fx$. Within intuitionist mathematics there exist only "constructive" proofs. "I am unable," says Heyting, "to give an intelligible sense to the assertion that a mathematical object which has not been constructed exists."[19] " 'To exist' must be synonymous with 'to be constructed.' "[20] In consequence, it will not be the case that there is a class of mathematical objects of which constructed objects are a proper subclass. Nor will a mathematical object be definable unless it is constructed or nameable.[21]

The limitations imposed by rejection of indirect proofs and of definitions other than constructive ones, as might be expected, do not gain the assent of classical mathematicians. Gödel objected to the fact that in the definition of constructable sets "not all logical means of definition are admitted; quantification is admitted only with respect to constructable sets and not with respect to sets in general."[22] According to him, sets which cannot be proved to be constructable can be defined, and there will be nondenumerably many sets definable in his sense (by expressions containing names of ordinals — an infinity of them — and of logical constants, including quantification over sets). He conceded that "it has some plausibility that all things conceivable by us are denumerable even if you disregard the question of expressibility in some language."[23] He goes on to remark that he thinks "the concept of definability satisfying the postulate of denumerability is not impossible but . . . that it would involve some extramathematical element concerning the psychology of the being which deals with mathematics," such as "comprehensibility by the mind."[24]

In order to assess the claim that mathematical developments are sometimes determined by extramathematical, i.e., philosophical considerations, we need a general characterization of a philosophical statement. For this purpose it is useful to examine some views which would be taken by everyone to be philosophical. Here it is especially useful to focus on views of the two schools about the nature of natural numbers — the "objects" in virtue of which statements of arithmetic and number theory are true. One of the obvious features of both Platonism and conceptualism is their failure to have been either established or refuted, and their total lack of promise of being so in the future. The prospect of their continuing irresolvability may reflect an *intrinsic* irresolvability, which is to say that they may be *in principle* not decidable by any new fact and therefore not decidable by recourse to fact. This possibility implies that they may not be truth-value statements. It is a perplexing feature of philosophical views, as contrasted with factual statements of science and everyday life, that a doubt about their truth-value status can arise, since they appear so convincingly to make factual claims.

The same doubt arises about claims which figure in what appears to be a strictly mathematical controversy between schools of mathematics. An explanation is called for. I shall try to show that the explanation of both is similar. Let us consider the two rival views, the one formulated by Plato and the other by Locke, on universals—in the present context, on natural numbers.

Russell put the Platonist position in the following way: "The statement 'two and two are four' deals exclusively with universals, and therefore can be known by anybody who is acquainted with the universals concerned and can perceive the relation between them which the statement asserts."[25] Numbers, if anything, said Theaetetus, "have real existence."[26] They and their relations, an infinite totality of them, constitute a world of abstract objects independent of us—"uncreated and indestructible"[27]—and open to our observation as surely as are the objects of sense. The task of the mathematician, as G. H. Hardy said, is to look into the special network of abstract entities that constitute the world of mathematics and note down his observations.[28] The theorems he proves are truths about nonempirical reality which force themselves on the trained mind and so produce the remarkable agreement characteristic in so many areas of mathematics. Gödel's proof that there are undecidable propositions is taken merely to show that within *that* theory they are undecidable, i.e., the axioms of the theory do not contain a *complete* description of the reality in question, but the reality described makes the undecidable propositions either true or false.

In opposition to this view Brouwer maintained that the natural numbers are mind-created. The numbers 1 and 2 are said to result from a "basal intuition of two-oneness" which consists in abstracting from the special character of successive mental states, and each number thereafter results from repetition of the process of using one of the elements of the original two-oneness to form a new two-oneness. Unclear as this account is, its intent is unmistakable: that the natural numbers be understood as mental products. It is clear also that the result of constructing natural numbers by the process of iteration can never be a *totality.*

There is one assumption common to both schools, which is, as Dummett put it, that "if a statement is true there must be something in virtue of which it is true."[29] The difference between them is over the kind of objects which make it true. Intuitionists hold that in the absence of a mental activity of construction, an existential proposition referring to numbers cannot be true, or false; and if true, it will be so at the date on which an entity exhibiting the property in question is constructed. All truths will be known truths, since proof will not consist in uncovering a prior existent fact about prior existing objects. But it will nevertheless be true in virtue of the objects it refers to. Brouwer expressed his divergences from other schools in terms of the entities each "recognizes."[30] He objected to such expressions as "the set of all real numbers between 0 and 1," "the set whose elements are the points of space," "the set whose elements are the continuous functions of a variable," on the ground that they fail to denote anything.

About natural numbers, then, there is no dispute over whether there are such objects. What appears to be in dispute is the *truth* of the claim, "Numbers exist even though no minds exist." The classification of both this view and counterclaim, "Numbers cannot exist apart from a mind," as *philosophical* is hardly in question. They therefore provide paradigm examples for the investigation of the character of philosophical views in general. One fact is immediately evident about these two special examples: that when each of the disputants who understands a number word, say "two," has before his mind a certain object, he cannot hope to settle its character by appealing to a more careful introspective scrutiny. "Being mind-dependent" and "being mind-independent" are not features exhibited on the face of the object, the way redness is exhibited on the face of a red image. The disputants are therefore forced to support their positions by argument.

In philosophical literature more argumentation is to be found for the Platonic view than for Lockeian conceptualism, and very little support is provided by philosophical mathematicians. I shall try to detail here a few arguments that may be, or may have been, in the minds of the proponents of the two views. First of all, taking intuitionists at their word that to be is to be constructed, it follows that there are but a finite number of natural numbers unless an infinite mind exists which has constructed *all* of them. This latter alternative is not open to them if an infinite totality is impossible. Kronecker's remark that God made the integers cannot be true if such a creation is impossible in principle. Allowing, however, that the intuitionist acceptance of "the potential infinite" implies that "to exist" means "to be construct*able*," there are again difficulties. If "possibility of constructing" denotes a psychological capability, then it would be "medically impossible,"[31] to use Russell's language, for numbers to be constructed indefinitely unless the race does not die or unless an eternal God with this capacity exists. Supposing that God does not exist or that the race does die out, but that rocks, trees, gravestones remain, there could not be two, three, or any number of them. To maintain that these have a number is to give up the mind-dependency of numbers. Numbers would be independently existing, abstract entities. And inasmuch as every number has a successor, there would be infinitely many of them.

Against this argumentation the intuitionist can say that the Platonist is in no position to go beyond argument—to verify by experience that the objects before both their minds when they grasp a proposition of arithmetic can exist independently of their apprehension. The Platonist is in an egocentric predicament[31] with regard to what is before his mind—he cannot, by experience, establish the existence of numbers when not before his mind. As for the statement, "There is an infinity of natural numbers," the intuitionist can maintain that all that is required is a proper interpretation of it to see that it expresses a truth: it asserts that for every natural number constructed another can be constructed. What is denied is that it asserts the existence of an infinite totality.

One striking feature of this dispute, and of philosophical disputes in general, is that advocates of rival views need not give way to each other. No matter how conclusive the argument against a view appears, it need convince no one but its proponent. Nor will an appeal to facts compel acceptance of one view or the other—and not because philosophical opponents are obtuse or hold their views in irrational disregard of the facts. There are no facts which decide, for example, between Leibniz's, Berkeley's, and Locke's views on the nature of physical objects. Similarly, there are no facts available, or theoretically possible, which decide whether or not the domain of individual variables, say, in number theory, consists of entities which exist in the absence of minds. Quine asserts that the acceptance of an ontology is like the acceptance of a scientific theory.[33] But if this was the case it should make a difference to the truth-value of some mathematical statements whether their subject matter was mind-dependent or not. Quine is explicit that there is something in virtue of which a theorem is true. He writes: "a theory is committed to . . . those entities to which the bound variables of the theory must be capable of referring in order for the affirmations made in the theory to be true.[34] Gödel says of set theory that it "describes some determinate reality."[35] It is an odd situation that mathematicians are unable to come to an agreement on what it is that makes their statements true. And this would indicate that very little, or nothing whatever, hangs upon an agreed on subject matter. It is therefore questionable whether an ontology in mathematics is comparable to a scientific theory. What, then, is the peculiar character of the view that natural numbers are independent existents, and of the contrary view that natural numbers are mind-dependent? If we can assess Wittgenstein's general view with respect to these paradigm philosophical positions, namely, that they are idle in mathematics, we shall be better able to assess conflicting positions regarding the law of excluded mean, indirect proof, and set theory.

The two contrary views are expressed in what might be called the fact-stating idiom: they are assertions ascribing a feature to natural numbers. But this is not to say they are matter of fact propositions, for it can scarcely be doubted that intuitionists and Platonists wish to be understood as asserting the "essential" features of natural numbers, i.e., as asserting something necessary. They express themselves with the assurance one has in asserting that a yard is three feet, or that lions are felines, and are not shaken by arguments against their positions. To see, then, what these philosophical views come to we should note some important features of necessary propositions. One is that they are not *made* true by some fact and another is that they are not about words. To illustrate with a proposition free from questions surrounding the philosophical propositions under discussion, consider "Lions are felines." Its truth can be known without observing lions. No empirical fact about lions has any bearing on its truth—something that cannot be said of "Lions are carnivores," which is also expressed in the fact-stating idiom. All that is required to know that it is true is the verbal fact about the words used to express it, in the English language the use of the words "lion" and "feline." To know that the sentence "Lions are felines" expresses a necessarily true proposition is to know that " 'feline' applies to what 'lion' applies to" expresses a factually true verbal proposition. It is an empirical fact of the English language that the first sentence expresses a necessity. Its equivalence to the fact that the second sentence expresses a truth about the use of "feline" and "lion," shows that it does not assert anything about what the words apply to—no knowledge of lions is required. The same verbal fact verifies that it expresses a necessity and that the second sentence expresses a factually true verbal proposition.[36] It should be noted that the sentence "Lions are felines" does not state a verbal fact; it does not mention, and is therefore not "about," the words "lion" and "feline," as is the sentence "The word 'feline' applies to whatever 'lion' applies to." It does not *state* the verbal fact required for knowing that what it expresses is true. What it states is a (nonverbal) necessary proposition, which is not to be confused with the verbal and factual proposition that "feline" applies to what "lion" applies to. Nevertheless, though the necessary proposition is not about lions nor about the word "lion," the fact that the *sentence* expresses a necessity is equivalent to the fact that a related sentence about the use of words expresses something in fact true. In an oblique way its import is verbal, but it is not itself a verbal proposition.

If this account of necessary propositions is correct, then even though the sentence "Natural numbers are mind-dependent" expresses a necessary truth; it cannot be construed as expressing a fact about numbers. It is ontologically idle—giving no information about the nature of what there is—since were it true that it expresses a necessity, this truth would rest on a verbal fact about the use of the words "number" and "mind-dependent." Here it is instructive to compare it with the sentence "Lions are felines," or "A yard is three feet." Unlike these, it is not a fact of English that it expresses a necessity, for it is not a fact that "mind-dependent," as English is used, applies to everything "natural number" applies to. Nor is it the case that "independent abstract entity" applies to what "natural number" applies to. Sentences for neither view express anything necessarily true.

How then are we to understand the claims of intuitionists and Platonists that they are stating the essential features of natural numbers? Both know the linguistic conventions, and both know that their sentences do not express necessary propositions. Yet they argue as if in support of the truth of a view. The verbal aspect of what they are doing is concealed by the fact-stating idiom in which they announce them. When the philosophical mathematician says "Numbers are to be reckoned among the things that are,"[37] he is *inventing* a subject matter — in name if not in fact — to correspond to substantive terms which do not have a use to refer to things one can point to. As Wittgenstein put it, "When we perceive that a substantive is not used as what in general we should call the name of the object, . . . we can't help saying to ourselves that it is the name of an aethereal object"[38] (whether or not the object exists only if a mind exists). "What you want is . . . a new notation, [but] by a new notation no facts of geography are changed."[39] It appears to me that what here looks to be argumentation for a position is to be interpreted as a means of persuading one to accept a convention where none exists. Actual usage is mute on the connection between "natural number" and "mind-dependency," and also on whether "number" and "independent entity" are connected. This being the case, there is leeway for argument that will incline one to accept a new convention. In what follows I take argumentation by each school, which on the surface purports to establish a necessary truth about numbers, as showing, not that a necessary truth *is* being expressed by the sentence uttered, but that it *should* be. Proceeding in accordance with the analysis of "Sentence S expresses a necessary proposition," I shall treat the assertion that a sentence should express a necessity as having a verbal point, to introduce a new way of speaking. The point is concealed by the declarative form of "Numbers are mind-dependent," "Numbers are independent existents." But since these are not in fact correlated with any accepted convention, I shall take them to present in a concealed way a preference for a notation.

In various ways the preferences are idle. The fact that there is no resolution of the dispute between intuitionists and Platonists is reflected in the verbal fact that no new convention has been generally accepted. So the philosophical labor of trying to resolve it has had no fruits within mathematics. But supposing the dispute were resolved, the labor required would seemingly still be "an idleness." For it is hard to suppose that anything in mathematics would change. The notation would remain unaffected. The historical dispute over " $\sqrt{-1}$ " was resolved in favor of its introduction, and the course of mathematics changed. But such terms as "mind-dependent entity," "independent existent," and their equivalents seem to have no place in mathematics.

The views at issue are idle in another way. Whether the arithmetical symbols in the sentence "$2 + 1 = 3$" denote entities of any kind, and whether the bound variables in "All primes greater than 2 are odd" do so, the propositions expressed by them are not made valid or invalid by their failure to be "true of something." As for the mind-dependency of numbers, $2 + 1 = 3$ is such that its opposite is logically impossible, whether one takes the Platonic view about numbers or the Berkeleian view that any general term stands for a particular (dependent) idea. Both views "leave mathematics as it is."

The idea that there is a logical dependency between these views and the mathematical developments with which they are associated is dispelled on closer scrutiny. Although it is natural to associate a philosophical view about the essential nature of numbers with the mathematical development its proponents engaged in—the view that natural numbers are mental constructions with taking the natural numbers to be primitive, and the view that they are independent entities with defining natural numbers as predicates taken in extension, i.e., as sets—the two are logically independent. For the notion of a natural number could be primitive without numbers being either the mind's creation or the mind's discovery. Also, a subjective philosophical view about predicate terms is compatible with defining numbers as sets. The relation between the fundamental ideas of a branch of mathematics and their philosophical analysis seems to be no closer logically than that between "numbers are sets" and "Jupiter is the largest planet." Furthermore, although on the philosophical view held by intuitionists construction is a mental process and its result is a mind-dependent entity, a constructivist requirement can be framed independently of this view. Heyting says "it must be clear what it means that a given operation is the construction of a certain object,"[40] and asserts that construction is a mental operation. But the requirement that a construction be effective can be met without subscribing to the view that it is mental. E. W. Beth asserts that "axiomatic set theory is the final result of the development of Cantor's strongly Platonist concepts,"[41] but at the same time he admits that it is compatible with radically opposed conceptions.[42]

Nevertheless, there are parts of mathematics which are done differently according as one philosophical view or the other is subscribed to, and some parts of intuitionist mathematics have no counterpart in classical mathematics. Intuitionist mathematics is not merely what remains of classical mathematics as a result of eliminating objectionable concepts, operations, and methods of proof.[43] These facts suggest that philosophy does not "leave mathematics as it is." The question is: In what way are these differences determined by a philosophical view? S. C. Kleene speaks of a development of mathematics being "based on a philosophy of mathematics,"[44] and of a position apparently within intuitionist mathematics being taken "on philosophical grounds." I wish to hold that the relation of the rival philosophical views we have discussed is a causal or associational one, not a logical one; that these views are no more integral to a mathematical development than Newton's theological views were to his physical theories. There are other points of divergence between classical and intuitionist mathematicians whose status—whether philosophical or mathematical—is not clear, and which are not logically neutral. These must be considered separately. Whether the divergent positions eventually connect through some causal link with Platonism and conceptualism need not be investigated here. That there is a merely contingent relationship between the philosophical views and certain statements expressed in wholly mathematical terms in one development or the other can be made relatively convincing.

To illustrate, consider the Platonist view that numbers are abstract entities existing independently of a mind with respect to the statement that numbers are classes of classes. It is plain that these are not logically related. However, misconceiving the philosophical statement as asserting a fact about numbers, and misconceiving similarly the statement that classes are independent existents, make it natural for Platonists to couple the expressions "number" and "class." The definition of a natural number as a class of similar classes is only expressible in a logical language quantifying over classes. (In a lower order language numbers will be primitive.) In consequence of it, it was possible to incorporate arithmetic in a system of logic. Since Frege's class logic was found to involve antinomies, Russell's system, in avoiding them through a types theory, had to add a postulate asserting the existence of an infinite set in order to make sure there is no greatest cardinal number. Thus, in the sense that the philosophical view that numbers are independently existing entities has been a motive force behind an analysis of numbers as classes, which itself was embodied in the fabric of mathematics, it has indeed not been idle. It had the effect of encouraging the axiomatization of foundations supposedly required to make mathematics logically secure, which in turn gave impetus to the addition of a new branch, proof theory. Hilbert's program of proving the consistency of arithmetic was given urgency by the class paradoxes. However, I think this is hardly the sense in which mathematicians of the two schools suppose their respective work is based on a philosophy of mathematics. If they suppose their work to be logically connected with the rival philosophical views I have considered here, then I believe them to be in error.

Nevertheless, there exist disagreements between logicists and intuitionists which are framed in the current language of mathematics — something which cannot be said of the disputes over the mind-dependency of numbers. These concern claims which have a logical relation to a mathematical development, yet resemble in important respects philosophical views. To these I now turn. If the claims at issue are classified as philosophical, then we must say that philosophy does not leave mathematics as it is. How they are to be classified, and therefore whether or not Wittgenstein is right, is unimportant if we can get clear on what their points of similarity to philosophical theories are. I shall try to show that, like philosophical theories, their import is misconceived. It will be recalled that the sentence expressing a "view" about numbers was taken to express a necessary proposition, and that since there is no accepted linguistic convention establishing that it in fact expresses a necessity, it was interpreted as introducing in a concealed way a linguistic innovation. In my opinion the same description holds for claims at issue between mathematicians which are apparently *within* mathematics since they can be expressed in mathematical terms. Although they make no mention of language, and appear to state essential features of "mathematical structures," as in the case of opposing philosophical theories, what is at issue is a terminological decision (like the decision on

" $\sqrt{-1}$ "). The difference is that once a decision is come to, this makes a difference to the course of mathematics. Sometimes it is open to a person to throw a pair of semantical dice, with quite different consequences dependent on the outcome. To carry the analogy to the context of the logicist-intuitionist controversy, the throwers here weight the dice—decide how the dice are to fall. But this is done without awareness that the course of mathematics is being changed by a linguistic decision rather than by a perception of a fact of ontology.

In the remainder of this paper I shall try to apply this thesis, which it is needless to say is not Russell's or Brouwer's, to various sources of controversy: the nature of real numbers, the existence of certain sorts of sets, the legitimacy of certain operations and of indirect proofs. It is instructive to begin with the Russell-Frege account of a natural number as a class of similar classes. On first meeting this account my own reaction was that Russell and Frege had assigned a new meaning to the term "number" (inasmuch as the dictionary was silent on this matter), rather than that they had explicated its conventional meaning. Doubtless they were governed by a condition for proper explication of a familiar concept which Carnap much later made explicit: that the analysis supply a corresponding exact concept by means of "explicit rules for its use, for example, by a definition which incorporates it into a well-constructed system of . . . scientific concepts."[45] It is clear that this procedure replaces the familiar concept by another. R. L. Goodstein remarks that Russell and Frege "found . . . a new concept,"[46] which is to say that they offered a new definition of a word (although under the guise of analyzing a familiar idea). The definition, which represents a *decision,* is not an idle one. It sets the future course of language.

I wish now to examine some of the propositions which occur within mathematics but have the earmarks of philosophical statements. They are at the center of a controversy which is carried on as though one of two contrary propositions is mistaken. Their affinity with the two philosophical statements we have considered is clear: the question as to their *truth* cannot be settled by mathematics itself, any more than the same question about a philosophical statement can be settled by appeal to fact. So long as they are not shown to issue in a contradiction there is no deciding between them. The fact that attempts to justify a decision on their truth have been fruitless suggests the possibility that no mistake has been made, and that disputation over their truth is idle. If I am right in supposing that this possibility obtains, then we have an explanation of the intractability of the disputation: the nature of what is in dispute has been misconceived. It would also be a possible explanation of Wittgenstein's claim that a philosophy of mathematics is idle. But the propositions in dispute do not leave mathematics as it is, inasmuch as they entail differing consequences. In this sense they differ markedly from the philosophical propositions discussed here, which are not logically connected with a mathematical development. My thesis is that propositions of the following list present concealed decisions governing the use of language (or derive logically from others which do) and that with the acceptance or rejection of the decisions, different bodies of mathematics result.

The number of the set of real numbers between 0 and 1 is greater than $\aleph_0$.

$2^{\aleph_0} > \aleph_0$.

There is no set of real numbers greater than the set of integers but smaller than the set of all real numbers.

Given any class of mutually exclusive classes (non-null) there is at least one class having exactly one element in common with each of the classes.

There are functions which cannot be effectively computed.

A real number $a_1\ a_2\ a_3\ \ldots$ can be generated by a succession of free choices of 0 and 1.

In describing the controversy over these propositions I shall use the language of the protagonists, that is, the idiom natural to it, in which "entities recognized" or "concepts admissible" by one side or the other are supposedly at issue. Central to the controversy are questions which are framed as questions about sets and set-formation. Putting them in this way is I think misleading, and I shall try to indicate how "acceptance" of a truth disguises making a linguistic decision. According to Cantor, a set G exists which has as members all objects x for which S(x) holds. The existence of the Burali-Forti paradox forced a modification of this axiom of set-formation[47] (the axiom of inclusion), so that sets could be introduced only if they are subsets of pre-existing sets: given a set H, there exists a set U having as members all objects x for which $x \in H$ and S(x) holds. Brouwer says that since the existence of a collection of sets has to be postulated to begin with and since the only objection classical mathematicians can bring to the introduction of a new set is the discovery of a contradiction, in practice the result has been to avoid formation of such sets while continuing to operate with other sets introduced on the basis of the old axiom of inclusion.[48] The linguistic consequence is that such expressions as "the set of all real numbers between 0 and 1," are acceptable, the new language of the theory of powers was created, and with it the wherewithal for expressing Cantor's continuum problem: whether there is a set of real numbers greater than the set of integers (with number $\aleph_0$) but smaller than the set of all real numbers, i.e., whether the power of the continuum is the second smallest infinite power.[49]

By unrestricted iteration of the operation *set of,* classical mathematicians are able to obtain Cantor's ascending orders of infinity. The totality of sets obtained is itself treated as a set, and a number is assigned to it. If, for example, the totality of subsets of a set is not finite and not 1–1 correlatable with the natural numbers, classical mathematicians say its number must be some χ greater than χ_0. Galileo said that infinite sets are not comparable as to size, that, for example, one could not say of the cardinals 1, 2, 3, 4, . . . that their number is either greater than or equal to that of the cardinals 1, 4, 9, 16,.... He said this while recognizing that 1 could be paired with 1^2, 2 with 2^2, etc. "The cardinals are 1–1 correlatable with their squares" is now a generally accepted description, which is to say that the phrase "1–1 correlation" has been extended to cover χ_0 correlations. The intuitionists' proviso is that " χ_0 correlations" denotes merely an unending process, and they do not go on to compare the sizes of infinite sets which cannot be 1–1 correlated. Their constructability requirement compels them to stop with the lowest order of infinity, χ_0. And this is the number, not of a totality of things existing all at once,[50] but of an unending sequence ("the potential infinite") whose elements can be computed separately.

It is clear that this requirement entails a different account of real numbers. Cantor's definition of a real number, say between 0 and 1, as a convergent sequence of rationals, and Dedekind's definition of it as a section of rationals, are replaced by "law of constructing a series of digits after the decimal point, using a finite number of operations."[51] A real number is also definable according to intuitionists as a "free choice sequence," a sequence resulting from a wholly irregular way of picking out an indefinite number of elements. On this account, a real number can be generated by a random device such as the throwing of a coin, each digit being 0 or 1 according as the coin falls heads or tails. Digit by digit development of a decimal by free choices is very different from development in accordance with a law; it has been objected that the operation yields only a daily changing collection of terminating decimals,"[52] and no more *results* in a real number than does, for a different reason, *throwing endlessly.* Goodstein says "it seems to me that only [where a law exists] can we speak of a real number, the . . . law itself."[53] As Wittgenstein put it, "A real number *yields* extensions but is no extension. A real number is an arithmetical law which endlessly yields the places of a decimal fraction."[54] In this discussion we have a good example of the concealment, by the fact-stating idiom, of a recommendation on how the expression "real number" should be used. "Real number" is to be applied to what is calculable (according to Kronecker and the French semi-intuitionists, to what is namable). The disagreement over its use remains unsettled, but opting for one decision or the other results in a different theory of real numbers. The same remark applies to the term "function." The question, "Are there noncomputable functions?", although so framed as to make no mention of words, is, according to Goodstein, not over the existence of a function but about how the term "function" is to be used.[55] Is it to be used where there is no computation procedure?

That conditions which intuitionists impose on the application of the terms "real number," "set," "function" have consequences for real number theory can now be usefully illustrated. The different conclusions drawn by Cantor and non-Cantorians from the diagonal process may appear to reflect a difference of opinion over their validity. But I think it will be evident that something arbitrary is involved, that the conclusion represents a decision. Mathematicians of each school will agree that denumerably infinite sets of real numbers can be constructed, and that for every such set a real number between 0 and 1 can be constructed which is not in the set. That is, the diagonal process can be used to generate, for every array of decimal sequences, a decimal different from any decimal occurring in the array. The difference lies in what each school then goes on to say. Cantor claimed to have proved by it the existence of a nondenumerable set, viz., the set of all decimal sequences. For his proof proceeds by *reductio ad absurdum* from the hypothesis that one has an enumeration of all decimal sequences. The diagonal process generates a sequence not in the enumeration, and in doing so shows the hypothesis to be contradictory. The question is whether in showing that there cannot be an enumeration of the totality of real numbers one has shown that there is a nondenumerable totality of them. In some axiom systems there is a "power set axiom" which postulates the existence of all subsets of a set, in the present case that all the sequences of decimal fractions form a set. This set can then be proved to be nondenumerable. The question is whether the diagonal process, without the axiom, provides the set.[56] Limitations intuitionists impose on the operation *set of* preclude such sets. The diagonal process is taken merely to show that an enumeration of all real numbers is impossible. In consequence "function which enumerates the real numbers" has no use.[57] But intuitionists stop short of allowing a use to "set of all real numbers." In claiming to have proved the set of real numbers to be nondenumerable Cantor takes the sentence "The real numbers are nondenumerable" to assert something necessarily true. In conformity with my earlier account of sentences of this sort, this is to say that "nondenumerable" applies to the class "real numbers" applies to. This, in my view, is to opt for a convention, for which the diagonal argument is the justification. I say Cantor opted for a convention rather than proved a truth, because there is another possible explanation of what the diagonal process does, and does not, justify saying, namely, (a) that from any sequence of decimal fractions another can be constructed which is not in the array, (b) in consequence "enumeration of the real numbers" has no use in the language of set theory, (c) that it does not require giving "nondenumerable set of real numbers" a use.

The exposition given thus far of views of classical mathematicians serves also as an exposition of Russell's views. In his Preface to *Our Knowledge of the External World* he says of the theories he puts forward in that book that *"except in regard to such matters as Cantor's theory of infinity,* no finality is claimed for them."[57] This claim to finality has been brought into question by the still extant division between classical and intuitionist mathematicians on precisely this matter. At any rate, the usual description of the division is that it is basically a difference over the existence of infinite totalities. If we look to the language of classical mathematicians we can, I think, find the linguistic analogy which their language accentuates. The language is that used to describe empirical reality, the language by which we assert truths about things and classes of things perceptible to the senses. Wittgenstein pointed out that the question "How many?" could be answered by "3" or by "infinitely many."[58] The answers suggest that "infinitely many" equally with "3" is a number designation. Talk of transfinite cardinals is modelled directly on that of natural numbers. Cantor defines equality between finite cardinals and extends it to infinite cardinals. The existence of a cardinal number with property P is defined to mean that a set having that cardinal exists. "On the basis of these definitions," Gödel says, "it becomes possible to prove that there exist infinitely many different cardinal numbers or 'powers,' and that, in particular, the number of subsets of a set is always greater than the number of its elements. . . . Owing to the theorem that for each cardinal number and each set of cardinal numbers there exists one cardinal number immediately succeeding in magnitude and that the cardinal number of every set occurs in the series thus obtained, it is possible to denote the cardinal number immediately succeeding the set of finite numbers[59] by χ_0 (which is the power of the 'denumerably infinite' sets), the next one by χ_1, etc. . . ."[60] Proof of this theorem requires the axiom of choice, a proposition which presents no puzzlement in regard to classes of objects we meet with in sense-experience. The source of the language of sets is to be found in the language of everyday. Stressing its features—such features as its subject-predicate structure—bolsters the Platonic philosophical view and encourages decisions which introduce linguistic innovations into mathematics, such as the similar use of "3," " χ_0," and "2^{χ_0}" as names of numbers. Platonists take the proposition "There are sets with 2^{χ_0} elements" to be true of a nonempirical reality. But their implied claim that the sentence expressing it, as well as the sentence expressing their philosophical view, stands for a necessary truth, is not backed by an established convention. Instead, it introduces a convention which stresses a similarity between "set of all real numbers" and "class of lepidoptera," between "3" and "2^{χ_0}." The difference is muted—such a difference, for example, as that one cannot sensibly say a larger number is nearer to χ_0 than a smaller one. The view that a mathematical development is based on a philosophy of mathematics arises from a misconception and it arises because a philosophical position and disputed mathematical statements have in common the fact that concealed linguistic decisions in each are prompted by analogies with ordinary language. That there is a misconception is most strongly suggested by the following questions: How is Russell to show the intuitionist that "series of natural numbers" means something more than "unending sequence" — that it denotes a totality with the smallest infinite power χ_0? How is he to convince the intuitionist that one of the two sentences "There are ten 7's in the expansion of π," "There are not ten 7's in the expansion of π" expresses a truth? And how is the intuitionist to show Russell that in an indirect proof it is illegitimate to come to an existence-conclusion in the absence of a means of exhibiting what is said to exist? To none of these questions is it relevant to turn to mathematics for an answer. I hold that reasons given do not logically entail one answer as against another. They are means of persuading the acceptance of a language decision.

This thesis may appear especially unconvincing as applied to the controversy over indirect proof and the law of excluded middle which figures in it. About a question of logical validity it would seem that one of the two opposing positions must be mistaken. A perception of a difference from usual questions of validity is evident in the following: "Brouwer demands of the mathematicians a profound change of their habits of thought on grounds which for them are not wholly convincing. . . . So long as they apply the methods stigmatized by Brouwer carefully and consistently, they do not have to come to contradictory results. Therefore, the position of Brouwer and his followers is much more difficult than that of the founders of modern analysis who also have pointed out the necessity of jettisoning various customary methods of reasoning [e.g., arguing as though every continuous function could be differentiated]. In such cases, one could conclusively convince his opponents of their errors through counter-examples. Brouwer's counter-examples, however, are not so convincing."[61] And in fact the prospect of resolving the dispute is as unpromising as is the Platonist-conceptualist controversy over universals. Why this should be true is suggested by the kind of support the two schools marshal for their positions on what they both conceive to be the universal validity of the law of excluded mean and of a standard form of proof employing it. In what follows I shall try to show that the controversy in a concealed way concerns a matter of terminology.

It is interesting that intuitionist objection to the "admissibility" of certain "concepts" is often framed as an explicit objection to terminology. For example, it is asserted that "set of real numbers between 0 and 1," "totality of integers," "numbers greater than χ_0" are *meaningless,* and that there will be an answer to Cantor's question about the power of the continuum as soon as it can be interpreted so as to have meaning.[62] Likewise, they give as a ground for rejecting indirect proof as generally valid that sentences of the form $(\exists x)fx$ which appear at the end of a proof-sequence are meaningless if there is no method of exhibiting the thing whose existence they purport to assert. Heyting says: "I am unable to give an intelligible sense to the assertion that a mathematical object which has not been constructed exists."[63]

What is curious about this assertion is that as language is used within mathematics these expressions are not meaningless. Further, the practice of intuitionists belies that they are. For despite saying that the final sentence "$(\exists x)fx$" occurring in a classical proof-sequence of sentences is meaning-less, intuitionists attempt to prove the truth of $(\exists x)fx$ constructively. They also attempt to "reconstruct" classical mathematics in intuitionist terms. Have they by a constructive proof demonstrated the *same* thing as was proved nonconstructively? If so, how could they know this if "$(\exists x)fx$" in the classical context was meaningless?

To apply the term "meaningless" to many phrases and sentences now in use might be thought to be a mere mistake. But this is not plausible. Intui-tionists' use of this term is motivated: its point is to exclude certain forms of expression in classical mathematics, and in addition, to curtain off from view the innovations in terminology which they themselves have introduced and incorporated into their mathematical practice. What is not evident to them is that they have put into operation a notational preference rather than discovered a fact about what exists or a fact about a class of propositions (that the law of excluded mean does not apply to them). In support of this thesis I cite their assertion that "to exist" means "to be constructed." Just as Hume could defy anyone to find a simple idea without a correspondent impression because by "ideas" he "mean(t) the faint images of [impres-sions],"[64] so the intuitionist can be sure there will be no nonconstructive existence proofs. It has already been decided that an existence proof will contain a construction of what is said to exist. On this Wittgenstein remarks: "One can merely say, 'I call an existence proof only one which contains such a construction'. . . . Intuitionists [who] say '. . . existence can only be proved so and not so', . . . have only defined what *they* call existence."[65] Note that it is a definition, not a truth, which alters the course of mathematics.

Russell's position can now be viewed as supporting the linguistic *status quo* (though certainly not conceived in this way by Russell). He maintains that as soon as he knows the meanings of sentences of the form "$(x)fx$" and "$(\exists x) \sim fx$" he knows that one of them states something true, though he may not know which.[66] That is, both sentences express *propositions*. Although the term "proposition" is not part of the apparatus of mathematical terms and has a minimal use in ordinary speech, whatever use it has is, I think, correctly characterized by Wittgenstein: "The word 'proposition' is equiva-lent to a calculus . . . in which $p \vee \sim p$ is a tautology (the law of excluded middle holds)."[67] That is, according to current conventions 'proposition' means what is either true or false. "If the law of excluded middle does not hold, then we have changed the concept of a proposition."[68] Intuitionists claim to have discovered propositions to which this logical law does not apply. Accordingly, their calculus of propositions does not include $p \vee \neg p$. At the same time, they say that existence-sentences which conclude proof-sequences expressing indirect proofs are meaningless. The first claim denies that $p \vee \neg p$ is a defining characteristic of propositions; the second appears to retain this criterion for being a proposition and to deny that these sentences express propositions. About the first claim, Wittgenstein's remark seems to me to be correct: that no discovery has been made of something to which the law of excluded mean does not apply but that "a new stipulation has been made."[69] As for the second claim, whether a sentence of the form "$(\exists x)fx$" expresses a truth or a falsity, like the question whether there are propositions to which $p \vee \sim p$ does not apply, is not to be settled mathematically. Both are matters of semantic decision. If the decision is in favor of its expressing something true or false, then indirect proof is admissible.

Arguments in favor of a position on these matters I take to be means of gaining acceptance of a linguistic decision. To illustrate, consider the logicist claim that ten 7's either occur or do not occur in the expansion of π. Suppose one gives as justification, as Russell would, that ". . . all members of the series from the 1st up to the 1000th . . . and so on, are determined: so surely *all* the members are determined."[70] This comes to saying that the law for expanding π makes it necessary that they occur or necessary that they do not occur. It should be noted that "it is necessary that p" and "it is necessary that $\sim p$" are not contradictories, that their relation is not that of P to $\sim$P.[71] In number theory if the assumption of p's truth leads to a contradiction there is no hesitation about inferring that p is logically impossible, i.e., $\sim\Diamond\sim(\sim p)$ — not merely that it is not necessary, $\sim(\sim\Diamond\sim p)$. We proceed as though $\sim\Diamond\sim p \vee \sim\Diamond\sim(\sim p)$ is an instance of P v $\sim$P. The decision has been made to treat them analogously to empirical propositions. The alternatives in "There either are or are not ten 7's in the infinite expansion of π" seems to "put two pictures before us to choose from . . . one [of which] must correspond to the fact."[72] The Platonist view that they are assertions about abstract entities reinforces the idea that these entities, like empirical objects, make one of them true — even though it is recognized that a necessary proposition has no truth-conditions. Russell argued for treating "the expansion of π" as standing for a sequence whose members are given in extension by arguing for the logical possibility of completing infinitely many operations in a finite time.[73] Such an argument, of course, lies outside any mathematical proof. It is truly idle in mathematics. But the decision made on the validity of $\sim\Diamond\sim p \vee \sim\Diamond\sim(\sim p)$, which may be *prompted* by it, is not idle — even though, like a philosophical claim, it cannot be shown to be true because a decision has no truth-value.

A.A.

NOTES

1. Alonzo Church, *Introduction to Mathematical Logic* (Princeton University Press, 1944), p. 33.

2. P. Bernays, "On Platonism in Mathematics," (trans., C. D. Parsons), in *Philosophy of Mathematics,* Paul Benacerraf and Hilary Putnam, eds. (Englewood Cliffs, N.J.: Prentice-Hall, 1964), p. 282.

3. "What is Cantor's Continuum Problem?" in Benacerraf and Putnam, op. cit., p. 271.

4. *Intuitionism: an Introduction* (Amsterdam: North-Holland, 1956), p. 8.

5. Ibid.

6. L. E. J. Brouwer, "Intuitionism and Formalism," (trans., Arnold Dresden), in *The Bulletin of the American Mathematical Society* (1913); reprinted in Benacerraf and Putnam, op. cit., p. 69.

7. P. Bernays, op. cit., p. 276.

8. *Philosophical Investigations,* p. 49.

9. Ibid.

10. *Remarks on the Foundations of Mathematics,* p. 157.

11. W. V. O. Quine, 'On What There Is,' in *From a Logical Point of View* (Cambridge, Mass.: Harvard University Press, 1953), p. 15.

12. Ibid., p. 14.

13. "Foundations of Mathematics for the Working Mathematician," *Journal of Symbolic Logic,* vol. 14, 1949, p. 14.

14. See A. Heyting, *Intuitionism: an Introduction,* ch. 7; and S. C. Kleene, *Introduction to Metamathematics* (Amsterdam: North-Holland).

15. Heyting, *Intuitionism: an Introduction,* p. 2.

16. Or some number of places not yet computed. By 1967 computation had been carried to 500,000 places. See P. Beckmann, *A History of* Π (Pi), 2nd. ed. (Boulder, Colorado: Golden Press, 1971), p. 181.

17. *Ergebnisse Eines Mathematishchen Kolloquiums (An Interpretation of the Intuitionistic Sentential Logic),* Vol. 4 (1933), pp. 39–40; trans., J. Hintikka and L. Rossi, in *The Philosophy of Mathematics,* J. Hintikka, ed. (London: Oxford University Press, 1969).

18. It is of interest that this system is equivalent to Lewis's system of strict implication if Bp is replaced by Np, and if to Lewis's system Becker's axiom $\square$ ($Np \supset NNp$) is adjoined.

19. Heyting, ed., *Constructivity in Mathematics* (Amsterdam: North-Holland, 1959), p. 69.

20. Heyting, *Intuitionism: an Introduction,* p. 2.

21. The requirement made by the French semi-intuitionists.

22. "Remarks before the Princeton Bicentennial Conference on Problems of Mathematics," in *The Undecidable,* Martin Davis, ed. (Hewlett, New York: Raven Press, 1965), p. 86.

23. Ibid., p. 86.

24. Ibid., p. 87.

25. *The Problems of Philosophy* (New York: Henry Holt, 1912), p. 164.

26. *The Sophist,* s. 238, Jowett translation.

27. *The Timaeus,* s. 52, Jowett translation.

28. "Mathematical Proof," *Mind,* XXXVIII (1929), p. 18.

29. M. Dummett, "Wittgenstein's Philosophy of Mathematics," in Benacerraf and Putnam, op. cit., p. 499.

30. "Consciousness, Philosophy, and Mathematics," *Proceedings of 10th International Congress of Philosophy,* Vol. I, fascicle 2; reprinted in Benacerraf and Putnam, op. cit., p. 79.

31. Russell held it to be only medically impossible, not logically impossible, to run through the series of integers. See 'The Limits if Empiricism,' *Proceedings of the Aristotelian Society, XXXVI (1934-35),* p. 143.

32. R. B. Perry's term.

33. Quine, op. cit., p. 16.

34. Ibid., pp. 13-14.

35. "What is Cantor's continuum Problem?," in Benacerraf and Putnam, op. cit., p. 263.

36. This account of the relation between a necessary proposition and a verbal fact is given in various places by Morris Lazerowitz. See especially *The Structure of Metaphysics,* pp. 266-71; *Studies in Metaphilosophy,* pp. 46-66; *The Language of Philosophy,* pp. 188-191.

37. Plato, *The Sophist,* s. 238, Jowett translation.

38. *The Blue Book,* p. 47.

39. Ibid., p. 57.

40. *Constructivity in Mathematics,* p. 70.

41. Evert Willem Beth, *Mathematical Thought* (Dordrecht, Holland: D. Reidel, 1965), p. 161.

42. Ibid., pp. 161-163.

43. Beth's comparison of the two developments, ibid., p. 89.

44. "Foundations of Mathematics," *Encyclopedia Britannica* (London, 1973), vol. 14.

45. *Logical Foundations of Probability* (Chicago: University of Chicago Press, 1950), p. 3.

46. *Essays in the Philosophy of Mathematics* (Leicester: University of Leicester Press, 1965), p. 113.

47. See "Intuitionism and Formalism," in Benacerraf and Putnam, op. cit., p. 71.

48. Ibid., p. 73.

49. Attendant questions can also be formulated, e.g., the question whether from current systems of axioms for set theory it is demonstrable, disprovable, or undecidable which infinite cardinal is the number of the set of all real numbers; also its partial answers: that the hypothesis that its number is χ_1 (the next cardinal after χ_0 in magnitude) is consistent with the axioms, proved by Gödel, and that its negative is consistent with them, proved by Paul Cohen.

50. Hilbert's words.

51. L. E. J. Brouwer, op. cit., p. 74.

52. *Essays in the Philosophy of Mathematics,* p. 104.

53. Ibid.

54. *Philosophische Bemerkungen,* p. 228 (translation mine).

55. *Essays in the Philosophy of Mathematics,* p. 100.

56. For this point, see R. L. Goodstein, "Wittgenstein's Philosophy of Mathematics," *Ludwig Wittgenstein: Philosophy and Language,* A. Ambrose and M. Lazerowitz, eds. (London: George Allen & Unwin, 1972), pp. 275–276.

56. As Wittgenstein put it, "a combination of words is withdrawn from circulation." (See *Philosophical Investigations,* p. 139.)

57. Pt. 7; italics mine.

58. *Philosophische Bemerkungen,* pp. 162, 209; *Philosophische Grammatik,* p. 463.

59. As Russell put it, 'the first infinite number . . . beyond the whole unending series of finite numbers.' See *Our Knowledge of the External World* (Chicago: Open Court, 1914), p. 181.

60. "What is Cantor's Continuum Problem?" in Benacerraf and Putnam, op. cit., p. 259.

61. Beth, *Mathematical Thought,* op. cit., pp. 84–5.

62. L. E. J. Brouwer, "Intuitionism and Formalism," in Benacerraf and Putnam, op. cit., p. 74. Gödel's remark that "The power of the continuum is the second smallest infinite cardinal" has been given several different meanings by intuitionists, all quite different from the original hypothesis (see "What is Cantor's Continuum Problem?", op. cit., p. 261.)

63. *Constructivity in Mathematics,* p. 69.

64. *A Treatise of Human Nature,* bk. 1, pt. 1, s. 1.

65. *Philosophische Grammatik,* p. 374 (translation mine).

66. "The Limits of Empiricism," p. 145.

67. *Philosophische Grammatik,* p. 368.

68. Ibid., p. 368; "Eine neue Festsetzung getroffen."

69. Ibid.

70. *Remarks on the Foundations of Mathematics,* pp. 139–40. Wittgenstein comments: "That is correct if it is supposed to mean that it is not the case e.g. so-and-so many'th is *not* determined."

71. Ibid., p. 141.

72. Ibid., p. 139.

73. "The Limits of Empiricism," p. 144.

XV

On a Property of a Perfect Being

In this discussion I wish to present in outline an hypothesis about the nature, or better, the *hidden* nature, of philosophical utterances; I will then go on to apply this hypothesis to a metaphysical-theological claim. The attempt to construct an hypothesis which will bring to light what a philosophical statement comes to, behind the appearance it presents, is justified by the unnoticed but blatant fact that philosophy cannot show a single *resolved* disagreement. In a discipline that employs reason and argument this fact clamors for attention which, as yet, it has not received. It is an enigma whose existence implies that we do not know what we are doing when we do philosophy, however skillfully we may do it. Until we arrive at a correct understanding of this enigma we are eyeless in our discipline. To mention one well-known theory, the claim that there are abstract entities is as far from being freed from disputation as it ever has been in its long and active history, which goes back to the beginning of philosophy. One strange though not unique feature of this dispute is that everyone knows the answer: in the present case, that there are abstract entities. For the literal meaning of a general word like "goat" or "tree" counts as an abstract entity. How are we to understand a disagreement in which everyone knows what the facts are while its intensity continues unabated?

The hypothesis to be developed here construes a philosophical assertion as presenting an academically, or fantasied, changed piece of language, one not meant for practical, everyday use. The reconstructed nomenclature is presented nonverbally, in the form of discourse in which things and occurrences are described. This creates the vivid semantic appearance that language is being used to convey esoteric cosmological information, rather than being used to introduce idle semantic innovations. This hypothesis about the nature of philosophical utterances has the virtue of providing an explanation of the infinite durability of philosophical debates. No fact is in contest. All that happens in philosophy is that a non-workaday verbal preference counters a contrary non-workaday verbal preference. In this connection Wittgenstein's observation comes to mind: "The confusions which occupy us in philosophy arise when language is like an engine idling, not when it is doing work."[1] Aristophanes seems to have divined what was at work in philosophy when he put Socrates in a suspended basket. As a speculation it may be added that a philosophical statement gives expression to, and in return receives support from, dramatic unconscious material in the depths of the mind. This is a speculation which only a psychoanalyst is in a position to check by clinical evidence.

Consider now the application of this hypothesis to a familiar metaphysical concept, one that is involved in the Anselmic conception of a Being than which a more perfect is inconceivable. This is the idea of a most powerful Being than which a more powerful is inconceivable, a Being which has power to an infinite degree. It is of some interest to note, as an aside, that one proposition entering into the so-called cosmological argument is that an infinite totality *is impossible,* which is required for the proposition that there must be a First Cause. The Anselmic conception instead uses the idea, later developed by the mathematician Georg Cantor, of the *completed,* or *consummated,* infinite, the idea of a set all the theoretically possible elements of which are *actual* elements. Aristotle spoke of the infinite as that which is potential, and Cantor argues that the potential infinite is an actual infinite totality. The Being of the Anselmic conception has power to an *actual* infinite degree, than which a being with a greater degree of power is a logical absurdity. How are we to decide between the claim of the cosmological argument, which denies the possibility of an infinite totality, and the claim of the ontological argument which implies the existence of the completed infinite? Is maintaining that there is a most powerful being than which a more powerful is logically impossible like maintaining that in the sequence of integers 1, 2, 3, . . . there is a greatest integer than which a greater is logically impossible? The second implies a contradiction, that is, $(\exists n)n + 1 \ngtr n$, although the notion that the infinite sequence 1, 2, 3, 4, $\ngtr$ . . . is a completed totality would seem to imply this. If we have a contradiction here, we also have one in the notion of a consummated infinity of degrees of power. What has happened? What makes it possible for astute thinkers to reject the idea of a completed infinite in one argument while maintaining it in a related argument?

To understand this perplexing state of affairs, let us look at Zeno's contention that all numbers are finite. His reported argument is that if there is a number of things, there must be just as many as there are, no more and no less. This is to say that there must be a definite, or *finite,* number of things. Hence, the numbers 1, 2, 3, 4, . . . count as *finite numbers.* It is readily seen that the expression "finite number" has a use in the language only if "non-finite number," or "infinite number," also has a use. Otherwise the term "finite" would not have a use to distinguish between numbers. The meaning of "finite number" would then be nothing in addition to the meaning of "number." The term "finite number" requires its antithesis "infinite number" and would lose its present use without it. One obvious consequence of this semantic fact about antithetical terms is that if "finite number" has a use to name or refer to a number, its antithesis "infinite number" would also have a use to refer to a number. The *possibility* of there being a certain number implies the existence of that number, unlike the possibility of there being, e.g., a unicorn, which does not imply the existence of a unicorn. To put the matter linguistically, in mathematics the fact that an expression has a use to refer to a possible number implies that it refers to an actual number, which makes it unlike such terms as "unicorn." To apply this consideration to the cosmological argument, the phrase "infinite number of causes" would *not* express a logical impossibility, and the argument would rest on a mistaken claim about the use of an expression. Now, if we assign numbers to degrees of power, then the notion of a being that has power to an infinite degree, than which a more powerful is inconceivable, implies the notion of a *greatest degree* of power. And this in turn implies the existence of a greatest number in a sequence which, because it is unending, can have no greatest number. We have here, indeed, a baffling pair of antithetical terms: they cannot function without each other and they do not function with each other. How is this to be explained?

One mathematician, E. T. Bell, has stated that there are no *finite* numbers, there are only numbers. It is clear that what he meant to convey by his words is that the term "finite" has no actual use to characterize *numbers,* which is not to deny that it does have a use to characterize series and sequences, as also does the term "infinite." The claim that "finite" does not apply to numbers throws light on Zeno's contention that all numbers are finite. It helps us understand what Zeno was doing with the word "finite." He creatively, by semantic fiat, identifies "definite number" with "finite number," and he does this by stretching the use of the word "finite." Doing this in the nonverbal, ontological form of speech creates the idea that he is *characterizing* the natural numbers.

The surreptitiously altered use of "finite," which makes the word applicable to numbers, provides a justification—or better still, a pretext—for applying the word "infinite" to numbers. This is done in order to furnish an antithesis for the term "finite number." One game played with the term "finite number" pulls in its verbal wake a related game played with the term "infinite number." It thus turns out that the phrase "all powerful being than which a more powerful is inconceivable" is a bogus description; it does no more than create the semantic appearance of describing an attribute of a kind of being.

The psychology that is bound up with the semantically doctored phrase "most powerful being than which a more powerful is inconceivable" is not hard to divine. On the surface, at the conscious level of his thinking, the idea which the metaphysical theologian appears to be presenting by his words is that of a cosmic colossus of unrivalled power, greater than that of any rival colossus. This is the picture that comes to mind, the picture it is natural to associate with the made-up descriptive phrase, although the picture is not the descriptive import of the phrase, which has been given no use to describe anything. Freud speaks of the difference between the biblical, popular picture of God, as that of a mighty, superhuman figure (whose throne is the sun and whose footstool is the earth), and the abstract, hazy conception of the Anselmic metaphysician. What clouds our understanding of the metaphysical "conception" is also what prevents our apprehending the idea of a prime number than which a greater prime is inconceivable: the conception implies a contradiction. But the notion, or rather the invented phrase that supposedly denotes it, undoubtedly serves as a basic reassurance formula against a threatening world in which we live and which in the end brings us death. In his *The Future of an Illusion*[2] Freud wrote:

> Now when the child grows up and finds that he is destined to remain a child forever, and that he can never do without protection against unknown and mighty powers, he invests these with the traits of the father-figure; he creates for himself the gods, of whom he is afraid, whom he seeks to propitiate, and to whom he nevertheless entrusts the task of protecting him. Thus the longing-for-the-father explanation is identical with the other, the need for protection against the consequences of human weakness; the child's defensive reaction to his helplessness gives the characteristic features to the adult's reaction to his own sense of helplessness, i.e., the formation of religion.

Intolerable, crushing anxiety has to be warded off or in some way held at bay, and this is one of the main functions of the belief in God, the creator of all that is.

It is easily realized that a mind characterized by obsessive traits will not neglect the thought that even a super-titan might, conceivably, meet defeat at the hands of a super-adversary or encounter a cosmic upheaval with which he is unable to cope. The same disconcerting possibility applies to the new titan who might turn out to have shortcomings and who could be vanquished by a still more powerful titan, and so on. The only way to eliminate such dreaded possibilities is to transform the conception of a powerful being into one than which a more powerful cannot be conceived. This is the conception of a being who cannot, even in theory, be overcome by a more powerful being or meet a situation that is beyond his power to control: he is all-powerful and can do anything that is theoretically possible. But his semantic inventor achieves his freedom from recurring anxiety by a semantic ploy, one which at the same time prevents the expression "most powerful being" from having a descriptive use. By adding the phrase "than which no more powerful is conceivable" to "the most powerful being," he exalts with the emotional part of his mind the being normally described by "most powerful" and at the same time lays to rest, or at least is able to contain, any anxiety that might tend to well up in him. Semantically, however, he unwittingly destroys its use to describe the attribute of a being. The explanation of Freud's complaint that the metaphysical theologian's idea of God is obscure and clouded is that the phrase "most powerful, than which a more powerful is inconceivable," like the phrase "greatest integer, than which a greater is inconceivable," looks to be descriptive while in fact being a descriptive blank. Freud's notion was that the man whose thinking is not influenced by the "wiles of philosophy"[3] will be able to see this without much trouble. The observation which irresistibly comes to mind is that the philosopher has about as much chance of avoiding the "wiles of philosophy" as Laoccoan and his sons had of freeing themselves from the coils of the Apollo-sent serpent.

In place of the descriptive function in the language it is represented as having, the philosopher's phrase "than which no more powerful is conceivable" would seem to have a threefold job. One is to create the deceptive but emotionally charged idea that the concept of a Cosmic Colossus is being presented, a God who rules the universe and towers above all other beings. In this respect its job is to create a public fantasy, a fantasy that is consciously shared with others. There is a second job which we may surmise with considerable assurance. This is to give expression to a cluster of affectively toned ideas in the unconscious: the magnified image of the male parent, the father who is the provider, protector, educator, and first titan in the life of the child. Wittgenstein has observed that philosophical utterances frequently are indistinguishable from factual utterances. The form of words in both may be the same, as in the two occurrences of the sentence "I alone exist." One states a matter of fact, and would be true if said by the last survivor of an atomic holocaust. The other declares the logical impossibility of others existing, and this amounts to introducing a revised grammar for the first person pronoun, a grammar which prevents it from having any application. In the solipsist's special language, second and third person pronouns have no place, and only singular first person pronouns remain, but no longer have their conventional use. To return to the sentence "God is a being than which a more powerful is inconceivable," understood as presenting the child's picture of the father, it uses "inconceivable" in its psychological rather than its logical sense. It is not to be construed as asserting the logical impossibility of a more powerful being, but rather as asserting its factual impossibility. Understood in its logical sense, i.e., in the sense in which the term "inconceivable" equates with "logically impossible," the term prevents the sentence from having descriptive sense.

It will be useful to revert to the idea of the extended infinite, and consider several attempts to defend it. An implied if not explicitly stated claim of at least some Cantorian mathematicians is that finitists base their rejection of the idea of an extended infinite on a psychological proposition.

This is that we are unable to imagine or conceive an infinite array, e.g., of pennies. From this psychological premise the critics of the extended infinite proceed to the conclusion that an infinite collection cannot exist as an entirety. The counter-contention is that this is like arguing that since we cannot imagine an array of 377^{19325} pennies, such an array cannot in principle exist. The rejoinder by those who embrace the Cantorian idea is that what *we* cannot conceive a super-prodigy could conceive, i.e., he could imagine an array of objects described by the words "the set of 377^{19325} pennies." It is the same with what is referred to by the expression "infinite array of pennies," except that the word "God" is substituted for the word "prodigy." God is able to comprehend what lies beyond the grasp of even a super-prodigy.

Some philosophical mathematicians allow that not even God can run through, or finish counting, an infinite array. He can perceive all of the elements of a totality in the way in which lesser minds perceive a collection of pennies. But if He embarked on the task of counting them, not even He could finish the task. An infinite mind could comprehend the entire sequence of natural numbers

$$1, 2, 3, 4, \ldots$$

as well as the consummated infinite geometric series

$$1 + \tfrac{1}{2} + \tfrac{1}{4} + \tfrac{1}{8} + \ldots ;$$

but not even an infinite mind could finish enumerating the terms of either. It may be of some interest to note that Leibniz was of two minds about the infinite. At times he held that the idea of the infinite implies a contradiction, in which case it would not be open to comprehension by any being. At other times he held that God could entertain an infinite totality of terms, which is why He could see that a truth of fact was really a truth of reason: He comprehends the infinite array of predicates entailed by the subject-term of a proposition.

One difficulty in what might be called the theological defense of the extended infinite lies on the surface and needs hardly any discussion. This is that it begs the question. It assumes the possible existence of an infinite mind in order to justify the claim that an infinite totality of objects exists as a consummated whole. The notion of an infinite whole is involved in the notion of an infinite mind, that is, a mind that can encompass "in one glance"[4] an infinite extension. And if the notion of an infinite extension defeats our powers of conception, so also does the notion of a mind that can contemplate such an extension in its entirety. A related, and perhaps more important, point is that in order to be able to say with literal sense that an infinite mind contemplates what we cannot even in theory conceive, we must be able to say what it is that the infinite mind contemplates. But the theological proponent of the consummated infinite maintains by implication that anything less than an infinite mind, i.e., a finite mind, however prodigious its powers, cannot in principle encompass in thought an infinite totality of entities. He thus implies that we can have *no idea* of what it is like for a set to have an infinite number of elements. The inference to be drawn is that phrases like "the entire set of integers" and "the totality of elements in the series $1 + \frac{1}{2} + \frac{1}{4} + \ldots$." have been assigned no application in the language: they have no use to describe. They are verbal counterfeits passed off as having a descriptive use in the language of mathematics.

Wittgenstein has said: "What cannot be imagined cannot even be talked about."[5] It is hardly to be supposed that Wittgenstein was referring to huge collections, like $377^{19^{325}}$, which elude our mental grasp. For we obviously *can* "talk" about them. We can, for example, calculate how long it would take to spend $377^{19^{325}}$ pennies ten thousand at a time, or how large a container would have to be in order to hold all of them. In his later writings he states that the term "infinite" does not have a use to refer to the huge or the colossal.[6] The mathematician turned metaphysician, in saying that we cannot, but that God can, encompass the infinite, is not saying that the infinite is too huge for us to contemplate but not too huge for God. The "cannot" and the "can" that are being used here have their logical sense. We may infer that he is unwittingly and picturesquely highlighting a verbal fact, namely, that expressions in which the term "infinite" occurs have no use to describe magnitudes. It will be clear that, although such an expression as "an infinite number of pennies" carries with it the semantic appearance of referring to a huge collection, it is descriptively empty. The expression "infinite number of terms," as applied to series and sequences, suggests the idea of a number which applies to a set of terms. But "has an infinite number of terms" means nothing different from "has no last term," which does not carry with it the idea of a *number* of terms. In showing a preference for the expression "has an infinite number of terms" over the expression "has no last term" it may be gathered that what the philosopher of mathematics wishes to do is to heighten the likeness between the use of the term "infinite" and the names of numbers, and to minimize the unlikeness between them, for whatever gain this may have for him.

If, on the one hand, the phrase "the totality of the infinite sequence of integers" has no use to refer to a set of elements, then it refers to nothing which might be the object of God's contemplation. If, on the other hand, the phrase does actually have a use in the language to refer to a set which is the object of God's contemplation, then it describes what is in principle a possible object for us to contemplate. But since it is logically, in principle, impossible for us to apprehend or imagine an infinite extension, it follows that expressions like "infinite set of elements" and "the consummated series generated by the formula $1/2^{n-1}$ " have no use in the language to give the number of either a set or a series. It is not hard to see why not even God can run through an infinite series or sequence of terms, and why neither God nor we can contemplate an infinite totality of elements. Spinoza observed that not even God can bring it about that from a certain cause no effect shall follow, and we might add that not even God can *conceive* of a cause which has no effect. It is language which erects the barrier to both action and conception. The phrase "cause without effect" has no descriptive use, and it therefore has no use to describe anything which could be thought or brought about. It is linguistic usage that prevents the existence of an infinite extension, or its grasp by a mind. And also it is linguistic usage which prevents counting an infinite number of objects.

M.L.

NOTES

1. *Philosophical Investigations,* p. 51.

2. Sigmund Freud, *The Future of Illusion* (London: The Hogarth Press and the Institute of Psycho-analysis, 1943), trans. by W. D. Robson-Scott, edited by Ernest Jones, p. 42.

3. Ibid., p. 50.

4. Paul Bernays, "Comments on Ludwig Wittgenstein's *Remarks on the Foundations of Mathematics,*" in *Philosophy of Mathematics, Selected Readings,* edited by P. Benacerraf and H. Putnam, p. 520.

5. *Notebooks, 1914–1916,* p. 84e.

6. *Wittgenstein's Lectures, Cambridge 1932–1935,* pp. 189–190.

XVI

The Philosopher and Daydreaming

Freud has said: "Happy people do not indulge in fantasies, only unsatisfied ones do. Unsatisfied wishes are the driving force behind fantasies; every fantasy contains the fulfillment of a wish, and improves on unsatisfactory reality."[1] Unlike children who do not try to conceal their fantasies from others, adults, who are expected to have outgrown the fantasy stage of their development, feel embarrassed by their wishful thoughts and so conceal them from others. They enjoy flights of fancy in the privacy of their minds, and betray themselves only indirectly or by inadvertence. Some years ago a colleague told me that he thought he should be awarded a Nobel Prize. I was astonished at his having such an idea, especially since he had done nothing outstanding in his field and was known best for the faculty parties he gave. It requires no stretch of the imagination to suppose that he did not live with impoverished fantasies. Freud tells us that psychoanalysts do not have to infer or guess that adults create fantasies for themselves. They obtain direct access to them from people who come to them for treatment. Freud has written: "These people are the neurotics; among other things they have to confess their fantasies to the physician to whom they go in the hope of recovering through mental treatment. This is our best source of knowledge, and we have later found good reason to suppose that our patients tell us about themselves nothing that we could not also hear from healthy people."[2]

Healthy people have daydreams, just as healthy people have nocturnal dreams, because their wishes are frustrated by reality and have to be put aside. But a wish that is dismissed or suppressed is not thereby extinguished, and it continues to demand satisfaction. In a world which grants us so few satisfactions we have to settle for less than the full amount, so we fall back on fantasies and dreams. Conscious fantasies, such as being made a Nobel Laureate or of performing great feats of strength (Superman) are not the only kind of fantasies. There are also unconscious fantasies. These are repressed material in the mind, material of whose existence we are in complete ignorance. Such ideas can present themselves to our conscious awareness only in disguised, unrecognizable forms; and only a special method, devised by Freud, can get behind the disguises and reveal the underlying, emotionally charged content. Unlike a conscious fantasy, which can lose its importance for us and be eroded by time, an idea that is under repression acquires immortality and expresses itself in hidden forms over and over again. This fact is perhaps the source of the fabled phoenix, which springs to life from its own ashes. The difference between a conscious fantasy and one that is under repression is that we hide our conscious fantasies from others and our unconscious fantasies from ourselves. The colorful New York Village character, Margaret Anderson, is reported to have said: "Reality is my greatest enemy. I have fought it successfully for thirty years." We may guess with reasonable assurance that the reality she fought successfully was composed of primitive wishes which she held at bay with the mechanism of repression.

With regard to daydreams Freud has written:

> You will remember that we said the day-dreamer hid his fantasies carefully from other people because he had reason to be ashamed of them. I may now add that even if he were to communicate them to us, he would give us no pleasure by his disclosures. When we hear such fantasies they repel us, or at least leave us cold. But when a man of literary talent presents his plays, or relates what we take to be his personal day-dreams, we experience great pleasure arising probably from many sources. How the writer accomplishes this is his innermost secret; the essential *ars poetica* lies in the technique by which our feeling of repulsion is overcome, and this has certainly to do with those barriers erected between every individual being and all others. We can guess at two methods used in this technique. The writer softens the egotistical character of the day-dream by change and disguises, and he bribes us by the purely formal, that is, aesthetic, pleasure in the presentation of his fantasies. I am of the opinion that . . . true enjoyment of literature proceeds from the release of tensions in our minds. Perhaps much that brings about this result consists in the writer's putting us in the position in which we can enjoy our own day-dreams without reproach or shame. Here we reach a path leading into novel, interesting, and complicated researches. . . .[3]

Unexpected as it may be, philosophy is one of these researches.

The appearance academic philosophy presents is that of being a high-level investigation of the world, but this appearance turns out to be the philosopher's daydream, one which he can share with others. The appearance is so realistic that only rarely has anyone expressed doubt or suspicion, and then usually by indirection. W. V. Quine, for example, goes out of his way to affirm that philosophy is not fictional: "The question what there is is a shared concern of philosophy and most other non-fiction genres."[4] And Freud's biographer, Ernest Jones, has written: "Time and again I have emerged from a course of reading in philosophy with the conviction that the authors were really avoiding specific problems by converting them into ten-uous sophistries that have very little real meaning."[5] Jones quickly dismissed his suspicious thought, and without further investigation went over to the defense of philosophy, which consisted mainly in belittling his own capacities for abstract thought. To give still another instance of uneasiness about philosophy, Peter Winch has remarked: "Philosophy is certainly an activity which needs constantly to be defended. Indeed it is hardly conceivable at all—except as a constant struggle against sophistry." These words hardly apply to nonfictional investigations of the world, and no attempt was made by Winch to explain why the doing of philosophy involves a constant struggle against sophistry. What we have is a plaintive whisper that is quickly stilled.

If we let ourselves be made thoughtful by the remarks of these thinkers and look with care at the words philosophers use to express their theories, we can begin to realize that the philosopher's use of language is not like the ordinary or scientific use of language. The philosopher uses language not, as it seems, to describe features of things but to create the illusion of describing features of things, and also, underneath, to give expression to unconscious wishes. With his special use of language he creates a gratifying illusion which wins him the respect of others and at the same time gives release to mental tensions brought about by affectively toned complexes of ideas that are active in the submerged part of his mind. This he does by the magic of hidden semantic maneuvering. The hypothesis about the nature of philosophical theories to be developed in the following pages is that they are structures composed of three interacting components. Uppermost, at the conscious level of the mind, is the appearance that a philosophical utterance, such as "A physical thing is a cluster of sense data," makes a declaration about the existence or nature of a phenomenon. At the preconscious level of the mind a piece of gerrymandered terminology is presented in a mode of speech designed to create the consciously entertained idea of a scientific pronouncement. And at the unconscious level the words are secretly understood to give expression to a repressed fantasy.

There are two things that might be called the central enigmas of philosophy. These are the endless disputes characterizing every part of philosophy,[7] and the complete absence of established results, however minor. It is an interesting and curious fact that philosophers are not seriously troubled by these, and for the most part seem to be oblivious to them. If Quine is right in his claim that "philosophy is an aspect of science and is continuous with it,"[8] then there is no question but that philosophers would be disturbed and *seriously* concerned. The impression, which with time gains strength, is that they prefer not to see what is plainly before their eyes. The maxim I wish to lay down here is that no hypothesis about the nature of philosophical theories, that is, about how they are to be understood, is correct if it does not also give an explanation of the intractability of philosophical disagreements and the complete absence of firm philosophical results. If we look at the various explanations as to what philosophical statements are about, statements such as "Motion does not exist," "Time is unreal," and "All desires are selfish," we can only conclude that philosophy is a subject that requires a kind of intellectual myopia for its practice. It is plain that the correct explanation cannot fail to be iconoclastic and disconcerting to philosophers. The explanation, which philosophers have opposed with the greatest hostility, is that under the influences of likenesses and unlikenesses in the functioning of terminology they unwittingly change or re-edit language in actual use. They do not use language to describe or make statements about things, despite appearances to the contrary. The semantic emendations effected by philosophers are presented in a form of speech which produces the vivid, if delusive, impression that they are announcing theories about features of reality.

On this account, we can understand why recourse to an examination of nonlinguistic, i.e., material, fact is not relevant to the solution of a philosophical problem. It makes intelligible, for example, why the fact that Diogenes walked back and forth before the scholars who came to Zeno's lecture was not thought to refute his conclusion that motion does not exist. The reason is that the statement "Motion is impossible" does not deny the existence of motion. The statement is not about a ubiquitous and familiar phenomenon. The general hypothesis about philosophical theories proposed throughout these chapters explains why the question as to whether motion is real can be argued interminably without anyone's perception being different from anyone else's. We can also understand why an examination of conventional linguistic usage, and getting a clear view of the working of our language,[9] do not resolve disagreements between philosophers. Thus, it enables us to understand why it is that seeing how the word "motion" functions in the language does not dissolve the philosophical problem about motion. On the present account, actual usage is no more in debate than is material fact. The picture of philosophy that comes into focus is that of a kind of verbal theater: the actors that present themselves are masked, re-edited expressions and the backdrop is unaltered everyday language. The reality behind the intriguing intellectual illusion that the statements of philosophy reveal cosmic truths or bring to light what has been called "depth grammar" is artificially stretched or contracted or rejected terminology.

By means of an appropriately altered piece of terminology, not meant for practical adoption, the philosopher creates the delusive appearance of discovering a truth about reality, and at the same time he gains an inner consolation for himself. Chapter I, verse 1 of the Gospel according to St. John reads, "In the beginning was the Word," and it can indeed be said that the word has lost none of its ancient magical power. The philosopher, Titan of the Word, knows how to bemuse his own intellect as well as ours by means of the magical possibilities hidden in the language. To imitate

Wittgenstein, philosophy may be said to be the bewitchment of the mind by the art of hidden maneuvering with nomenclature.

To illustrate the hypothesis about philosophy in a concrete way, consider Hume's celebrated 'discovery' that causation is nothing more than the constant conjunction of independent occurrences. This claimed finding is represented as being the outcome of an empirical examination of what everyone takes for granted, such as that water extinguishes fire. In language that is appropriate to a scientific investigation, Hume invites us to "turn our eyes" to occurrences which, to all appearances, are instances of causation, and we shall be satisfied that we have been taking a mirage for the real thing. In consonance with Hume, Russell has written that the controversy about causation is "one of empirical fact: Do we, or do we not, sometimes perceive a relation which can be called causal? Hume says no, his adversaries say yes, and it is not easy to see how evidence can be produced by either side."[10] It turns out, however, that Hume's mirage is produced by words and not by the world. This can be seen from the following consideration.

Anyone who says, "α is not really ϕ, it only appears to be," implies that he knows what it would be like for α really to be ϕ. Read literally, his words imply that he can say what it is that α lacks, which if possessed by it would make it ϕ. In saying that α only appears to be ϕ he implies that the appearance pictures α as having what in fact it lacks. He implies, in other words, that he can identify what the appearance pictures that is not to be found in the reality. If he is unable to do this, then whatever it is that he wishes to convey by his words, he is not telling us that α only appears to our senses to be ϕ. He is using an ordinary expression to say something other than what the expression is naturally taken to refer to. Indeed, it turns out that a philosopher is not using language in the ordinary way when he declares, for example: "Water is not heated by fire, it only appears to be. If we use our eyes with care we shall see that all that really happens is that water heats *of itself,* independently of the presence of fire." If we question him, we find that he cannot describe a circumstance which, if it obtained, would make him grant that fire is the cause of the water heating, that it really heats the water and not merely appears to heat it. To put the matter generally, he is unable to tell us what is required to make an occurrence one in which a causal *transaction* takes place. He is unable to describe the feature whose absence makes him deny that causation occurs. This means that he cannot *identify* anything *in the appearance* of a causal transaction which pictures a theoretical reality. On the surface, the philosopher's talk is the talk of appearance and reality, but the fact is that he only pantomimes such talk. His use of language, whether mistaken or contrived, is not to describe either a phenomenon or the appearance of a phenomenon.

Once it is seen that the philosopher is not using his words to express an experiential proposition, e.g., the words, "Nothing is the productive cause of anything," "Causation is no more than the constant conjunction of independent occurrences," it is natural to think that he is using them to make a statement about the use of causal terminology in the language. Construed as verbal in import, they are to the following effect:

(1) "x is cause of y" does not mean the same as "the occurrence of y depends on the occurrence of x,"
(2) "dependent occurrence" has no descriptive use in the language,
(3) "x is cause of y" means the same as "y regularly occurs with x."

If we take the skeptic to be stating facts about the accepted meanings of terminology, he strikes us as somehow having got a wrong notion about the use of causal language. He appears to have the strange idea that "causation" has the same meaning as "constant fortuitous joint occurrence." But his use of language for the purpose of everyday communication makes it evident that he knows better, i.e., that he is aware of the linguistic fact that "x is cause of y" does not have the same use as "y regularly but accidentally occurs with x." The words "x is cause of y" do not apply to cases of long-run gambling success. It is implausible to suppose the skeptic to be laboring under a mere verbal misapprehension, one which does not intrude itself into his everyday use of language, and from which he cannot be detached by having his attention called to it. If we look with care at the skeptic's three-fold claim, a peculiarity emerges which suggests that he is changing rather than merely misdescribing language.

It is a simple matter to see that the expression "independent occurrence" has a use in ordinary speech only because "dependent occurrence" is an expression which describes actual or hypothetical states of affairs. If "dependent occurrence" were deprived of the use it has, without some sort of linguistic reparation being made, "independent occurrence" would lose its descriptive function in the language. To think that the word "dependent" has no application to occurrences commits one to thinking that the descriptive force of "independent occurrences" is identical with that of the word "occurrences." For if "dependent" had no application to occurrences, actual or hypothetical, "independent" would not serve to distinguish between kinds of occurrences and would not have its present place in the language. In Emerald City where the only color is green there would be no word for green, because the word "green" has a use only when it serves to distinguish amongst colors. It does this kind of work only if provision is made in the language for its use in expressions of the form "This is not green."

It is unnecessary to go into further reasons for thinking that the causal skeptic is not making a persistent mistake about the conventional use of terminology. The unavoidable alternative would seem to be that he has unwittingly re-edited language. To put the matter shortly, what has happened is that the word "independent" (Hume's term is "loose and separate") has been artificially stretched by semantic fiat so as to apply to all occurrences, dependent as well as independent. Parenthetically, it is to be remarked that the everyday term remains unchanged and is used by the causal skeptic in his nonphilosophical talk the way Everyman uses it. It is as if the philosopher had two dictionaries, one of which he consults for familiar, ordinary purposes and the other for a special esoteric purpose. No philosopher is a reformer of language, and he makes no sort of attempt to transport the word from his philosophical dictionary to Webster's dictionary. He introduces us to the stretched use of the word in order, it would seem, to create the illusion that he is presenting a theory about the way things work. Given that he is not making a mistake about language and that the use he makes of causal language creates the idea that he is announcing a scientific theory about the way the world works, it is reasonable to conclude that his intention, whether conscious or not, is to create an illusion. Undoubtedly there is more to the skeptic's view than has been brought to light here, more, that is to say, than just a piece of academically gerrymandered language and an illusion that is bound up with it. It is a creation of the mind and must, we are constrained to think, serve a psychical need. Like a dream, or a painting, or a poem, it undoubtedly caters to an unconscious wish. We may permit ourselves a guess at one of the fantasies linked with causal skepticism. When I was a student, one of my philosophy professors remarked in a classroom lecture that if he were the lawyer for the defense in a murder trial, he would invoke Hume's arguments against the proposition that one thing can by an action *produce* a change in another thing. No lawyer, of course, would dream of using Hume's arguments in a court of law, but in dreams, where life does not impose its practical restraints, matters are different. In a dream or in a fantasy Hume's arguments may well play the role of a defense against an inner accusation. The Egyptian *Book of the Dead* speaks of "the silent act of thought," and in the unconscious a criminal wish is equated with the criminal deed. This explains why some people confess to crimes they have not committed. Dostoevski, who had remarkably perceptive insights into the human mind, relates cases of this sort in *Crime and Punishment*; many such confessions fill police records. Oedipal crimes, enacted in the darkest part of the mind, or in unconscious fantasy, produce guilt feelings no less than actual crimes committed with conscious awareness, and the subjective accusations to which they give rise produce tension and must be deflected. A philosophical lawyer might well invoke Hume in his defense against an unconscious charge.

A criticism of a remark I made in *The Structure of Metaphysics* provides a further illustration of the kind of games philosophers play with words. The remark is to the effect that a philosopher dreams with words. In a review of the book which appears in *Mind,* Professor C. H. Whiteley writes:

> . . . when Lazerowitz says that metaphysicians "dream with words" (knowing quite well that they are awake when philosophizing) is it fair to say that, under

cover of a pseudo-description, he is proposing an *ad hoc* alteration in the meaning of "dream" in order to gratify an unconscious spite against metaphysicians? This, of course, would be caricature; and Lazerowitz's theory is likewise a caricature which vividly reveals some features of his subject, and also distorts it.[11]

The plain implication of this criticism is that the word "dream" has been altered so that the statement "Philosophers dream with words" is introducing an altered use of the term rather than using it in the customary way to describe an activity. A number of philosophers have directed a *tu quoque* form of argument against the general thesis that philosophy introduces redistricted terminology rather than uses it descriptively in the accepted ways. What these philosophers apparently fail to see is that on their own accounting the thesis about philosophy does not say anything about the nature of philosophy and would be no cause for concern about a respected discipline. Whiteley also seems to have failed to realize that if, according to him, the statement "The philosopher dreams with words" comes to nothing more than proposing an *ad hoc* alteration in the meaning of "dreams," then the statement would not only express a caricature of philosophical thinking but would say nothing whatever about it. The statement would neither reveal a feature of the subject nor distort it.

To see what Whiteley has done, no more is necessary than to consult a standard dictionary. The *Oxford English Dictionary,* for example, gives *reverie* (a form of conscious thinking) as one of the meanings of the word "dream." Everyone who is brought up in the English language, including Whiteley, employs the word "dream" in this way, and the plausible conclusion to come to is that, in what Moore calls a "philosophic moment," Whiteley unwittingly plays a game with language in which he confines the word "dream" to part of its actual range of application. His contracted use of "dream" is such that "is asleep" now applies to whatever "is dreaming" applies to. Thus "dreams" is deprived of its application to reveries and the like.

One psychological gain from this contracted use is not difficult to surmise: a fantasied refutation of a distressing view which is hard to incorporate into our normal way of thinking about philosophical activity. When fact becomes threatening it is not unusual to vanquish it with fantasy. The philosopher's magical Excalibur is a manipulated word.

NOTES

1. Sigmund Freud, *Collected Papers,* Vol. 4., "The Relation of the Poet to Day-Dreaming," p. 176.
2. Ibid.

3. Ibid., pp. 182–183.
4. W. V. O. Quine, *Word and Object,* p. 275.
5. Ernest Jones, *Free Associations,* p. 60.
6. *Mind,* LXXIII (1964), p. 608.
7. Formal logic seems to be an exception, but formal logic has become part of mathematics.
8. W. V. O. Quine, "Philosophical Progress in Language Theory," *Metaphilosophy* I (1970), p. 2.
9. See Alice Ambrose's "Commanding a Clear View of Philosophy," *Proceedings and Addresses.* The American Philosophical Association, XLIX (1975–1976), reprinted in revised form as Essay III in the present volume.
10. *A History of Western Philosophy,* p. 669.
11. *Mind,* LXV (1956), p. 252.